CAMAS PIONEERS

Historic Profiles of Prominent Camas Families

A Non-Fiction Book

by Sally Alves

Camas-Washougal Historical Society

ISBN: 979-8-218-64083-5 (Paperback)

Edited by Rene Carroll and Madeline Mesplay.

Cover and Interior Design by April Pereira, Lymantria Press.

First printing edition 2025.

Camas-Washougal Historical Society
PO Box 204
Washougal, WA 98671
www.2rhm.com

Printed in the United States of America

CONTENTS

STATEHOOD AND THE GOOD LIFE

THE CAMAS MILL

INTRODUCTION
An Overview of Camas History

IN 1864, HAMILTON J. G. Maxon and his wife Arabella received Donation Land Claim #47 from Abraham Lincoln for 640 acres on the Washington side of the Columbia River ten miles east of Portland, Oregon, in what is now downtown Camas and the paper mill site. Several real estate transactions took place regarding this property over the years before the land was sold in 1882 by B.F. and Hattie Dennison of Portland to Horace Belding, a migrant from Iowa. Belding planned to use the land for farming and built a small log home at the corner of 1st and Columbia, close to the Columbia River.

A scant year later, Belding was approached by D. H. Stern who represented the LaCamas Colony Company, primarily owned by Henry Pittock, owner of the newspaper in Portland, Oregon. Pittock had been searching for a site to place his future paper mill to provide a source of paper for his newspaper. Belding's property was perfect for shipping on the Columbia River, and for generating power from LaCamas Lake, a lovely, pristine body of water that sat on a plateau above the river. The deal for 641.60 acres closed on May 12, 1883, with a selling price of $6,416.00, a considerable sum for those days. Soon, the news spread of the new paper mill and workers from all over the United States and abroad came to LaCamas eager to work at the mill.

A town site was soon platted next to the mill, streets, homes, and stores were constructed to accommodate the new arrivals, and the little farming community blossomed into a town. Professionals arrived including store owners, schoolteachers, doctors and lawyers to add to the development of

LaCamas. After the turn of the century, a railroad and electricity came to LaCamas. At that time the name was changed to "Camas" because of post office confusion over two other towns in Washington with similar names. The word "Camas" came from the Camas Lily that grows abundantly throughout the area.

Today, Camas is a thriving city with modern schools, commercial buildings, and homes. The paper mill now called "Georgia Pacific Corporation" continues to be a major player in town, but other important hi-tech industries have also found their homes in Camas. Descendants of the early pioneers still live in the area and are thankful that their courageous ancestors had the vision to trek across the rugged Oregon Trail in order to develop this wonderful community.

death experiences, and their battles for land and profit. It was all there in the dramatic story of early Camas.

The driving force behind the beginnings of the town was, of course, the paper mill. This smoking giant was the lifeblood of the community back in 1883 and for all the generations that followed.

Midway through this project, I suddenly realized that by relating these individual true stories of the town's early people, I was, in essence, writing a history of Camas. So, here is that history, dear readers.

The story of Camas Pioneers and their paper mill town on the mighty Columbia River.

PROLOGUE

WHILE RESEARCHING INFORMATION for my "John Roffler, Camas Craftsman" book in 1990-1991, I found my interest growing in the overall history of Camas, once called LaCamas, Washington. This, in turn, led me to research the individuals who had helped in the development of the town and surrounding countryside.

As soon as my "Roffler" book was completed, I began to explore these other early pioneers, their unusual histories, and what had drawn them so many, many miles across the rugged Oregon Trail to settle by the Columbia River in the Oregon Territory, now called Washington State.

My investigation began with the earliest settlers who were the homesteaders and farmers of Grass Valley and Fern Prairie in the mid 1800's. My research continued with the beginnings of the Camas paper mill and those who came to develop and work in this exciting new Camas industry. Then, I focused on the folks who platted the town, the early town leaders. Next came the merchants who opened their businesses in the raw, muddy streets in order to provide goods and services to the mill workers and their families. Lastly, I researched the educated professionals who arrived to teach the children, tend to the sick, and give legal advice to those in need. I was impressed by the overall intelligence of this incredible, diverse mix of early settlers who came from so many different places and backgrounds to formulate this fledgling town into a solid, thriving city.

Along the way, I was caught up in the human spirit of this pioneer drama. I began to share the joys and sorrows of my pioneers, their triumphs and failures, the beginnings and endings of their loves, the sorrows of their

METHODOLOGY

RESEARCHING A BOOK of this kind can take years, and in my case, it did. I began by visiting the local historical society, museum, and library, digging deeply into their files, books, documents, old newspapers, photographs, and anything else that could give me early Camas history and the important players in its' development. From this research I made up a master list of early pioneers. When I ran across material that corresponded to my list, I made copies of that material and placed it in notebooks that I set up with each of the pioneer's names, alphabetically on index tabs.

My research base broadened to the county museum and library, and the genealogical society's records for births and deaths. Then, to the records at the county courthouse for marriages, census figures, land records, etc. Next, I traveled across the river to Portland and the Oregon Historical Society for area information. I photocopied all material relating to my "pioneers" and placed the copies in my notebooks.

I began to gather old local newspapers from long ago and borrowed a microfilm of early LaCamas Post newspapers from 1887-1892 that I had hard copied into a bound book. I purchased copies of area history books and borrowed oral interview tapes that related stories of Camas old timers. I visited all the areas' pioneer graveyards, taking photos of my "pioneers" tombstones. I also made the rounds of old homestead sites and buildings previously owned by my list of pioneers. Adding to my understanding of the area's early beginnings, I avidly read any "Abstract of Titles" I could get my hands on. These AOT's told stories of East Clark County property from the time of presidential land grants to more recent times.

Once I had all this material gathered together, I began to write the first drafts of my pioneer stories based on the information that I had amassed. Once each draft was completed, I searched for any living relative of that pioneer, and in most cases, I was successful. I vowed that no chapter would be published until I had the final approval of the pioneer's descendants, if any could be found. Then, I conducted interviews with the living relatives to glean more information and to collect any old photographs they would let me borrow. I had negatives made and promptly returned the treasured photographs. Some chapters are detailed, others are not but it was important to include everyone.

The whole process was very painstaking and costly, but I was determined that this book would be totally accurate in its content, and of great value as a historical resource for the community. However, once the book was completed, I spent a good year trying to get a grant or financial aid to have it published.

Unfortunately, I was unable to do so at that time. Years have gone by with my book and research materials in storage boxes. Unfortunately, my computer crashed, and I lost the whole manuscript except for the hard copy. So, when I was recently contacted by the Camas–Washougal Historical Society expressing interest in publishing my book, I decided to re–input the whole book from my hard copy and put it on disk. So, finally, my "Camas Pioneer" book will be published with all proceeds from the sale going to the Camas–Washougal Historical Society with my blessing, because finally, so many years later, I know that all my work, time and cost involved in this lengthy project, has not been in vain.

DREAMS OF A NEW LAND

THE EARLY FARMERS

HENRY MONROE KNAPP

Authors Preface: On a cold, windy Sunday in late December 1991, almost one hundred and forty years after Henry Monroe Knapp had staked his land claim in Grass Valley, I drove my car one mile due north from four-corners to the intersection County Roads 119 and 122. To the west of the intersection, on one corner of the old Knapp property, sat the ruins of the one-room Grass Valley School. As I photographed the small brick building, I could only imagine what had transpired here. Looking southward up the hill to the barely visible Pacific Rim Highway, I felt suspended in time, somewhere between what was destined to happen in the future to this lovely, historic alley, and all that had gone before. I closed my eyes and visualized the huge, stately residence of Henry Monroe Knapp, his vast fields rich with crops, a team of horses prancing down the long spacious driveway, pulling a highly polished carriage and a small schoolhouse alive with laughing pioneer children. As I stood there in the stillness of that very special moment, the wind suddenly quickened and whispered through the tall, timothy grass, like ghosts across the valley.

❧

CAMAS GRASS VALLEY pioneer, Henry Monroe Knapp, was born in Wyoming County, New York on January 16, 1829. At the age of twenty-one, the distinguished and eloquent Henry came overland to the Oregon Territory, Arriving in October 1850, he lived for a time in the tiny, rural community of LaCamas and was listed in the 1850 census as living in House Number 87. His distant neighbors in this farming community were Joseph Gibbons in House Number 86 and Hamilton J. G. Maxon in House Number 88. Love came to Henry when he was twenty-four. At that time east Clark County was sparsely populated because the Oregon Trail migration was just beginning. That did not stop Henry from immediately becoming involved in politics, becoming Clark County Auditor in 1852-1853. It also did not stop him from meeting and wooing one of the few lovely ladies in LaCamas, twenty-four-year-old Rachel Fisher, the daughter of Michael and Eliza Fisher of Missouri. She was very impressed with Henry, who was already becoming known in the area, and on May 26, 1853, the two married. Rachel was born January 28, 1829, in Hardy County, Virginia and had lived most of her life in Missouri with her parents and siblings, Solomon, Ann Jemima, Adam, Job, and John. In 1850 the adventurous Fisher children said goodbye to their surprised parents and left Missouri traveling westward to Oregon when they learned that opportunities were greater there. Ann Jemima was married to William Mortimer Simmons and the long, grueling six-month journey took its' toll with two of their five children dying along the way.

When they finally arrived in east Clark County, the Fisher children filed land claims around what is now 164th Avenue and Cascade Park. The oldest son, thirty-one-year-old Solomon, established a thriving riverboat landing in 1851, that henceforth became known as "Fisher's Landing" on the Columbia River at the foot of 164th Avenue. His land claim was west of 164th Avenue and north to Mill Plain and although he built a large home close by, Solomon never married. William and Jemima Simmons filed their land claim on February 10, 1851. It stretched from the Columbia River north to Mill Plain, east of 164th. Adam Fisher's claim lay to the north, taking up most of what is Cascade Park today. However, in 1857 Adam married Portlander, Elizabeth Ann Dort and moved to the Oregon side of the Columbia River to raise their soon-to-be ten children. Job helped his brother Solomon build the boat dock but did not complete his land claim, so it was later canceled by the land office.

In August of 1853, newly married Henry and Rachel Knapp filed for a Donation Land Claim of 320 acres next to the claim of John Hicks at Grass Valley. Grass Valley was so named because of the acres of timothy grass that grew so abundantly there. Henry traded in his LaCamas property and began building up his new Grass Valley homestead for his new bride. He kept busy with his many acres of farmland, horses and cattle plus his political and civic duties.

During the Indian Wars of 1855-1856 Henry served under Captain William Kelly in the Clark County Rangers, Second Regiment of Washington Volunteers. These activities kept him away from home for long periods of time, but the couple still managed to have six children in the next ten years. First born on May 14, 1854, were twins, James and Sarah, who lived for only four years and died on the same day, October 13, 1884. Their son Pliny born January 11, 1857, had died on September 12, 1857, at the age of nine months. How heartbreaking it was for Henry and Rachel to lose their first three children before the age of five. In 1859 another son, Oliver H. Knapp, was born. The 1860 Clark County Census listed the Knapp family as H.M. Knapp, thirty-one years of age and a farmer, Rachel E. Knapp, thirty years old, one year old Oliver Knapp and a farmhand, John Adams who was thirty-five.

Henry continued to be busy with his political life and was elected County Assessor in 1860 and served on the Territorial Legislature in 1859 and 1866. Being a very strong Democrat, he felt that no Republican could be trusted. It is of written record that he gave a powerful speech on Territorial Suffrage "the woman's right to vote" while serving in the legislature. Unfortunately, he became ill during his speech and was unable to finish. However, one and all agreed it was a remarkable oration. In the meantime, Rachel was busy at home delivering a daughter, Olive Georgina in December of 1860. Three years later in 1863 a sixth child, Ella Adelia Knapp arrived.

Henry Monroe Knapp (Source: Deb Knapp)

However, on December 18, a few weeks after Ella's birth, Rachel Fisher Knapp passed away. She had endured the overland trip from Missouri by wagon train, had survived the rigors of clearing land in a new territory and building a homestead, but the trauma of giving birth to six children in the family home and burying three of them finally did her in. Rachel and her three dead children are all buried in the Fisher Cemetery. On her headstone, Henry wrote "Gone But Not Forgotten." At the age of thirty-four, Henry was left to care for four-year-old Oliver, three-year-old Olive Georgina, and baby Ella. Times were tough for those early pioneers. Most babies were born at home with no doctor present and many women died in childbirth or shortly after.

Although full of sorrow at losing Rachel, Henry wasted no time in marrying again. In 1865, barely a year after Rachel's death, Henry married his fourteen-year-old housekeeper, Anna A. Huffman. She had arrived in Clark County with her family from Whitesides County, Illinois and was swept off her feet by the dynamic Henry. Anna assumed the responsibility of raising Henry's three children, plus her own bundle of joy, Andrew, who was born in 1866. Andrew grew up to become LaCamas Postmaster in 1887 and married Grace Belding in 1888, the daughter of another early settler, Horace Belding.

In 1866, Henry Knapp donated one little acre at the edge of his property for the future construction of a small, log school building that he aptly named "Grass Valley School." It was the first school in east Clark County. Henry made this decision because his children were becoming of school age and along with the other children from Grass Valley, had no local place to attend school.

A second child was born to Henry and Anna on April 2, 1868, and he was named Henry Adelbert Knapp after his father. The 1871 Clark County Census lists the Knapp family as Henry, age forty-two and a farmer, Anna was twenty, Oliver twelve, Olive Georgina ten, Ella eight, Andrew five, and Henry A. Knapp was three.

In 1874, the first LaCamas post office named "South Plain" was established in the Henry M. Knapp farmhouse in Grass Valley, four miles northwest of LaCamas. This occurred nine years before the official town site of "LaCamas" was platted in a virgin forest in preparation to clearing the site for a paper mill and adjacent village. Henry was to be the only postmaster ever appointed to the South Plain post office.

A third child, Charles, was born to Henry and Anna in 1878, ten years after Henry Adelbert's birth. Although I could find no record of Charles' death, it is said that he died quite young after becoming an invalid. Life was difficult for pioneer children in those days with many dying from sickness or disease.

On June 15, 1878, Olive Georgiana died at the age of seventeen and was buried in the Fisher Cemetery alongside her mother and siblings who had passed before her. Olive's death left two living children of Henry and Rachel, nineteen-year-old Oliver and fifteen-year-old Ella. Oliver married Mary A. Allison and worked for many years at the paper mill. A photo in the

December 7, 1934, Camas Post shows Oliver and other employees of Crown Zellerbach Paper Company being honored for their lengthy service. Oliver died in 1939 at the age of eighty.

Rachel's youngest, Ella Knapp, lived a long, full life, marrying twice. Her first marriage was to Adam Schwoebel of Mill Plain on May 17, 1879. Their first two children were Charles born in 1880 who died before his ninth birthday and Elizabeth who arrived in 1883 but died before her fifth birthday. They had three more children, Adam, Ida, and Mildred Belle. In May 1895, there was an article in the Vancouver Independent stating that Adam had unsuccessful surgery for cancer of the stomach and passed away at the age of forty-five. Two years later, Ella married A.C. Rinehart, a widower. They had one child, Juanita. Ella died in September of 1915 and was buried next to her first husband and two children in the Fisher Cemetery. On Adam Schwoebel's headstone, it reads "One by one Earth's ties are broken

Adam Schwoebel, Ella Adelia, and Nellie Knapp
(Source: Deb Knapp)

as we see our love decay. And the hopes so fondly cherish, brighten but to pass away."

The 1880 census tells the story of Henry Monroe Knapp's family. Henry was fifty-one and a farmer, Anna was twenty-nine and "keeping house", Andrew was fourteen and Henry A. was twelve both "at school", and the baby, Charles was two. There were also three hired farm laborers, George Briggs, Humphrey Coffey, and Horatio Price.

Henry Knapp Sr. continued to be active throughout his life in community and family affairs. He was responsible for starting Mill Plain Grange No. 24 and LaCamas Grange No. 74 and was elected Deputy Master of the Oregon State Grange in 1874. In the next fifteen years he helped in the formation of many other granges and was elected to the Washington State Grange's Executive Committee on September 10, 1899. In political matters, he was present for the signing of the Washington State Constitution and to this day, his photo along with other 1889 legislators hang at the state capital in Olympia.

Henry died on July 10, 1892, when he was sixty-three years old. He was remembered by his many friends and constituents as having a flowing black beard, worthy of the fullest confidence, true to his convictions, unswerving in his integrity and upright in his dealings. At the time of his death, the Knapp homestead was a fertile 475 acres with a huge three-story home where large parties were held quite regularly with the guests staying overnight, a tradition in the old days when folks arrived by horse and buggy after a long ride. There were acres of prunes, many horses and other livestock. The ranch sold timothy hay, prunes, cream, and butter.

Two years after Henry's death, Anna married George Briggs, a former farmhand on the Knapp ranch. Their property on Prune Hill became known as "Briggs Addition." By that time all the children were grown and married, including Henry Adelbert Knapp who was twenty-six. Anna Knapp Briggs died in 1928.

Henry Jr. had grown up on the family homestead pretty much in awe of his powerful father and the many dignitaries who visited the ranch. At the age of fourteen, he was forced by his father to go to the Green Valley School along with his brother, Andrew so that they might attain an education. Henry preferred working long hours on the ranch helping to harvest the crops and doing chores. The school had recently hired a very intelligent, lovely sixteen-year-old teacher named Sarah Deborah Woolf, who boarded with the Knapp's in their large home. Henry was attracted to Miss Woolf but love sometimes has to wait because education and work took precedent over Henry's social life. But, seven years later in 1889, twenty-one-year-old Henry married twenty-four-year-old Deborah, as she was called.

The Woolf family had a pioneer legacy, arriving in Vancouver's Fruit Valley from Iowa in 1881. Her father had made the tough trip alone across the Oregon Trail to establish himself before sending for his family. His wife, Margaret Harsh Woolf packed up all of their belongings and left Iowa with her seven daughters, Lou, Maggie, Mary, Ida, Cora, Deborah and Lottie also make the dangerous trip to join her husband. Imagine a woman traveling that perilous trail for six months by covered wagon with seven young daughters. What an adventure that would be for any of us today!

Luckily, they all arrived safely, and Deborah was invited to teach at the Grass Valley School and married Henry A., three years prior to his father's death. Before he died, Henry Sr. gave each of his son's forty-five-acre parcels of the old homestead. Henry A.'s portion included the one-acre Grass Valley School site. In 1896, Henry and Deborah built a fine home on their piece of valley land. Two of their four children were born on the old homestead and two were born in their new home, most without the benefit of medication or a doctor. Claude was born in 1889, Cecil in 1894, Veva in 1896 and Hilda in 1897.

Henry Adelbert Knapp and Sarah Deborah Woolf Knapp (Source: Deb Knapp)

In 1902, Henry Jr. began to suffer from ill health and had a long sick spell. He was unable to do ranch work so he sold forty four acres to his mother, Anna Knapp Briggs, and moved to the now bustling community of LaCamas. He retained ownership of the one-acre school site. Although LaCamas was not incorporated until 1906, the town had grown so quickly because of the paper mill, employment opportunities were at a high level. Henry got a job at the mill and worked there until 1913.

Around that time a local builder named John Roffler constructed a six-bedroom two story home for the Henry's family at 637 N.E. Everett Street. The Knapp's new home was of the Queen Anne Free Classic style with Classical Revival details. It had multiple columns and broad porticos on the first level and to this day is considered a good example of the Queen Anne style.

The home was nestled in trees with outbuildings in the rear to house the animals. There was a "Roffler Rock" cast cement block wall bordering the front walkway with steps leading to the house. An early photo shows Henry and Deborah sitting out front.

After retiring from the mill in 1913, Henry was appointed Postmaster at the Camas Post Office under the Wilson Administration. He kept that position until 1921 when he was hired as a janitor at Central School located at 640 N. E. Everett Street right behind his Camas property. In 1992 the school had converted to being a nursing home called "Highland Terrace." Deborah Knapp died September 11, 1939. Through all of her seventy-one years she had been a pillar of strength to family and friends, as well as writing a diary of her early years in Iowa and her long trek across the Oregon Trail. Henry Adelbert Knapp followed Deborah in death on December 17, 1950, at the age of eighty-two.

Both of Henry's son's married Canadian ladies. Cecil wed Sophia and Claude married Winnifred Fike. Claude and Winnifred had three children, Donald, Catherine and Hugh, all born at home, and lived in a rented house at 1st and Everett. Claude became a contractor in town, taking over for John Roffler in his building of many fine homes in Camas, including the Duvall House. Early on Don and Hugh helped their father in the contracting business. Claude also constructed the main sewer system in town in 1925, a major project hand dug by forty workers. His next project was the Art Deco "Granada Theatre", after which he built the Camas-Washougal Recreation Center and the Chamber of Commerce Building. Claude died September 16, 1942, in Portland at the age of fifty-three with his wife Winnifred dying in 1961. Claude's son and grandson, Hugh and Roger Knapp became noted lawyers in Camas and were active in civic affairs. Donald was a gifted science student and attended Reed College. After graduation he held a good job at the paper mill for many years.

Cecil was a pioneer in his own right, driving the first truck and hauling freight, including liquor shipments from Portland. He was a licensed drayman for Walter Marchbank who owned the livery stable. Claude later spent forty-eight years at the paper mill. His wife Sophia suffered badly from rheumatism and was almost confined to her bed as an invalid. They went to Canada for treatment but returned to Camas in 1929 and moved into a home at 637 N.E. Everett Street for the rest of their lives. Sophia died September 16, 1966. Cecil remarried and lived well into his 90's. The house on Everett Street fell into disrepair, but early in the 1990's, new owners took over and restored the home to its' former glory.

Although Veva Knapp married Don Mitchell, Hilda Knapp never married. She became Postmaster for a short time in 1931, and passed away in 1973. In 1925 the log Grass Valley School was demolished to make room for a new, strongly built brick building that remained a thriving school for Grass Valley children until 1936 when Grass Valley School District 28 consolidated with the Camas School District. After so much history with so many children, the school was closed for good. Charles Farrell purchased the one-acre site from Henry Knapp, and then the Farrell's sold it to Paul Rainey in 1957. Although somewhat restored at that time, the building when I viewed it in 1992 stood deserted and deteriorating, perched at its' lonely watch at the corner of the field as if waiting for its' inevitable future. As it turned out, a developer bought the property and bulldozed the structure down. The developer allowed the Camas Washougal Historical Society to pick up and store the bricks from the building for a future historic monument honoring the first school in east Clark County.

Early in the 1920's, the grand old Knapp family homestead in Grass Valley burned to the ground. It was a sad day for those who remembered what a showplace it had been in the old days. Henry Monroe Knapp's fine homes, outbuildings, prune trees and plantings exist no more. In 1992 I walked the fields above the old Grass Valley School but could find nary a trace of what had been. It appeared almost like the Knapp homestead had never existed and only recorded history will prove that indeed, the events that transpired on those many acres of land were a colorful and exciting part of east Clark County history.

THE JOEL COFFEY FAMILY

Author's Preface: Anyone who takes the first step in blazing new trails deserves recognition. Homesteading property in east Clark County in the 1850's was no easy proposition. First you had to conquer the Oregon Trail and that meant six months of hard travel from St. Louis to the Oregon Territory over difficult terrain in a covered wagon with obstacles arising each day. Many did not make it and were buried along the way. When you finally reached the Columbia River, you broke down your wagon and rafted down the rushing rapids holding onto all of your worldly possessions for dear life and towing your cattle. When you finally reached what is now the Port of Camas-Washougal, you faced dense forests and hostile Indians who did not want you to take their land. Joel Coffey was a man who faced all of these odds and won. He did it with five children who mourned the recent loss of their wife and mother. "Raw Courage" would be a good description of the Coffey family who settled in Fern Prairie in 1852.

JOEL COFFEY WAS born June 15, 1789, at Wilkesboro, Tennessee, the son of Chesley Coffey and Margaret Baldwin. His noted grandparents were Chesley Coffey and Jane Cleveland who came to Virginia with Sir Walter Raleigh. The family was related to Samuel Houston of Texas.

On April 19, 1818, Joel married Sarah "Sally" Mackey, the daughter of Lewis Mackey and Elizabeth Ashbrook of Rutherford County, North Carolina. Sally was six years younger than Joel, born in 1795. Their wedding took place in Maurey County, Tennessee. During the next several years, Joel and Sally raised four sons and four daughters. Firstborn was Amanda in 1829 in Tennessee, then the family moved to Boonville, Cooper County, Missouri where the rest of the children were born. On March 15, 1831, twins Terrel and Alexander arrived. Mary Louisa came along on August 9, 1833, then Elisabeth Angeline on May 8, 1836. Three other children, William, Chesley, and Derrinda were born in Missouri, but it is not known what happened to them, there is no further record of their lives that could be found for this book.

In 1851, when Sally was fifty-six, she passed away leaving Joel with five grown children in their late teens and early twenties. The grieving family could not bear to stay in Missouri, so left their home in 1852 and traveled westward over the Oregon Trail. After a hard, rigorous trip they arrived in east Clark County.

Although there were a few settlers in the small farming community of LaCamas, most of the western migrants staked their land claims in Grass Valley to the west and Fern Prairie to the north of LaCamas. Joel Coffey received his 159.7-acre Donation Land Claim at Fern Prairie in 1854. His property was adjacent to Lewis Van Vleet's, who later became his son-in-law. Joel's twin sons, who were twenty-three at the time, also filed Donation Land Claims. Terrel received the 159.9 acres adjoining his father's and Hiram Strong's. Alexander homesteaded several parcels close by. It is said that the Coffey family, at that time, owned about every foot of land upon which the city of Camas is now located, and their boundaries extended on to Prune Hill.

In 1853, twenty-four-year-old daughter, Amanda, married New York born William Hosmer who was one year her senior. The same year her younger sister twenty-year-old Mary Louisa married Webster Abbot. On December 10, 1855, with his family safely settled in their new homes and with two of his three daughters married, Joel Coffey passed away and was buried in Fern Prairie Cemetery as one of the earliest interred there. The year of their father's death, Terrel and Alexander joined the Washington Volunteers and fought in the Indian Wars of 1855-1856. Their captain was William Strong in Company A, First Regiment.

Elisabeth A. Coffey, who was sixteen when her family settled in Fern Prairie, was a warm, lovely young woman of twenty when she met her soon-to-be husband, Lewis Van Vleet. Louis had arrived in the area on August 6, 1855, securing his homestead next to the Coffey's. He was born in New York in 1826, became well educated and through hard work and thrift, attained a sizable sum for beginning a new life in the west. He was immediately attracted to the gentle but genial Elisabeth, and she in turn, was impressed by the dashing New Yorker and so their courtship began. They were married on February 3, 1856, in Oregon City by the Reverend Harvey K. Hines. Louis and Elisabeth had seven children including Louisa V. Wright who later became the first doctor in the area. On April 12, 1905, Elisabeth Van Vleet, the youngest Coffey child, was the first to die. She was grieved by her many children, and much was written about the sunshine she brought into other's lives. Author's Note: Please see Van Vleet/Wright Family Section.

In 1856, Alexander Coffey was a very good-looking man of twenty-five with blue eyes, black hair and a dark complexion. He was a farmer by trade, but his military experience had excited him and after the Indian Wars he served in the Second Regiment of "Washington Mounted Rifles" under Captain Hamilton J. G. Maxon. When he was not involved in the military, he raised cattle and even had his own cattle brand. Such a fantastic man would have made a great catch for any young woman, but unfortunately, Alexander never married. In 1882, he was elected sheriff of Clark County. He also studied to become a civil engineer and that was a tremendous undertaking in those days. He died August 8, 1913.

In 1870, Terrel married Mary Patterson, and they moved to Pendleton, Oregon. The couple had three children, Terrel, Jr. who died at age eight months, son James born in 1855, and Earl in 1887. One of his sons became a plain river boatman, then entered the U.S. Navy and held a responsible position of "Master" of a troop transport vessel. Under the tension of his strenuous life, he broke down and became hopelessly insane in an eastern hospital. Terrel's other son was pronounced "not curable" from the ravages of Tuberculosis, known as "consumption," in those days. He went to New Mexico in the hope of regaining his health.

Terrel was financially on "easy street", but the sunset of his life had been darkened by the physical misfortune befalling his two sons. Terrel died on March 7, 1919, in Pendleton almost an octogenarian in age and was buried near his home. Camas attorney, J. D. Currie and Dr. Armstrong, were requested by a Pendleton lawyer to proceed to Portland and witness Terrel's will.

Mary Louise Coffey Abbott lived until August 18, 1922. She was buried with the rest of the family including Joel and Alexander, and except for Terrel, in the Van Vleet plot in the Fern Prairie Cemetery.

Another Camas Coffey, Henderson, was born August 14, 1860, in Missouri and was related to the Joel Coffey family. In 1888, he married Orpha, the daughter of Horace Belding, the pioneer who sold Henry Pittock the land where the paper mill and the town of Camas are now located. When the Coffey's married, Orpha Belding Hartzel was a widow with two children. Henderson and Orpha had two children of their own, Claude born in 1889 who died at the age of one year, and Edna who was born in 1891.

At the time of Claude's death, Henderson and Orpha built a Rural Gothic Vernacular, otherwise known as Western Farm Style home at the top of what is now Garfield Street. The Henderson Coffey's were original members of the little mission Catholic Church out at LaCamas Lake that was later called St. Thomas Catholic Church.

In the Camas Post "Riverview Notes" on February 2, 1891, it states that Mrs. Coffey had grip and was an "inmate" of the Prune Hill Hospital. Orpha died in 1894, the day after giving birth to a stillborn child. Henderson Coffey died on November 18, 1925. Alf Coffey planned for all the Coffey funerals.

Around the 1940's or 1950's, siding was added to the original Coffey house on 14th Avenue. The blue Coffey house was still perched at its' original location atop Garfield Street in 1992 with Bob Hartman as owner. Bob stated that the home was the original Mill Manager's house, but only history knows that fact. In any case, the Coffey's were a prominent family in Camas' history.

LEWIS VAN VLEET &
DR. LOUISA WRIGHT

Author's Preface: One of the earliest pioneers in the Fern Prairie area north of LaCamas was Lewis Van Vleet. He "trail-blazed" his way to the west in 1854 taking up a Donation Land Claim next to Joel Coffey. Lewis married Joel's daughter, Elisabeth Coffey and the two owned a large ranch, beautiful home and family cemetery on their homesteaded property. Their daughter, Louisa Van Vleet made her own mark as the first physician in the area and possibly the first woman doctor in the State of Washington. Lewis Van Vleet was a U.S. Deputy Surveyor and served in the Territorial Senate and House of Representatives. The Van Vleet family were strong and effective pioneers.

❧

L EWIS VAN VLEET was born October 21, 1826, on the family farm in the state of New York. He was the seventh of thirteen children born to Peter P. Van Vleet and Lois Swarthouse Van Vleet. Peter's roots went back to Holland when one of his ancestors immigrated to America in the early 17th Century. A farm was established between the Seneca and Cayuga Lakes and generations of Van Vleet's were born in the tiny Dutch farmhouse.

When Lewis was seven years old the family moved to the yet undeveloped region of Ridgeway, Lenawee County, Michigan, was designated as a territory. During the previous year, Peter Van Vleet had scouted out the area to determine whether there was promise for a home site in the new settlement. He was pleased with what he found and returned to New York, packed up his family and headed to Michigan. The trip was a difficult one traveling by canal at first, then using a team and wagon over barely visible trails for the rest of the way.

The new arrivals found the Michigan settlement quite primitive as compared to the sophistication of New York. They set to work clearing the land, building houses from the felled trees and planting crops. Once those tasks were completed, the families in this remote area found it necessary to do everything needed for daily life. The women spun wool for garments, prepared flax, made their own candles, and cooked in a big brick oven. The men farmed the land, raised cattle, and hunted for wild game. Traveling salesmen, tailors, and shoemakers would pass through occasionally.

Lewis attended school three miles from his home, learning reading, writing, spelling and arithmetic. He was an excellent student, demonstrating a good business head at an early age. However, he continued to live at the Michigan homestead helping his father until he was twenty-one. With five dollars in his pocket Lewis headed back to New York where he learned the cooper's trade in Oswego. He practiced his trade, carefully saving his money until he was able to attend the Oswego Academy where he majored in business.

What motivated Lewis to leave the upscale, bustling city of New York to endure a long, hard trip to the Oregon Territory can only be speculation. What we do know is that he left New York in August of 1852 and traveled to Missouri. In April of 1853, when Lewis was twenty-seven, he hitched up an ox team and joined a wagon train headed for the west. He arrived in Oregon City in August of 1853. Lewis spent a couple of years in Portland listening to tales of others filing Donation Land Claims on the Washington side of the Columbia River. Settlement started there in 1844 when David C. Parker arrived with his wife Ann and their children, John, James, George, and Eliza Ann, on the northern shores of the Columbia River about ten miles east of Portland. On October 14, 1845, Parker staked a land claim covering hundreds of acres that was recorded at the Clarke County Courthouse. It was the first claim filed there. David built a log cabin, planted potatoes, and possibly platted a township.

At the time, Lewis Van Vleet became interested in the Washington side of the Columbia River, Parker had been granted a license to establish a ferry from the head of Lady Island to above the mouth of the Washougal River. He built a small dock on the Columbia River that was initially called "Parker's Ferry." Riverboats from Portland soon made Parker's Landing a regular stop on their trips upriver. The story of Parker's success fascinated Van Vleet and on October 25, 1855, he filed a Donation Land Claim approximately two miles away from the river in an area called "Fern Prairie." A few others had already settled in the area including Joel Coffey in 1854 and James Parker on May 1, 1855. According to the Clarke County Book of Records, Van Vleet's property was located at T.2N.,R.3E. Today's location would be Highway 500, two miles north of Camas. The current address is N.E. 267th and N.E. Robinson Road.

After cutting down some towering evergreen trees on his property, Lewis built a sturdy log house and surrounded it with fruit trees. He put up a fence and considered raising cattle just as his father had done in Michigan. Van Vleet also got involved in the Yakima Indian War of 1855-1856 serving under Captain William Strong. Two of his war buddies were Terrel and Alexander Coffey, twin sons of his neighbor, Joel Coffey.

Lewis was a very good-looking man, tall and erect with piercing blue eyes and black hair. He enjoyed life to the fullest and his outgoing personality soon attracted Elisabeth Angeline

Van Vleet Lewis and Elizabeth Angeline Coffey-Van Vleet (Source: TRHM)

Coffey, youngest daughter of Joel Coffey. Elisabeth was born in Missouri on May 8, 1836, and, in 1852, she traveled with her father and siblings across the Oregon Trail. Her mother had died the year before, after raising eight children. The family settled on a Donation Land Claim in 1854 north of Parker's Landing. Lewis Van Vleet arrived a year later, fell in love with the warm and witty Elisabeth and the two married on February 3, 1856.

After marriage to Elisabeth and discharge from the war effort, Lewis became involved in politics. From 1856 until 1859 he represented Clarke County in the Territorial Senate. In 1856, he was appointed U.S. Deputy Surveyor and served in that capacity for forty years, a real record in those times and in these times. He also served as Justice of the Peace from 1857 to 1859, 1861 to 1862, and 1863 to 1864. Lewis was reappointed to the post on

November 6, 1867. In 1860, after completing his terms in the Senate, he was elected as Clarke County's representative in the Territorial House of Representatives.

Although his work as a public servant took Lewis away from home for long stretches of time, he and Elisabeth raised a family with Lois arriving Christmas Day 1856. Sadly, she died five months later on May 13, 1857. After his daughter's death, Lewis earmarked one acre on the corner of his land as the Van Vleet burial grounds and they laid little Lois to rest there. Later the burial ground was donated to the Fern Prairie Community with an agreement that the community would continue to maintain all of the graves on the site including Van Vleet's.

This agreement was still in effect in 1992 when I researched this chapter. In 1858, David Parker died and Lewis was named as administrator of Parker's estate, possibly because of his position as the U.S. Deputy Surveyor. Lewis was in the "right place at the right time." In any case, he surveyed the property and filed the papers in the courthouse in Vancouver. As payment for handling the estate and surveying Parker's holdings, Lewis ended up with a valuable parcel of land at Parker's Landing.

Disposition of the rest of Parker's property became a major disappointment to his widow, Ann Parker. During probate, it was brought to light that although Parker had filed a Donation Land Claim in 1854, it had never been legally recorded. It was twelve years after Parker's death before the claim was finally settled. In 1870, disposition of the estate was concluded with one half going to Ann and the other half to be equally divided between Parker's three sons and daughter. Through legal maneuvering, the daughter, Eliza Ann Parker Wiley, ended up with title to her mother's half of the property. By the turn of the century Eliza and her husband had lost all the land due to foreclosure for nonpayment of loans they had taken out, using the property as collateral.

God blessed the Van Vleet's with their second child on November 7, 1858, when Harriet arrived. The 1860 Clarke County Census lists Lewis as thirty-one, although he was really thirty-four and a surveyor, his wife Elisabeth as twenty-four and baby Harriet was two. Also living on the Van

Vleet farm were two laborer's, Elisabeth's brother, Terrel Coffey and Russell Burt.

In addition to his farming, surveying work and political life, Lewis took on another responsibility in the early 1860's. He became connected with the Land Department of the Northern Pacific Railroad Company appraising land grants of that corporation. In those days one could be a U. S. Surveyor and also work in a similar position for a private corporation without fear of "conflict of interest."

Lewis had been a member of the Michigan Order of the Masons since 1847 and joined the Oregon City group when he arrived in the west. So, it was no surprise when he became a charter member of the new Washington Lodge when it was formed in Vancouver in 1857. He remained active with the Masons until his death. During the years of 1861 and 1862 Lewis and Elisabeth began building a new Fern Prairie home. They had long since outgrown the rustic log home in the orchard. The new Van Vleet home was

Lewis Van Vleet (Source: TRHM)

designed on a very grand scale with only the finest materials used in its' construction. Lewis bought new equipment in Portland and had it shipped to the building site. Then trees were cut down, lumber carefully prepared with all of the work completed by hand. Windows and doors were crafted in Boston and shipped around Cape Horn. Lewis loved large warm fires, so a huge fireplace was designed by a brick mason from Vancouver. When the house was completed, it was a marvel to behold, admired by people from all over the territory. The Van Vleet's named their new home "The Oaks."

Before beginning the house project, Lewis constructed a large strongly built eastern-style barn. It was initially used for storage of materials and as a workshop for the new home. Once the house was completed, the barn reverted to farm usage. By this time Lewis not only raised dairy cattle but also many head of beef cattle. Buyers often came to look over his herd. Lewis would go to the pasture, give a beckoning call and the cattle would come running at a fast clip toward their beloved master. It appears that Lewis' kind spirit was recognized even by his devoted animals.

In the 1860's Lewis could be seen driving his ox team and wagon loaded with butter over Woodburn Hill on his way to Parker's Landing where it would be put on a steamer for Portland. He did not travel through the LaCamas area because there was very little there at the time. On October 30, 1862, a third daughter, Louisa "Lutie" Van Vleet was born at "The Oaks." She survived all childhood illnesses and grew up to be Dr. Louisa Wright, the area's first physician. A year later five-year-old Harriet died on November 16, 1863, and was buried in the family plot. It was another sad time for Lewis and Elisabeth, three daughters born and only one surviving.

However, Elisabeth was blessed with a fourth daughter, Edith, in 1865, and three years later, in 1868, Stella arrived. In 1868 Lewis helped organize and was president of the Clarke County Agricultural and Mechanical Society along with fellow founder, Silas D. Maxon. The 1871 Clarke County Census lists Lewis as forty-three, although he was forty-five and as a "hotel keeper" whatever that meant. Maybe it was because he had so many children and helpers, he felt he was running a hotel. Elisabeth was listed as thirty-four, Louisa was eight, Edith was six and Stella was three. Also living with the family was their German cook, Philip Littize.

Right after the 1871 census, Lewis Van Vleet packed up his family and left "The Oaks" moving to Kalama in Cowlitz County. It is hard to imagine why the family would leave their beautiful home and farm in Fern Prairie with two of their children buried in the cemetery there. Perhaps the move was politically motivated because it was 1872 when Lewis was elected by the citizens of Cowlitz County as their new representative to the Territorial House of Representatives.

While residing in Kalama, the Van Vleet's became the parents of two sons, Lewis on May 18, 1875, and Felix on January 11, 1878. Soon after Felix's birth the family moved again, this time to Portland, Oregon until 1882 when they returned to their farm in Fern Prairie. Edith was seventeen, Stella was fourteen, Lewis was seven and Felix was four.

I would like to return a moment to 1870 and the final disposition of David Parker's property. As stated before, Lewis was awarded Parker's Landing as his fee for administering the estate. He then platted streets and lots establishing the town of "Parkersville." In the following years, stores and homes sprung up, most facing the river. The first store was J.E.C. Durgan who ran a general store and post office. A. J. Wiley and Eliza Ann Parker Wiley, David Parker's daughter, owned a farm complex behind the town. Parker's widow, Ann, lived with her daughter and son-in-law on this farm.

Things were booming in Parkersville in 1880 when Mr. Durgan donated land for a town site at what is now Washougal. He hired Alexander McAndrew to map and plat the property and then built a residence and store building there, closing his business at Parkersville. A wharf was also constructed and soon riverboats were making regular stops in the new town of Washougal.

In the meantime, Fritz Braun had decided to build a hotel at Parkersville. When the hotel was half completed and ready for windows, Braun got into a property dispute with Van Vleet and literally picked up his hotel building and moved it to Durgan's new town. It was easier to move buildings in those days to make room for progress. Braun named his new hotel the "Commercial House." After Braun left Parkersville, a giant exodus by other store owners took place and the little city that almost was became a ghost town, much to Van Vleet's chagrin.

While the Van Vleet's were moving around, oldest daughter, Louisa "Lutie" was busy teaching school at the one-room schoolhouse in Grass Valley. Although she was only thirteen years old with an elementary education, she decided to give teaching a try in 1876. Her salary was $25.00 per month and Lutie meticulously saved toward tuition at Oregon Medical School. Her dream was to become a doctor, a profession unheard of for women in those days.

After Lutie completed her studies at Oregon Medical School she went to the University of Michigan where she earned her medical degree in 1885 at the age of twenty-three. Her first practice was in Missoula, Montana, but she soon came home to LaCamas where she set up her practice in 1887. This was four years after the formation of the LaCamas Colony Company, the building of the paper mill and the platting of sixty blocks of downtown LaCamas. Her practice was an immediate success, and she was kept busy delivering babies and tending to sick patients within a wide radius from LaCamas to Yacolt. Her mode of transportation to patient's homes was by either riding sidesaddle on her horse or by using a horse and buggy.

The new druggist in LaCamas was William Spicer and he took quite a fancy to the young, talented Dr. Van Vleet. After a courtship they married and soon had three children, Cecil, Lewis and Edith Spicer. However, their marriage did not last and Lutie found herself raising three children alone while running a medical practice. During those difficult times there was one man who offered a sympathetic shoulder for the young doctor to lean on. Jim Wright owned a livery stable at the corner of 1st and Clara Streets. His pasture included all LaCamas south of 1st Street to the river, called the Overlook Addition. Early settlers reported that when one wanted a rig and Jim was not around, they had

Dr. Louisa Van Vleet (Source: Deb Knapp)

permission to go to Jim's pasture, catch a horse, harness it and drive away. They would pay Jim when they returned. Business in those days was based on trust and honesty.

Jim was a widower with five children when he and Lutie became friends. Later he owned a drug store and was a city councilman. He loved to hunt with hunting friends Rufas Blair, Henry Karnath, and Joe Ernst, and had newspaper photos taken of his catches that included cougars, deer, and elk.

Feeling that she had made a good choice in picking out a second husband, Lutie married Jim. However, what appeared at first to be a good solution to her problems quickly turned sour. Cecil Spicer reported in a 1976 interview that Jim was an unkind stepfather to the Spicer children and his treatment of Lutie was equally harsh. As soon as he could manage it, Cecil left home to live with his grandparents, the Van Vleet's. He was able to attend the University of Washington where he received a master's degree in chemistry, then legally changed his name to Cecil Van Vleet.

In the meantime, Lutie bravely struggled with her bad marriage. She became a member of the school board and served there for twelve years. She was the first person to ignite interest in building the big, new high school erected at the top of Garfield Street. She also served as City Health Officer and was nominated for mayor. Although she did not campaign, she lost by just a single vote. In an age when men "ruled" this was indeed an accomplishment. Dr. Wright was considered as a "ministering angel" to the folks who knew and loved her because of her kindly, sympathetic manner. As a citizen she was always on the side of progress and worked hard for the betterment of the community, materially, intellectually, and morally.

Around 1890, Louisa bought the Parkersville property from her father and had a house moved to that location. She connected the house to Ann Parker's old home and the combination became a very comfortable abode.

Lewis Van Vleet, Jr. married Olive Clark of Camas in 1901. They lived in Fern Prairie for five years, then moved to Portland where they had a son, Lewis III in 1906. Lewis III died an early death in 1936, at age thirty, and his mother, Olive, died in 1941. Lewis Jr. lived to be eighty-two, passing away in 1957.

Elisabeth Angeline Van Vleet, the mother of the clan, died in Portland April 8, 1905, and was buried in the family plot alongside her deceased children. She was fondly remembered for her genial smile, compassion, humor and wit. Lewis Jr. penned a beautiful poem dedicated to his mother at her funeral. Five years later on April 15, 1910, Lewis Van Vleet Sr. followed his wife in death. The funeral service for this remarkable pioneer was held at the Methodist Church in Camas. Then a solemn procession crossed the quiet countryside to the old Van Vleet Cemetery where he was laid to rest beside his wife. Lewis Van Vleet left a legacy of fifty-seven years devoted to the development of the western United States.

In 1912, Louisa retired from her medical practice at the age of fifty years and moved permanently into her home at Parker's Landing. She loved the big house that looked out onto the Columbia River. That same year her sister Edith died at the age of forty-seven. She had never married. Although Stella Van Vleet Freeman lived her life in Portland, she was well known by Camas' residents.

On Memorial Day 1913, Jim Wright was harnessing up the horse to go to the Camas Cemetery with Louisa and her daughter. Louisa emerged from her house wearing a white apron that apparently frightened the horse who bolted and kicked Louisa under her chin, breaking her neck. The blow killed Dr. Wright, and her funeral was held at her home in Parker's Landing. It was attended by many folks in the area including Native Americans who came in canoes. She was buried in Fern Prairie Cemetery within sight of her birthplace and near the heart of the region where she had served so well. Louisa was lovingly eulogized in the county's leading newspapers. Jim Wright lived until 1945 when he died at the age of eighty-two and was buried in the Camas Cemetery.

Cecil Van Vleet returned to Camas for his mother's funeral decided to take up residence at his mother's Parker's Landing home. He operated a dairy farm at that location during the 1920's and 30's. He was married for thirty years to Elsie Moore and after she died, he married Mary Van Vleet in 1953. He was a teacher at schools in Oregon, Washington, and California for thirty years.

In 1919, Felix Van Vleet, Dr. Wright's brother, was shot in California by a police officer while trying to break up an argument. He was also buried in the Van Vleet family plot. One of the Van Vleet grandchildren, Alfred, was killed in an airplane accident at Bremerton, Washington in 1929.

The old Van Vleet homestead in Fern Prairie was owned by the Oliver Langford family from the 1920's to 1930's when it burned to the ground. The property was later owned by W. E. Schmitt. Cecil Van Vleet sold the Parkersville property in the 1970's to the Port of Camas-Washougal with the stipulation that he and Mary could live there if they wished. Cecil died December 4, 1977, and Mary moved to Vancouver shortly afterwards. She was quoted in a 1978 article as saying, "Cecil and I talked about donating the land to the people for public use as a park, but we could not afford to just give it away. Still, I hope that the Parkersville land will be used as some sort of park. "

Dr. Wright's historic Parkersville home stood until 1978 when Port officials worried that its' deteriorated condition constituted a safety hazard. They held off the bulldozers at that time because local historians petitioned to save the historic building, but the home mysteriously burnt down sometime later.

Today the site of Parker's Landing is on the National Register of Historic Places. The land has been developed as a park by concerned local citizens and the Port of Camas-Washougal, complete with rose gardens, a gazebo and a kiosk with panels relating to the history of the site. There is also a brick Van Vleet Plaza encased in the old footprint of the house. The park proudly sits as a fitting memorial to both David Parker and the Van Vleet family.

HORACE BELDING &
D. MONTGOMERY PAYNE

Author's Preface: Looking through old land records, it is interesting to note that in 1864 after Hamilton J. G. Maxon and his wife, Arabella received Donation Land Grant #47 from Abraham Lincoln for 640 acres, several transactions took place before the land passed in 1882 to Horace Belding. The land covered all of downtown Camas and the mill site. A scant year later, Horace sold the property to the LaCamas Colony Company and the rest is history. Horace was a thrice-married man with six daughters, a deceased son, and a stepson. His daughters were to marry into other noted pioneer families including the Payne's, the Marchbank's, the Coffey's and the Knapp's. This story relates how his stepson's life ended in a terrible and public manner. But, most of all, this chapter is a classic example of several early pioneer families, how they met, married and shared common goals in east Clark County.

❧

BORN MARCH 16, 1828, to parents Ezekial Belding and Susan Choate in Oppenheim, New York, Horace Belding came to the little fledgling community of LaCamas in 1882 from Story County, Iowa. Horace was fifty-four years old and a widower from his first marriage to Ohio born Mary Davis who died in 1871 at the age of thirty-five. Her death left Horace responsible for raising nine-year-old Orpha Rosana, eight-year-old Susan Nina, and three-year-old twins, Julia Etta and Thomas.

After Mary's death, Horace married a Missouri woman named Mrs. Bayly who had a son, Lester born in 1872. In November of 1875, the Belding's had a daughter, Lena or "Linnie" as she was called. In 1879 Orpha Rosana, who was seventeen, married Singleton R. Hartzel and moved to Kentucky where they had a daughter, Vera Olive. In 1880 the second Mrs. Belding passed away as did one of the twins, twelve-year-old Thomas.

That same year, grief-stricken Horace left Iowa with his surviving children and stepson and headed for California where opportunities seemed brighter, and memories could dim. The Hartzel's decided to accompany the Belding family and a whole lot of them left by train westward to California. After two years in California, the families took the steamer to Portland, Oregon. When they arrived, Horace was told about some choice land for sale in a little community called LaCamas on the Washington side of the Columbia River, ten miles east of Portland. He promptly bought over six hundred acres from Portland residents, Judge B.F. Dennison and his wife, Hattie, on November 8, 1882, and moved all of his family, including the Hartzel's to LaCamas.

Although Horace had been a schoolteacher in New York, his occupation in Iowa and LaCamas was that of a farmer. He fully intended to farm his 600 plus acres and built his first home, a modest wooden structure at the corner of 1st and Columbia within close proximity to the Columbia River. The rich land seemed ideal for farming. Later in 1882, Horace met and married the third Mrs. Belding, twenty-seven-year-old Nancy Murray, a woman half his age.

Early in 1883, D. H. Stearns representing the newly organized LaCamas Colony Company, approached the Belding's offering to purchase their 600 plus acres including the home site. Henry Pittock, the primary owner of the LaCamas Colony Company felt the land was a perfect location for his future paper mill and proposed town. The Columbia River was nearby for shipping, and water-power could be generated from the three lakes that sat on a plateau above the town and a creek that ran from the lakes to the river. Realizing they could make a tidy profit from the transaction, Horace and Nancy agreed to sell with the deal closing May 12, 1883. The selling price for 641.60 acres was $6,416.00 or $10.00 per acre. Part of the agreement was that the Belding's could occupy their home for one year and remove any timber that had already been cut.

The Belding's were considered well-to-do by folks in the farming community because of the profit they had made on the land sale. They were able to complete a lovely, new home by 1887 at 2nd and Burton Street, just southeast of the mill. Their new residence was quite pretentious for those days, a Western Farm Style two-story dwelling with a white picket fence surrounding a yard filled with flowers. At that time Julia was nineteen, Lester fifteen and Linnie was twelve. Lo and behold, when Horace was sixty-two, he and Nancy became the parents of a daughter, Effie Virginia and on Christmas Day 1892, Myrtle Belding was born.

Horace's oldest daughter, Orpha became a widow when her husband, Singleton Hartzel died sometime during 1887 or 1888. With two young children to support, eight-year-old Vera Olive and four-year-old Bertha Violet, Orpha wasted no time in marrying Henderson Coffey who was related to the Fern Prairie Coffey family. Henderson and Orpha built a home at the top of Garfield Street that was still standing in 1992. They had a son, Claude in 1889 who died one year later and a daughter, Edna was born in 1891. After giving birth to a stillborn child in 1894, Orpha passed away. Early deaths were often the norm with pioneer families.

In 1883, when Horace sold his land to Henry Pittock, Horace's daughter, Susan "Nina" Belding was twenty years old and teaching school in Grass Valley, an area to the northwest of LaCamas. Grass Valley had been settled in the 1850's and was considered more "civilized" than the new paper mill town. Homes were large and spacious, often with three stories and had

Susan "Nina" Belding-Payne (Source Post-Record)

numerous outbuildings including large barns and vast planted areas with rows of fruit trees. Neighbors often got together for parties and overnight stays.

Early Washington legislator, Henry Monroe Knapp, took a land claim in 1853 and owned one of the largest ranches mentioned above. In 1866, he donated one acre at the corner of his property for a small, one-room log schoolhouse. Nina Belding took over as schoolmarm in 1882, following in her father's footsteps as an educator. Teaching meant moving from the family home in LaCamas to Grass Valley, but any regret she felt soon turned to joy when she met the brother of one of her students, who was to be her future husband. Twenty-three-year-old William Henry Payne was the son of homesteader D. Montgomery Payne who owned a large parcel of land northwest of the Knapp property.

D. Montgomery Payne was another pioneer critical of the early development of east Clarke County. He began his life on February 10, 1823, in Tennessee, the son of John Payne and Julina Spurr, natives of Virginia. His older brother Almon was born in 1820 and when they were quite young, their parents moved to Vigo County, Indiana. Almon married seventeen-year-old Minerva Bennett in Hancock County, Illinois on August 28, 1848. Three years later on February 29, 1851, Montgomery married twenty-two-year-old Indiana native, Sarah "Louisa" Barmore. Almon and Minerva had a daughter in 1851 and named her Julina after Almon's mother.

Montgomery and Almon began to hear stories about adventure in the Oregon Territory and although both were newly married, the close-knit brothers decided to migrate westward in 1852. Both families experienced the hardships of six months on the Oregon Trail with their wagondrawn ox team, but finally reached their goal of the Cascades. They rafted down the Columbia River and landed on the north bank in east Clarke County. Like so many others they were worried about the Indian Wars in Washington so at that time the Payne brothers felt Oregon was a safer place. Almon purchased land on Government Island in 1853 and Montgomery's family moved to Lane County, Oregon in 1854.

When the Military Bounty Land Act of March 3, 1855 came into being, Almon applied for 109 acres in Clarke County receiving Warrant #48098. He was also awarded other property in Clarke County although he still lived in Oregon. His acreage was part of the tranquil, fertile Grass Valley, so named because it was conducive to the raising of timothy grass. Almon continued to live in Oregon where all of their remaining children were born, Mary Caroline in 1855, Rufus in 1857, Harriet in 1861 and Minerva Jane in 1864.

During the same period, Montgomery and Sarah Louise raised a family of four in Lane County, Oregon near Cheshire at Franklin Post Office. John L.

Payne was born in 1856, followed by William Henry in 1858, Harriet in 1860 and Sarah Jane in 1862. When the Indian Wars ended in 1865, all the Payne's moved to their properties in Clarke County. Montgomery attained Homestead #816 that encompassed 160 acres in Grass Valley close to Almon's property and purchased additional land in the LaCamas area. Frank Edgar Payne was born in September 1869. The 1870 Clarke County Census shows forty-eight-year-old Montgomery, a farmer, thirty-eight-year-old Sarah, thirteen-year-old John, twelve-year-old William, eight-year-old Sarah Jane and ten-month-old Frank. Dennis Wylie was listed as a farm laborer.

It was common in those days for the daughters of pioneer settlers to marry at a very young age. Such was the case of Montgomery's two daughters with fifteen-year-old Harriet marrying William L. Pangburn in 1875 and seventeen-year-old Sarah Jane marrying William

Members of the Payne family circa 1907 (Source The Post-Record)

Horn in 1879. However, Sarah did not stop there. She later had two more husbands, William Brackett, and Jack Rowell. My research did not determine whether all her husbands expired naturally or met with some dire fate.

While Montgomery's daughters seemed to be living happy lives, Almon's children did not fare so well except for Mary Caroline who married John Wagonblast in 1873, and Minerva Jane who married Sydney Stamp in 1879 at the age of fifteen. Seventeen-year-old Rufus died in 1874, fifteen-year-old Harriet died in 1876 and Julina who was married to Jonathan Helterbrand, died in 1876 at age twenty-five, leaving five small children behind. All were buried in the Fisher Cemetery.

Almon Payne passed away at his Clarke County home on March 9, 1877, and was interred next to his three deceased children in the family plot at the Fisher Cemetery. He left his estate to his widow Minerva, who was the executor of his will. When Minerva died, the estate was to be split three ways between their surviving two daughters and Almon's brother Montgomery.

Montgomery was to hold his one-third in trust for the five children of Julina Helterbrand.

The next Clarke County Census in 1880 showed D. Montgomery Payne, a farmer at fifty-five, Sarah "keeping house" at forty-eight, John a farmer at twenty-two, William Henry Payne a farmer at twenty-one and Frank, eleven and "at school."

The fates of the Payne and Belding families were soon to intertwine. Nina Susan Belding began to teach school in 1882 at the Grass Valley School. With his brother Frank attending the school, William Henry Payne was destined to meet the lovely new schoolteacher, and promptly fell in love. The courtship period began.

Montgomery and Sarah's oldest son, John, had always been of a sickly nature. On June 16, 1883, he passed away at the age of twenty-seven. His headstone at the Fisher Cemetery reads "Afflictions sore for years I bore, physicians were in vain, at length God pleased to give me ease and free me from my pain."

Although still in mourning for his older brother, William Payne married Nina Belding one month after John's funeral on July 28, 1883. They moved onto a part of the homestead property and began to raise a family. Nettie Dell was born in 1884, Mae in 1887, Henry Lewis in 1889 and Elzie in 1894. In 1893 William's surviving brother, Frank Edgar married Mary Beseler. They had four children, Hazel, Esther, Wesley and John.

Horace Belding's niece, Grace Belding came to visit her cousin, Nina at the Grass Valley farm. She was introduced to the very handsome, Andrew Knapp, oldest son of Henry Monroe Knapp and Anna Huffman Knapp and what followed was another marriage on July 5, 1888.

One of the most successful businessmen in LaCamas was Walter Marchbank who arrived in town from Canada. He owned a livery stable and delivery business that was heavily involved in construction of the new city streets, and Walter later became a county commissioner. In 1889, Julia Belding, who lived with her parents in the family home at 2nd and Burton Streets, married Mr. Marchbank. The Marchbank's had six children, Frank in 1890, Bessie in 1892, William in 1894, Howard in 1898, Mabel in 1901 and

Edward "Ted" in 1908. In the 1890's the Marchbank's bought the elegant, eight-room Cowan House up on the hill to house their growing family. They added a porch, columns, and Roffler Rock in the early 1890's and the place was considered a modern showplace.

Lena "Linnie" Belding became the wife of Edward Norene on September 25, 1894. Linnie and her brother, Lester Bayly Belding had always been close, growing up with fond memories of the same mother. Linnie asked Lester to stand up for her as a witness to the wedding. Linnie and Edward had four children, Ruby, Noble, Lester who was named after his uncle, and Russell.

In 1895, Lester courted and married Sylvie Maud McCrosky, the daughter of Lemuel McCrosky. However, their marriage turned out to be a stormy one with Sylvie often seeking refuge from a violent Lester at relatives' homes. Today, this type of problem is called "domestic violence." Finally, in 1902, seven years after their marriage, Lester went crazy, murdering Sylvie, her mother, and another man, Frank Woodard in a fit of rage. He also seriously injured Sylvie's father. The multiple murders made front page headlines in the Portland Oregonian. A later story about Lester's execution in the March 28, 1903, Oregonian states "Belding's mother and father passed away years before and his only relative in this part of the country was his sister, Mrs. Ed Norene, referring of course to Lena. The story went on to say, "Belding's father at one time owned nearly all of the original town site of LaCamas."

Fortunately, as the article stated, Horace Belding did not live to experience the tragedy of the triple murders and his son's execution. He died of heart disease at age sixty-seven on April 29, 1895, seven months after celebrating Lena's wedding. The legacy he left besides three well married daughters, was his famous "land sale" to the LaCamas Colony Company. After Horace's death, his widow Nancy married Fred Tallman and moved away with her two daughters.

The old Belding home at 2nd and Burton was sold to the newly arrived James Farrell family who lived there for many years. There is a 1906 photograph of the Farrell family proudly grouped outside their lovely home.

The house was demolished when the Copeland Lumber Company built a new store at that location in the 1930's.

On September 13, 1899, D. Montgomery Payne died of heart failure at his home in Grass Valley. Dr. Louisa Wright was his attending physician. Montgomery had cleared the virgin land of Grass Valley, built his home, raised his family and in doing so, had reached the goal he set when he left Indiana. Sarah Payne out-lived her husband, Montgomery, by eleven years and was buried in the Fisher Cemetery next to her husband when she died.

Montgomery's surviving sons, William and Frank inherited a good portion of their father's land in Grass Valley. In 1916, William and Nina built a new home on their land and lived there until May 23, 1927 when they sold it with all their acreage to George and Katrina Bafus for $5000.00 For an additional $10.00 they included one Dodge touring car, one grey horse, one black cow, two wagons, one set of heavy harness except collars, one half set of driving harness, one grain drill, two plows, two harrows, one mowing machine, one disk, one old hay rake, one grindstone, one spraying outfit and all growing crops. I would venture to say that the Bafus family got a "real deal" from the Payne's. In 1992, Reuben Bafus still owned the property with the address of 3122 N. W. Lake Road. Frank's property had a 1992 address of 22821 S.E. 20th Street and was owned by Conrad Morashe. The year after William Payne sold his property to the Bafus family he died. Nina moved to Camas living alone at her 835 N.E. 4th Street home.

Frank Payne's son, Wesley got into trouble with the law during prohibition days by operating an illegal still and making "prune brandy" among other delights. He married Harriet Duman whose brother, Edgar Duman lived in Vancouver in 1992. Harriet Duman Payne was noted in the September 14, 1934, Camas Post article as winning a prize during a card party at the Fern Prairie Grange Hall. A 1932 article stated that Nina's son, Elzie Payne, sold his home on Martha Street to C. L. Johnson.

In 1934, Nina Belding Payne was interviewed for a December 7th Camas Post article in which she reminisced about life during the early days of LaCamas including when she taught school in Grass Valley. Her counterpart in LaCamas was Elizabeth MacMaster who taught in a "shack" on 3rd Street.

Nina stated that the hardest part of living in early Camas was getting supplies up and down the river. She said it was also difficult negotiating the muddy streets with all the stray livestock running to and fro. Nina died in 1943 and was buried next to her husband in the Fisher Cemetery. Their graves are marked with a magnificent marble headstone.

Walter Marchbank passed away in 1936, and Julia Belding Marchbank in 1955, after raising their six children. Walter and Julia are buried at the Park Hill Cemetery in Vancouver.

So, there you have it. Four pioneer families: The Belding's, Payne's, Coffey's and Marchbank's who by intermarrying so long ago, established a solid foundation for the Camas Community.

DREAMS OF LIFE IN A NEW LAND

THE FORMATION OF THE PAPER MILL

HENRY PITTOCK &
FRED LEADBETTER

Author's Preface: No story of Camas would be complete without including the LaCamas Colony Company's illustrious founder, Henry Lewis Pittock and his son-in-law early Portland entrepreneur, Fred Leadbetter. Pittock was a self-made man who arrived in Oregon penniless and without a job. Where he went from there is a tribute to his character and determination. He possessed the same fine qualities that were so typical of other LaCamas pioneers who heeded the call of a new paper mill and converged on the little town. Leadbetter charted a new course for the mill, taking it and the town through difficult times to success in the 20th Century. Both men deserve recognition for their fine achievements.

❧

Henry Lewis Pittock's story begins in London, England where he was born on March 1, 1836, the third oldest of eight children. His parents were Frederick and Susanna Bonner Pittock, both from Kent County, England. While still a young man Frederick immigrated with his parents to America but returned to England to learn the printer's trade, marry Susanna and begin a family.

In 1839, when Henry was three, his parents moved their family permanently to Pittsburg, Pennsylvania where Frederick began a lifetime of work in the printing business. Frederick and Susanna were of considerable means and able to afford a good education for their children, including Henry. One of his brothers became successful as founder of the Pittsburg Leader newspaper. Henry graduated from a preparatory school for the University of Western Pennsylvania and began work in his father's print shop. However, he was drawn to the west coast by letters written to the Pittsburg paper from members of a missionary colony in Oregon. For that reason, seventeen-year-old Henry and his brother Robert joined a wagon train heading west in 1853.

The arduous trip to Oregon took six months to complete and the two brothers arrived at their destination in October with Robert settling in Eugene and Henry going on to Portland. When Henry arrived in Portland, he had nary a penny to his name.

There is an adage that "once newspaper ink gets in one's blood it stays there forever" and it appears that Henry was no exception. Although he was broke and offered a job as a bartender in a Portland hotel, he did not hesitate to refuse the offer of employment. Henry was hopelessly hooked on the printing trade and was determined to get a job at one of the newspapers in town. Through persistence, Henry was finally hired as a printing assistant by

Henry L. Pittock (Source Find a Grave)

Thomas Jefferson Dryer who owned the Weekly Oregonian. The deal offered Henry was free board and room plus clothing in exchange for six months of service. Henry proved his worth and knowledge of the industry ten-fold and six months later Dryer renewed his contract, put him on salary and before long, Henry attained the title of Journeyman Printer.

Mr. Dryer was a busy man involved in a variety of outside interests and soon left the responsibility of getting out the paper to his able assistant. Henry never failed to meet the deadlines and was promoted to Business Manager of the Weekly Oregonian. In 1860 Dryer sold the newspaper to Pittock who at that time was twenty-five years old.

As the new owner/publisher of the Weekly Oregonian, Henry was determined to make the newspaper daily even though competition in Portland was fierce with three other dailies already being published. That did not deter Henry from purchasing a cylinder press in San Francisco and arranging for a news service out of Yreka, California. The first daily

Oregonian was published on February 4, 1861, and even though he suffered some financial ups and downs, Henry soon eliminated the competition. His success was due to always getting the paper out regardless of flood or fire and producing a quality product at the same time.

In 1852, one year before Henry Pittock made the trip from Pittsburg to Portland, seven-year-old Georgiana Martin Burton traveled the Oregon Trail with her parents, the E.M. Burtons. Although Georgiana was born in Missouri, the family journeyed from their most recent home in Keokuk, Iowa. Like so many others the Burtons had heard about opportunities in the west and unlike Pittock who had arrived broke, Mr. Burton had plentiful personal finances to support him upon his arrival in Oregon. Mr. Burton promptly built a flour mill in Milwaukie and became a well-known building contractor and prominent businessman in Portland.

With Henry's visibility as the Oregonian's successful new owner, it was inevitable that he would meet Mr. Burton within the Portland business community. That meeting would eventually lead to an introduction to Burton's daughter, Georgiana, who was growing into a lovely young lady. A courtship began and in 1860 twenty-five-year-old Henry married fifteen-year-old Georgiana. Although there was ten years difference in their ages, their wedded bliss was to last fifty-eight years and result in six children and fourteen grandchildren.

Henry and Georgiana were both community minded people. Georgiana helped found the Ladies Relief Society in 1867 and was active with the Woman's Union and the Martha Washington Home for single, working women. She loved to garden and tended to her flowers and roses with great care. Henry also loved the outdoors, often riding his horse in the Rose Festival parade and was one of the first to climb Mt. Hood. During that climb he made his famous quote of "the man who sits down never reaches the top." Henry was seldom ever caught sitting. Besides running his newspaper, Henry was deeply involved in any and all movements for bettering Portland's growth and development. He was also elected Grand Senior Steward for the Mason's in the State of Oregon.

Henry's fortunes continued to increase with the popularity of the daily Oregonian and in 1873 he incorporated his paper under the name of the

Oregonian Publishing Company. Other opportunities presented themselves and he diversified his business interests by investing in banking, railroads, steamboats, sheep ranching, silver mining and most importantly to LaCamas, investing in the pulp and paper industry.

According to the late A. O. Hathaway who was an old timer and pioneer, local lore relates that "Henry Pittock was out in a rowboat on LaCamas Lake, leaned over the side, looked at the water, and said, this would be a great place for a paper mill." Whether this is true or not, only history knows. But what is true is that Pittock and W.W. Buck had built and were operating a paper mill at Park Place in 1867 that was supplying the Oregon City Enterprise and the Oregonian with paper. However, because the Oregonian's circulation had increased so rapidly due to its' popularity, Henry needed a new source for his

Henry L Pittock (Source TRHM)

paper. He had only to look ten miles east to the north shore of the Columbia River to find his ideal location. This bountiful area was a small farming community of pioneers called LaCamas in east Clarke County. The three lakes and sloping land to the river seemed perfect for Pittock's plans.

Since the early 1850's, farmers like Henry Monroe Knapp and D. Montgomery Payne had homesteaded and farmed large acreages in Grass Valley to the north and west of the LaCamas site. One of the few settlers to purchase property in LaCamas was Horace Belding who had recently purchased 600 plus acres of prime riverfront land from Judge Dennison of Portland. Belding intended to farm the land and built a small wooden house where he settled his family in 1882.

Undaunted by the farms already established in early LaCamas, Henry Pittock set about forming the LaCamas Colony Company. On May 12, 1883, naming himself as president and D. H. Stearns as manager. Stearns had entered negotiations with Belding and others to purchase 2,600 acres of land in the area to find a town or colony and build a paper mill. He wanted to make use of the tremendous waterpower available that included the three lakes, LaCamas Creek, the land fronting both sides of the creek, and the Columbia River. The sales were made and at the direction of Stern's, a series of dams were built, and a 7,000-foot aqueduct was dug by Chinese workers to bring the waterpower from the lakes to the mill site for purposes of powering the paper machines.

The mill site was all trees, many had been uprooted in the big storm of 1876. A crew was hired to clear the land and under the supervision of architect S. P. Millard, three paper mill buildings were constructed close to the Columbia River. A sawmill was also built capable of cutting 30,000 board feet in one day.

Articles of Incorporation were filed in Portland in 1884, naming the new LaCamas paper mill business "The Columbia River Paper Company." Pittock was president and J. K. Gill, a Portland businessman, was vice president. William Lewthwaite was an officer in the corporation as well as the mill's superintendent.

While all of the paper mill activity was going on, the new town of LaCamas was being cleared of timber, platted, and laid out in blocks, lots and streets. Then sixty blocks of business and housing lots were offered for sale to the influx of early pioneers coming to work in the paper mill. It was reported that anyone of modest means could afford to buy a deed and start a business. One of the first to arrive was Aeneas MacMaster from Scotland via Canada. He opened a two-story wooden general store in 1883, and others quickly followed.

By 1885, the downtown area was bustling with three general stores, a drug store, a meat market, two hotels, a lodge and meeting hall and a dance pavilion. The largest building in town was a four-story flour mill built by O.C. Grove that added to the town's industry. Two church groups and a one-room school were part of the new community. Modest style homes were springing up downtown and in Cowan's Addition located on the first bench above the town. The new sawmill was straining to provide all the lumber needed for the new construction.

Although there were a few early settlers out by the lakes in small wooden houses, it was D. H. Stearns who decided to build a large villa on sixty-four acres on the north shore of LaCamas Lake. It was a fancy two-story home decorated with gingerbread trim located up on a hill overlooking the pristine water. Stearns and his bride, Clara Duniway Stearns of a prestigious Portland family, held large parties and gatherings at the villa for important out of town guests. Stearns named a downtown street "Clara Street" after his wife.

The Columbia River Paper Company and the town of LaCamas experienced a major setback in 1886, when a disastrous fire destroyed the paper mill and a large amount of finished paper. Damage was estimated at $95,000, a goodly sum in those days. Henry Pittock and his partners took the misfortune in stride, bought new, modern equipment, and rapidly rebuilt the mill. On May 3, 1888, the mill was back in operation, hiring a record number of workers and producing more paper than ever before.

The tide turned during the depression years of the 1890's when the Columbia River Paper Company suffered major financial woes that extended over a lengthy period. At one bleak point during

Fredrich "Fred" Leadbetter (Source Find a Grave)

these sinister years, the company was unable to pay their workers for several months and rumors spread that the company was nearing bankruptcy.

During the mill's darkest days, a new energized figure came on the scene. Fred Leadbetter, who had married Henry Pittock's daughter, Carolyn, leased the Columbia River Paper Mill. Leadbetter was a very sharp financial wizard who began buying bonds at ten cents on the dollar from the original bond holders who were more than willing to sell. He also bought the land around the mill and the lake for a minimal price. He added a sulphite mill and with his "go-getter" personality it wasn't long until his presence was felt in the industry. His actions lifted the Columbia River Paper Company out of its' financial mess, and made the paper mill the world's largest pulp and paper operation of its kind.

Although Fred and Carolyn's main home was in Portland, they built a small wooden summer home on LaCamas Lake's west shore in the late 1800's that looked northeast across the lake toward Stearn's villa.

Henry Pittock's son, Frederick, married Bertha Leadbetter in 1902 further entwining the two families. Bertha and Fred were the children of Charles and Anne Leadbetter. As a wedding present to the newlyweds, Henry hired a contractor to construct an elegant Queen Anne Victorian home just below and to the south of Stearn's villa. The two and a half story home had a three-story circular bay capped by a conical roof. The classic home was completed in 1903 and was named "Lakeside." It stands in the same location today as a National Historic site. However, in 1903 the eleven-room house on its' ninety-six acres was considered by the Pittock's as a "farmhouse." Frederick farmed the estate, raised dairy cattle and vegetables, built a chicken coop and planted a prune orchard. Fred and Bertha had five children and in 1919 moved back to Portland to give their children a more refined education that LaCamas offered. Anne's parents, Charles and Anne Leadbetter also owned a parcel of land next to the Pittock property that they called "Pomaria."

The Columbia River Paper Company of Camas and the Crown Paper Company of West Linn, Oregon merged in 1905 to form Crown Columbia Paper Company. With the merger, the Camas mill expanded and by 1907 had completed construction of a bag factory on the site.

In 1906, the Pittock Leadbetter families combined to build a 2000 sq. ft. bungalow style home that overlooked the town of LaCamas or Camas as it may have then been called. The house was of wood frame construction and had many of the expensive interior qualities that appeared in finer Portland homes. Originally the home was used by the two families as a summer residence, but it was later utilized by traveling dignitaries visiting the paper mill.

In the January 25, 1908, edition of the Camas Post there was a story titled "New Mill Here." The article stated "It has been rumored that Pittock and

Leadbetter's big lumber mill will be moved from Vancouver to Camas. Those in position to know have not confirmed the rumor but it is not to be expected that they will until everything is in readiness to make the change."

Around 1910, Pittock-Leadbetter bought the Camas water system from another pioneer, A.D. McKever, who operated his water towers close to Round Lake, one of the three Camas lakes. They used his facilities for two years and then developed their own system across the road from the lake slough, building the Butler Reservoir and installing a six-inch water line. Leadbetter later sold this system to the City of Camas in 1923.

With the advent of World War I, Fred Leadbetter volunteered for duty and became a captain whose responsibility was supplying spruce for fighter planes. As was his normal course of action, Fred threw himself into the war effort and left his managers to run his much-loved mill while he was away.

The Henry Pittock's began to design and build a huge mansion around 1909 that was nestled high in the northwest Portland hills overlooking the city of Portland. It took five years to complete, and the finished estate sported a greenhouse and an Italiante gate lodge and servant's quarters. The Pittock's moved into their new imposing home in 1914 when Georgiana was seventy and Henry seventy-nine. The residents of Portland were in awe of the beautiful architecture and modern conveniences of the new residence.

Also, in 1914, the Crown Columbia Paper Company merged with Willamette Pulp and Paper from Oregon, thus becoming Crown Willamette Paper Company. Business continued to flourish.

On June 12, 1918, Georgiana Pittock died at the age of seventy-three, leaving Henry and five grown children behind. A scant seven months later, on January 27, 1919, Henry followed her in death. It was a tremendous loss for friends, relatives, and the community. The couple continues to be remembered for their kindness, quiet reserve, compassionate nature and contributions to the city and state.

Fred Leadbetter returned from World War I, and early in the 1920's and made the decision to build a decent summer retreat at LaCamas Lake. He contracted local woodworker, Severt Ostenson to build a rustic log house that became known as "Fern Lodge." With their English lifestyle, the Leadbetter's kept a stable full of Arabian horses and played polo on their private polo field. There was a variety of water sports, and they hosted afternoon teas for the many distinguished guests who came to visit. A chauffeur driven limousine would deliver invited visitors to Fern Lodge for weekends of relaxation and fun.

In 1925, Leadbetter was approached by Crown Willamette to sell his mill and certain other lands. The price they offered was ridiculously low, but he accepted the offer, retaining those properties that surrounded the Pittock and Leadbetter estates. What he did not sell to Crown Willamette was the water rights and a paper mill is worthless without a large supply of water. When the CW officials realized that he had not sold them the water rights necessary to their operation they asked what his price would be. Leadbetter then gave them a very high sale price. When they scoffed at his sale price, he doubled the price. When they claimed he was out of his mind, he tripled the price. Shortly thereafter, Leadbetter sold his water rights at a very handsome profit. He retained one sixth of ownership in Crown Willamette and felt he was financially set for life.

In 1928, Crown Willamette merged with Zellerbach Paper Company and this marriage began Crown Zellerbach Corporation, a company that survived for decades spending millions of dollars in mill expansion and improvements. The new corporation took over more of the western end of the Camas downtown area in its growth plans including MacMaster's store which became the Perfection Twine company.

In the meantime, Fred Leadbetter was leading a life of leisure and travel using his profits from the sale of the Camas mill and water system. However, after a period he became bored with his lifestyle and began to buy paper mills in other locations. The stock market crash of 1929 caught Leadbetter off balance and although he lost a great deal of money, he somehow kept his mills afloat. He wisely invested in property in Las Vegas that later brought him great rewards. With this new financial windfall, Fred and Bertha built another summer home in British Columbia they called "Clowhom Lodge."

As the years went by, the Leadbetter's spent less and less time in Camas enjoying instead summers in British Columbia and winter vacations in

California and Arizona. Eventually Fern Lodge deteriorated from lack of use and care. Wood rot began to eat away at the log structure, the roof caved in, and the walls crumbled. In 1976, one of Leadbetter's daughters, Mrs. Nels Teren, had the house torn down due to vandalism. In April 1977, she sold her remaining 250 acres to the Shipler Land Company of Salem, Oregon after offering it to the City of Camas and Clark County at a very low price. Shipler bought the property for 2.3 million dollars and proceeded to have one of his companies, Shipler Logging Company, log of the valuable stand of timber. Shipler burned what remained of the lodge except for the three-story chimney that stood like a beacon of times past. And soon even the chimney was gone, bulldozed into a pile of rubble to make room for a housing development.

Lakeside and the property surrounding it remained in the Pittock-Leadbetter family as of 1992. This beautiful old home looks out to the eastern shores of LaCamas Lake, a symbol of a past era. Unfortunately, the view from Lakeside's windows is no longer shining clear water, lush forests, and rustic friendly Fern Lodge. Instead, the view is a bare slope with imposing modern homes and troubled murky waters.

In the spring of 1985, in a series of corporate maneuvers, Crown Zellerbach became the James River Corporation. In 1992, James River continued as a powerful but positive influence in the City of Camas, a major industry employing many of the city's residents. The James River Company sells a variety of paper products throughout the world.

When Fred Leadbetter passed away, he was eulogized as a man of foresight, ambition, and guts. Without his direction, the Camas mill most certainly would have been doomed to failure in the 1890's. And without Henry Pittock's vision and wisdom in selecting the LaCamas site for his new paper mill back in 1883 the Camas we know today may have never been. It is for that reason that we salute and thank both Henry Pittock and Fred Leadbetter for their enormous contributions to our community.

THE TIDLAND FAMILY

Author's Preface: When the LaCamas Colony Company was formed by Henry Pittock in 1883 with the object to "create a town or colony at LaCamas and make practical use of the magnificent water there" they were extremely lucky to find talented, intelligent workers like thirty-eight-year-old Louis Tidland. Louis and his son Edward rose to high positions within the company due to their management skills and creative ability. Their grandson Bob Tidland carried on the tradition and as of 1992, he owned one of the most successful business operations in the Camas area.

⚇

Louis Tidland was born in 1846 in Hasselby, Sweden and came to Camas in 1884 the same year "The Columbia River Paper Company" began operations. The new paper company was an offshoot of the LaCamas Colony Company that had been formed to provide paper for Henry Pittock's Oregonian and two other newspapers. Tidland was immediately hired and began what was to be many, many years of service with the company.

Because Louis was a hard worker and a man of strong convictions, he not only did well at the mill but also became deeply involved in community affairs. He soon became president of one of the LaCamas Colony Company's subsidiaries, the Domestic Water Company. Early businessman Aeneas MacMaster was treasurer and A. F. Mills was secretary.

On November 6, 1886, the paper mill was destroyed in a terrible fire. Tidland played a big part in rebuilding the mill along with J. J. Harrington who was the Finishing Room supervisor. They worked side by side along with others wielding hammer and saw until the mill was back in production on May 3, 1888.

Louis married Annie Faubion who was nineteen years his junior, having arrived in this world on February 10, 1865, in Kansas City, Missouri. The couple had five children, four sons and a daughter. First born was Edward H.

Tidland on November 7, 1888, then Josie on May 28, 1890, Charles in 1892, Chester in 1897 and Bart in 1902.

The Tidland family were strong supporters of the Baptist Church from its' earliest beginnings in Camas. Annie was one of the initial members of the church when it was formed in 1885, and the first meeting was held in the old flour mill on Columbia Street. When the flour mill burned down services were conducted at the schoolhouse on Third Street. Although Aeneas MacMaster was a Presbyterian, he invited other religions in 1886 to hold service in the newly constructed St. John's Presbyterian Church on Division Street. The Baptist congregation and other religious groups gratefully accepted his invitation. However, in the late 1800's the Baptist Church took over a new building constructed by the Evangelical Church but recently vacated. They entered into an agreement to pay off the mortgage, but hard times forced them to give up the building and they ended up renting out the hall above MacMaster's store for their services.

On May 10, 1888, Richard and Margaret Cowan and Samuel and Lottie Irwin dedicated the new Forest Home section of LaCamas for use as residential lots. A plat map of Forest Home shows thirty lots available for sale. Louis and Anne Tidland were starting a family and needed to build a home, so they were one of the first couples to buy property in Forest Home. Their lovely new home was located at N.W. 7th and Hill Street.

In 1889, Albert and Sarah Davis arrived in town from Wisconsin and looked for a home site. Albert was twenty-four and Sarah who was born in Pikes Creek, Canada was twenty-one. They bought a lot in Forest Home at the current address of 525 N. W. 10th Avenue and built a home there. Albert and Sarah had one child, Wesley born on October 8, 1888, then Bessie on October 21, 1891, and finally Charles in 1893.

The Tidland and Davis families became good friends through their joint and active participation in the Baptist church and because they were close neighbors. When the children started school, Josie Tidland was best friends with Bessie Davis.

Around 1900, the Davis family moved to a farm at LaCamas Lake and rented out their 10th Avenue Forest Home residence. Unfortunately, in 1902 the large Yacolt fire spread southward to the lake. Bessie was eleven years old and vividly remembers watching the fire out the kitchen window. In a 1985 interview she recalled that "trees went up like matches and my dad and fourteen-year-old brother Wesley had to wet down burlap sacks to protect the roof of the barn. My mother was in town at a lodge meeting and could not return home because of the fire. My father suffered smoke inhalation and almost died." After that bad experience, the Davis family left the farm and moved back into the Camas home.

Like many other LaCamas residents, the Davis family went to Portland to shop because although the paper mill town was growing the selection of stores was limited. In 1885 Aeneas MacMaster opened a much larger two-story general store that offered a greater variety of goods. When Aeneas passed away suddenly in 1888 Hugh MacMaster took over his father's business, expanding it even further. Cowan and Knapp also operated a general store in LaCamas at that time. However, because shipping costs on the Columbia River were so high, it was hard for store owners in LaCamas to compete with lower prices in Portland and still make a profit.

A typical shopping day would have the Davis family catching the Sternwheeler Ione to Portland leaving LaCamas at 7:00 a.m. The boat would stop at various islands and docks along the way to pick up passengers to stay overnight in Portland and return home the next day. The Davis family would do all their shopping and then check into the Portland Hotel. They enjoyed eating their meals at the hotel's dining room because you could get a good meal there for twenty-five cents. The Davis children thought the best part of the meal was the fresh bakery bread. There was no bakery in LaCamas, so store bought bakery bread and cakes were a real treat. Another way to travel to Portland was by horse and buggy, trotting down the ten-mile dirt road, now called Evergreen Highway, to catch a ferry boat across the river. On the other side passengers would have a short buggy ride from the south bank of the Columbia River to downtown Portland. The Davis family sometimes took this route for a change of pace.

In 1902, Louis Tidland was engaged as a gatekeeper for the paper mill's water supply. He built a family home on what was then called "Lake Road" and the new home was easily visible to those passing by. That home was later owned by another pioneer, A. D. McKever and his family.

On August 16, 1905, Louis Tidland bought all of Lot No. 3 and three acres off the east side of Lot No. 4 of Forest Home from Colby and Estella Long. At that time, he owned all of Block No. 7 in Cowan's Addition and Lot No. 8 of Block 26 in Cowan's Addition. Shortly after the Forest Home transaction, Louis deeded all the property to his wife Annie. At that time, he must have had a feeling or knowledge that he would soon pass on, because Louis Tidland died on October25, 1905 at the age of fifty-nine. His seventeen-year-old son Edward became head of the family. To help support the family of six Edward went to work in a blacksmith shop located on the northeast corner of what is now 4th and Garfield in the area where Brown's Funeral Home was located in 1992. The blacksmith shop had a chestnut tree that was popular with the locals. After four years of hard work, Edward Tidland became part owner of the shop.

In 1905, the Columbia River Paper Company merged with Crown Paper Company of West Linn, Oregon becoming Crown Columbia Paper Company. The paper mill expanded building a "Bag Factory" at the Camas site.

The year 1906 proved to be a banner one for Camas when the city was incorporated and elected its' first mayor, J. J. Harrington, who had been a good friend of Louis Tidland at the mill but who was now engaged in the real estate business. Another old friend, A. D. McKever built a wooden two-story building in Camas at the corner of 4th and Clark. The Baptist Church moved from MacMaster's Hall to McKever's Hall on the 2nd floor of the new building. The members set up benches, chairs, a few lamps, the pulpit, and a pump organ in the 40x50 space making the area into quite a nice chapel. They had been saving for several years to build their own church and in 1907 after raising $200.00 they purchased a lot on the corner of 6th and Clara and erected a church building. The new Baptist Church opened for worship on December 15, 1907, with Bessie Davis playing the pump organ.

The children in Camas attended a three-room school in town that taught grades one to eight. The school was small with several grades consolidated into one room. When students graduated from the eighth grade they had to travel to Vancouver, ten miles east, to continue their high school education. In 1908 Bessie Davis was sixteen and had finished the eighth grade but instead of continuing her education she went to work in the Bag Factory at the mill operating a printing machine. Her supervisor was James Duvall who was elected mayor Camas in 1910.

The railroad was completed in 1908, opening whole new vistas for those coming from the east. New settlers arrived in Camas daily, including O.F. Johnson, the first banker in town. For residents the railroad meant much easier access to Portland, Vancouver and beyond.

With his blacksmith business well in hand, Edward Tidland sought employment at the Crown Columbia Paper Company in 1909 determined to follow in his father's footsteps. Bessie Davis had already been working at the Bag Factory for a year and welcomed her old friend as a fellow employee. Their friendship blossomed into deeper feelings, and they began to court.

In 1910, electricity finally came to Camas. Up until that time everyone had to use kerosene lanterns to light their homes and buildings. Those who ventured out at night needed to carry a lantern or walk in the dark and that was very risky indeed.

On September 2, 1911, Bessie Davis and Edward Tidland married in a quiet ceremony for close family members and friends at the Davis residence in Forest Home. Sarah Davis spared no expense for her daughter's beautiful wedding, ordering flowers from Portland and a custom-made wedding gown for Bessie. Edward's brother Charles was best man and Genevieve Reed who later became Charles' wife was maid of honor. The newly married couple rented a home on N. W. 10th across the street from the Davis home. In 1916 they settled into their own new home at 914 N. W. 7th in Forest Home.

During World War I, Charles and Chester Tidland went off to fight the Germans but returned safely once the war was over. The folks at home had been very patriotic helping the war effort in any way they could with "victory gardens" and other projects.

In 1914, ownership of the paper mill changed again when Crown Columbia of Camas and Lebanon merged with Willamette Paper Company.

At that time, the mill switched from steam power to electric power operations. With his skill in mechanics, Edward Tidland received promotion after promotion in the new Crown Willamette Paper Company, becoming a "Master Mechanic" responsible for all new construction, all industrial trades including electrical, machinist, riggers, etc., the position known today as "Plant Engineer."

Ed and Bessie Tidland became the parents of a daughter, Frances Lydia in 1916, but she did not survive. During the next few years, they had three more children, Edward Chester, Barbara Louise and Charles Robert.

Edward Tidland (Source Roberta Tidland)

Annie Tidland was a vibrant fifty-nine-year-old in 1924 when she took the Forest Home and Cowan Addition properties Louis had given her and dedicated Tidland's Subdivision with twenty-four lots, streets, and roads. Tidland's Subdivision was officially recorded on May 25, 1925, in the Clark County Record Book.

Another change for the paper mill occurred when Crown Willamette Paper Company merged with Zellerbach Paper Company in 1928, a union that was to last for decades. That same year Ed Tidland was elected to the Camas City Council and served there for ten years.

During the Depression years of the 1930's, times in Camas were not as bad as the rest of the country. The paper mill was the saving factor, keeping operations humming and paying their workers on a regular basis. O. F. Johnson's bank, First National Bank of Camas, was the only bank in the county that remained open on a continuous basis during the Depression. The folks in town banded together with neighbor helping neighbor, friend helping friend, and those who worked at the mill helping those who did not have jobs. Food and clothing were shared with the less fortunate townsfolk. Annie Tidland died during the Depression on January 30, 1930, at the age of sixty-five years old.

After the Depression, Ed Tidland became Crown Zellerbach's mechanical problem solver and trouble shooter, a position of high esteem. In 1934 he received his 25-year pin from the mill and this fine achievement was written up in the December 7, 1934, Camas Post. In 1937 he was transferred to the Pacific Coast Supply Company, a division of Crown Zellerbach in Portland, Oregon. He worked as a salesman and trouble shooter for paper making machinery and equipment, traveling to other locations, finding ways to make the equipment work better. Ed was considered brilliant in his trade.

An October 13, 1938, Camas Post article announced "Ed Tidland, a councilman-at-large for nearly ten years tendered his resignation stating that his personal affairs make it impossible for him to complete his term. Mayor Province thanked him for his many years of service, especially his technical advice and assistance with the Water Department." As a further explanation here, Edward Tidland had started a gravel company known as "Tidland

Roberta Tidland 1925-2018 (Source CCHM)

Sand and Gravel" that was located just east of Oak Park Bridge. As a man of high integrity, Ed resigned from the city council because any sale of sand, gravel or crushed rock to the City of Camas would be considered a "conflict of interest."

In 1945, Ed Tidland invented and patented a pneumatic shaft. This was a collapsible metal core upon which large rolls of heavy paper could be wound without damage to the center paper, collapsed, withdrawn and used again and again. This was a revolutionary idea to replace the wooden cores that were hammered in and knocked out thus damaging thousands of feet of paper. The shaft would save time, labor and loss of product.

Ed and Bessie's youngest son, Charles "Bob" Tidland, joined the Navy in World War II and became a skilled mechanic in his six-year stint. While still in the Navy, he and his father collaborated on a second shaft design and secured the patent for that invention too.

Bob Tidland married Roberta June Wilson in 1946, and was discharged from the Navy in 1949. Upon discharge, he and his father started the "Tidland Machine Company" for the manufacture of the Tidland Pneumatic Shaft. The first shaft was built in the Camas Machine Shop owned and operated by Art Williams and Tony Pillar. Bob Tidland did most of the actual work on the shaft and when completed, it was placed in the local paper mill for testing. After the test proved to be a big success, Ed and Bob Tidland felt their long time dream had finally come true.

Although Ed Tidland had been the brainchild of this venture, Bob Tidland was the sole machinist, advertising and sales manager in the beginning. Bob worked long hours at the Camas Machine Shop and after hours constructed his own cement block building at a location just over Oak Park Bridge. In January 1951 the building was completed, and Tidland Machine opened for business. The company rapidly grew, adding many employees and fifteen months later Tidland Machine found it necessary to move once again due to a lack of manufacturing space, locating to a larger building in Washougal.

In 1954, Tidland's bought out Camas Machine Shop and took one of the owners, Art Williams, as a partner with the business, becoming Tidland Machine Company, Inc. In the years that followed the company continued to expand, operating two separate plants in Camas and Washougal.

Bob Tidland was elected to the city council in 1955 and served in that position for ten years just as his father had done. Ed Tidland passed away on June 30, 1956, at the age of sixty-eight. After his death Art Williams was elected president of the corporation. In 1957 a new 23,000 sq. ft. plant was built in Oak Park halfway between Camas and Washougal. The new modern plant produced a variety of specialty paper mill equipment and Tidland soon became a worldwide corporation employing over 150 people in the Camas area.

In 1969, C. R. "Bob" Tidland bought the remaining interest in Tidland Machine Corporation from Art Williams and became president. He changed the name to Tidland Corporation and set the company on a new course. Under Bob's direction, the company went on to add sales and manufacturing plants in New Hampshire, U.S.A., Sao Paulo, Brazil, Manchester, England, Ahaus, Germany, and Japan. Bessie Tidland lived to the age of ninety-seven, dying in 1988. She was a fountain of information for those who wanted to know about early Camas and was interviewed by Jon Larson of the Camas Post-Record in 1985.

In 1993, Tidland Corporation was continuing its' success with Bob Tidland as chairman of the board. Three generations of Tidland's have been community leaders as well as outstanding business entrepreneurs. The Tidland children and grandchildren are most certain to carry on the tradition begun by Louis Tidland in 1884.

The old Davis family home still stood on N. W. 10th Avenue in 1992, although slightly remodeled. It was owned for many years by the Hugh Ball family and local resident, Mildred Piontek, still lived there when I interviewed her in 1992. Louis and Annie Tidland's old home was demolished many, many years ago to make room for duplexes. Edward and Bessie Tidland's 1916 family home was still at 914 N. W. 7th in 1992 although looking a bit tired and weary but still retaining its' original character. As they say in historic circles, once a home or any old building is gone or demolished, it is gone forever. It is important to restore rather than replace these historic buildings because they are a part of history and once that is lost, that part of history can never be replaced.

J. J. HARRINGTON

Author's Preface: How do you choose who will be the first mayor of your newly incorporated city? Such was the decision voters of Camas had to make in 1906. Criteria could very well have included community leader, manager of the paper mill, intelligence, ability to provide and negotiate solutions to problems. With so many talented individuals in town, it was quite an honor when the electorate picked John J. "Jack" Harrington as the first mayor of Camas. This Irish immigrant possessed all of the above qualifications and really did "make good" in America.

❧

JOHN J. "JACK" Harrington came to LaCamas from Kenmare, Ireland in 1886 at the age of twenty-five. He was born in Ireland April 20, 1861. When Jack arrived in town the Columbia River Paper Company was going full steam ahead after two years of operation. Jack was hired at the mill and rented a room at the Mountain House Hotel. The room rates were one dollar per day and twenty-five cents per meal. The hotel's operation was more like a boarding house, but it was the best that Camas had to offer at that time.

Being from good Irish stock, Jack was a good worker and management at the mill soon rewarded his hard work by promoting him to foreman in the finishing room. Life seemed rosy for Jack until six months later when the paper mill burned down. It was a devastating blow to the town of LaCamas because so many depended on the mill to survive.

The mill's founder and owner Henry Pittock decided to rebuild as soon as possible because his Camas paper mill operation had been extremely profitable up to that point. Louis Tidland, Thomas Teeson and a man name Egbert had the contract to build the second mill. They hired Jack Harrington, Bede Butler, and Joseph Teeson as carpenters. The three men pitched in with hammers, nails, and saws to help in the construction effort. Pittock ordered new equipment, and the mill was back in operation by May 3, 1888. The new mill had two pocket grinders making about six tons of pulp per day. Sulphite was shipped in but was very scarce, so bleached rags were used to give the paper strength.

During the 1880s, there were badly rutted dirt roads and no railroad so the only transportation anywhere out of the area was by boat. In extremely cold winters when the river froze up the men from the mill had to haul the finished paper all the way to the Willamette River on sleighs.

As so often happened in the early days, twenty-nine-year-old Jack Harrington married a woman twelve years his junior. Emma Jane Wright became his bride on December 9, 1890, when she was seventeen. Emma was born in Baker City, Oregon on March 12, 1873, to parents who had ventured over the Oregon Trail. After Jack and Emma married, they wasted no time in starting a family. In 1891, a daughter, Vera, was born, in 1896, a son John arrived and finally, in 1899, they welcomed another daughter, Muriel. In 1904, five-year-old Muriel died and was buried in the Camas Cemetery.

The Harrington family home was located for decades at 536 N. E. 3rd Street in Camas. In the 1980's the home was moved to Washougal to make room for a commercial business at that prime 3rd Street location.

Jack Harrington continued to work at the mill while his family was growing up. The city of Camas flourished and in 1906 the Clark County Commissioners voted to incorporate a municipality to be known as Camas. J. J. "Jack" Harrington was elected the first mayor with a city council comprised of Henry Karnath, J. W. Conn, C. Litz, Walter Marchbank and James Farrell. W. Swank was a clerk and treasurer.

When the SP&S Railroad Company was building a new railroad line on the north shore of the Columbia River, Harrington put considerable pressure on the railroad company to build its' depot and warehouses at the downtown Camas site and not in Oak Park. It was then that Jack Harrington's diplomacy and persuasion skills were utilized to the fullest. On November 22, 1908, the railroad opened for freight and passenger business to the delight of Camas citizens and business owners.

There were many saloons in town as was normal in "old west" cities and it was difficult to police those who had too much to drink and roamed the streets of town in a drunken manner. Again, Harrington proved to be a good negotiator by making it the saloon owner's responsibility to keep the drunks off the streets or have their licenses revoked. His plan worked and peace prevailed.

A news clip in the 1908 LaCamas Post said, "Mayor Harrington has been in ill health for several months but is feeling better and just recently resumed his place at the mill." Jack Harrington completed his two terms as mayor shortly after the news story and John Cowan was elected as the city's second mayor. Once he was relieved of his mayoral duties Jack Harrington became a member of the Camas Realty Company firm. He continued with his paper mill work and was still a very busy man. In 1911 the Camas Post named Harrington as one of Camas' outstanding town citizens.

Daughter Vera was active in high school both musically and in sports and in 1911 she played on the high school girls' basketball team. After graduation Vera married another Irishman, Charles Duffin who was the only son of early pioneers Allan and Elizabeth Duffin.

Jack Harrington continued to be active in city affairs and in 1923 he and others felt there was a need for a savings and loan association in Camas. The group formed Clark County Savings and Loan making Jack the first vice president of the firm.

In 1939, the Harrington family was deeply saddened when son John W. Harrington died in World War II at the age of forty-three. Emma Harrington died in 1946 and Jack Harrington in 1953 when he was ninety-two years old. Daughter Vera Harrington Duffin died in 1969.

Jack Harrington had lived a long and fruitful life dedicating much of it to public service. He spent his final years at Ocean Park, Washington because he loved being near the ocean, feeling that he was just a little bit closer to his beloved native Ireland.

LORENZ & KARNATH
FAMILIES

Author's Preface: The paper mill in Camas has always been the strongest and most productive business enterprise in town. In fact, the paper mill was the reason for the beginning of a town originally called LaCamas, and then called Camas. A new industry sometimes generates the need for a new town and Henry Pittock's need for paper for his Oregonian newspaper made him decide to plat a new town next to his paper mill in 1884. Many of the newest arrivals to Pittock's new town were men who came to work at the mill. Nothing deterred these people from their life's work and generations followed in their footsteps. Two such families were the Lorenz and Karnath families. The paper mill town became their lifeblood where they worked, built their homes and raised their children. They loved Camas because it was a mill town.

❦

HENRY LORENZ ARRIVED in LaCamas from Wisconsin around 1888 at the age of thirty. He was born in Germany in 1858, but left Europe during the early 1880's with his sister Ida and younger brother Charles. The adventuresome three hoped to find fame and fortune in America and first settled in Wisconsin. It was there that Henry met his future bride, Anna Karnath who was born July 8, 1861, into a strong Catholic family in Madison, Wisconsin. Henry and Anna married and had their first child, a daughter Hilda on April 11, 1887, in LaCross, Wisconsin.

Henry and Anna and other family members heard the stories of those who were traveling westward to Oregon and Washington, finding happiness at the trail's end. They also heard stories about the new paper mill town and the opportunity to find jobs there. Determined to better their situation, they packed all their worldly goods and set out with their family on the six-month trek west, ending up in the small but growing community of LaCamas. The

Lorenz and Karnath families were surprised to see two churches in town plus a lodge, a hall, and a public pavilion.

In 1888, the LaCamas Colony Company's paper mill operation called Columbia River Paper Company was well established although there had been a major setback when the mill burned to the ground. However, by the time that Henry and Charles Lorenz arrived in LaCamas the mill had been rebuilt and both men were hired on as workers.

Henry and Anna purchased a parcel of land on top of the hill overlooking the mill. The property was located in a densely forested area north of what is now Crown Park. They built a fine two-story Western Farm style house exactly where N.E. 17th Avenue runs today midway between N.E. Everett Street and N. E. Division Street. In their new home they welcomed their first son, Fred who arrived on June 11, 1891, but sadly died eight months later in February 1892. Burying their baby in the Camas Cemetery, Henry and Anna inscribed the following on his headstone "We can safely leave our baby, our darling, in thy trust."

Henry and Anna (Karnath) Lorenz 1893
(Source Steve Lorenz)

On December 18, 1892, Amelia Augusta was born, and five-year-old Hilda had a new baby sister. Three years later Gustaf August Lorenz arrived on December 30, 1895. He was named after Anna's father, August Karnath who was born in 1824. Anna and Henry had another child that they named Freddie after their first lost baby, but this Freddie also died and was buried in 1897. On his small tombstone it reads "2/2." Two more sons were born to Henry and Anna, Henry Jr. in 1898 and Edward E. on May 17, 1899.

Anna Karnath Lorenz had three brothers all living in Wisconsin. They were August "Gus" Karnath married to Anna Stritsle, with six children. Her second brother was Charles "Henry" Karnath whose wife was named Lena, and Anna's third brother was John A. Karnath whose spouse was Winnifred. A fourth brother, William had died at the age of five in 1869.

Hearing about Anna and Henry's success in LaCamas, Anna's father and mother, the three brothers and their families also pulled up roots and headed to LaCamas with their spouses and children. Henry and John Karnath opened a butcher shop aptly naming it "Karnath Brothers Meat Market." They sold fresh, salt and canned meats and fish and game in season according to an ad in the LaCamas Post. In such a small community their meat business did very well.

The whole Karnath family joined St. Thomas Catholic Church that was located out at LaCamas Lake. Anna Karnath Lorenz was already a member of the congregation. August Karnath, the patriarch of the family died in 1897 and was buried in the old Catholic cemetery close to the church at the lake. "Mother" and son William were also buried there. Later, St. Thomas built a new Catholic church in town at N. E. 12th and Birch Streets and the graves at the lake were relocated to the Camas Cemetery.

In 1897, Henry Lorenz Sr. was one of fourteen charter members who established the Zion Lutheran Church at N. E. 12th and Division. The Lorenz family and their heirs became lifetime members.

During the early 1900's, both Henry and John Karnath served on the Camas Town Council. John also served as City Treasurer in 1908. Henry went into contracting, building streets locally as well as in Portland. He later worked for Crown Zellerbach who took over the Camas paper mill for twenty-five years. Gus Karnath was in the house moving business in Camas for thirty-two years. As the downtown business area grew, people moved their homes to make room for the business district. It is astonishing that in those days residents were able to move homes and stores with such ease.

Gustaf Lorenz's sister, Amelia Lorenz, married Paul Hinz who came to Camas in 1908 and built the Camas Hotel in 1911. It was originally called the Commercial Hotel and in 1992 was considered the oldest standing building in Camas.

As Gus Lorenz grew up, the resident Native American Indians disappeared, and a favorite pastime of Gus and his friends was to hunt for beads and arrowheads. They walked the woods around their home to attend school down on Garfield Street and did fun things like fishing or swimming at LaCamas Lake or watching the Columbia River steamboats navigating the currents up and down the river. In the early days transportation between Camas and Vancouver or Portland was mostly by boat, a six-hour one way trip. When the Model Ts came out a stage line of Model Ts would make the Vancouver-Camas loop on a dirt road. In 1908, the railroad came to town and traveling got much easier. Gus Lorenz did not know it at the time, but the railroad was to bring him his future bride.

Gus and Marie Lorenz 1920 (Source Steve Lorenz)

In October 1909, eleven-year-old Marie Meyers arrived in Camas with her family after a long train trip from Baltimore, Maryland. Her father Godfrey had come west to work with his son Gus Meyers who was already employed at the mill. With Godfrey were his wife, Florentine and Marie's brother, John, and sisters Florence and Amelia. When the Meyers family finally reached Camas, it was raining, the streets were muddy, and the raised wooden sidewalks helped just a little bit. Coming from the big, cosmopolitan city of Baltimore to the tiny town of Camas with its' small stores and huge trees was a bit of a jolt for the Meyers family. Marie's brother, Gus met the family at the train and escorted them to his place of residence, the Lorenz home. It was there that Marie met another Gus, fourteen-year-old Gus Lorenz, for the first time. The Meyers spent the night at the Lorenz home and then headed out for Aunt Bertha and Uncle Adolph Miller's farm in the country by horse and buggy to spend the winter.

Marie's father found work at the mill as the Karnath's and Lorenz's had before him, and the following March moved his family to a home in Camas just four houses away from the Lorenz family home. In 1992 the old Meyer home was located at 123 N. E. 17th Avenue and owned by Verna Hughes.

Gus Lorenz and Marie Meyers went to the same two-story elementary school although Gus was three classes ahead of Marie. One of Marie's classmates and friends was Ed Lorenz, the younger brother of Gus. Classmates of Gus were the Blake boys and Titus Butler. Handsome and popular Gus participated in football, basketball and baseball with great athletic ability between the years 1911 and 1914. His 1913 Camas Papermaker football team beat Vancouver, and they were very proud indeed. In 1911 Gas became a confirmed member of the Zion Lutheran Church.

Besides schoolwork, sports and church activities, Gus took a summertime job at the paper mill where his dad worked as at Beater Room foreman. When he was a senior, his class picked the school colors of red and black and those are the colors of Camas High School to this day. Gus watched the new high school being built brick by brick and in 1914, his class of five was one of the first classes to graduate from the new high school.

After graduation, eighteen-year-old Gus went to work full time for the paper mill making $1.85 per day. Although Marie Karnath was fifteen and still in school, she worked in the paper mill Bag Factory to earn extra money. It was at that time they started courting and for their first date they attended a high school football game. Another popular activity at that time in Camas was movies and roller skating at the old Granada Opera House across from MacMaster's store. Of course, both Gus and Marie were active members of Zion Lutheran Church on Division Street. In 1919, lovely Marie rode upon a special float in the Camas Fourth of July parade.

World War I broke out and Gus enlisted in the Army Signal Corps. He was luckily stationed in Vancouver so was able to come home every Saturday night to see his sweetheart, Marie. Gus and Marie were married on September 16, 1920, in a home they had built at 214 N. E. 14th Street. They set up housekeeping at their new residence and Gus returned to his paper mill work rapidly getting well deserved promotions. Gus and Marie soon had two children, Doris, and Howard. In 1924 Gus helped to organize the Camas Volunteer Fire Department and became its' first president.

As the years went by Gus served on the Camas School Board and the Camas City Council. He was a charter member of the American Legion Post and was active in Kiwanis and the Men's Garden Club. Marie was also involved in many activities including "fishing."

Gus's aunt Ida Lorenz died on November 29, 1922, and his uncle Charles Lorenz, died ten years later on June 23, 1932. Amelia Lorenz Hinz died in 1931 at the age of thirty-eight and August "Gus" Karnath passed away in 1932.

During the "Spree of 33," the 50th celebration of Camas and the paper mill, Gus Lorenz was one of many who grew bushy black beards. He had his picture in the Camas Post.

In the mid 1930's, Gustaf Lorenz lost his parents. Seventy-six-year-old Henry Lorenz Sr. passed away in 1934, and in 1938 his mother, Anna Karnath Lorenz, also died.

In 1941, Gus and Marie moved into a new house at 401 N. E. 17th, just north of the old family home. Gus loved beautiful flowers, and the Lorenz home was always surrounded by lovely gardens. Marie did her part with spectacular floral arrangements within the house.

Gus Lorenz during the "Spree of 33" (Source TRHM)

Henry Karnath died in 1943, and Gus's remaining uncle, John Karnath, passed in 1946.

Taking after his father, Gustaf Lorenz, Howard became an outstanding athlete at Camas High School and Willamette University in Portland. He married Beverly Howard who was quite gifted musically and involved in the community Christmas concerts. Howard became a well-known realtor in Camas. Gustaf's daughter, Doris, married Donn Carey, and the couple had twin sons on St. Patrick's Day. Donn Carey worked as a superintendent at the paper mill.

The old family Lorenz home continued to sit right in the middle of N. E. 17th Street until 1952 when the city bought the right-of-way to complete the street between Division and Everett. At the conclusion of the sale, the old house was demolished.

Gus finally retired from the mill after forty-five years of service, giving him more time to spend tending the Lorenz gardens with Marie and taking well-deserved fishing trips with friends. They also enjoyed their grandchildren and great-grandchildren plus any pets that happened to fly by.

In his later years, it was not unusual for city and school officials to come to Gus Lorenz for advice. He was well respected for his many years of contributions to the community and school district. Gustaf August Lorenz passed away on Sunday, August 6, 1989. He was eulogized for his honesty, integrity, leadership and vision. Marie followed Gus in death the following July.

Gus and Marie Lorenz circa 1970 (Source Steve Lorenz)

As of 1992, when this book was written, Howard and Doris, their children and grandchildren were still living in Camas following the good Lorenz family traditions. At that time the Gustaf Lorenz family home at 401 N. E. 17th was still and was owned by Linda Lorenz Stoller and her husband, Steve Stoller.

ARCHIBALD DUNCAN MCKEVER

Author's Preface: Most men have the opportunity for a formal education to begin their life, but most men are not orphaned at five years of age and forced to make their own way in the world. When one can still be a successful individual against these odds, we can only admire such a person's efforts. Without one day of formal schooling, A. D. McKever engineered LaCamas' first water system. Despite being a widower twice, this resilient man raised his children alone finally marrying one last time to a dear, old friend. Property owner, builder of buildings, engineer, loving husband and father; that was A. D. McKever. This is his extraordinary story.

❧

ARCHIBALD DUNCAN MCKEVER was born June 5, 1857, in a town on the banks of the Wabash River in Indiana. He never knew his father because at the time of his birth, his mother was a widow. It appeared that life was not to be easy for Archie when his mother passed away and left him an orphan at the age of five. His lone surviving relative was an aunt who took him in for the next two years treating him like a son. However, in 1864 his aunt also died and poor little Archie or A.D. as he preferred to be called in later life, was left a 100% orphan with no living relatives.

At the tender age of seven, A. D. went out into the farming community of Indiana to find work and a place to live. For a time, neighboring farmers took him in and let him work off his room and board. Although he was of school age and had a great desire to learn, the daily farm work prevented him from attending school. As the years went on, A. D. went from farm to farm, moving further and further south following the harvest. Soon memories of his Indiana birthplace faded as he grew into a young man heading for Texas. By the time he reached Dallas in 1880 he was twenty-three years old and mature far beyond his years.

In Dallas, A. D. found employment with a farmer named Daniels who owned a one-hundred-acre farm, raised cotton, corn and potatoes, and badly needed extra help. Mr. Daniels liked the young McKever and nicknamed him "Mac." A. D. was accepted as a member of the family with Daniels' ten-year-old daughter Martha Jane becoming like a younger sister to him. Although A. D. was thirteen years older than Martha Jane who was born March 26, 1870, the two formed a bond that was to last throughout their lifetimes.

The local schoolteacher also boarded with the Daniels' family, teaching at a one room schoolhouse about a mile from the farm. She soon realized although McKever was very bright he did not know how to read or write. Thus, began evenings of lessons conducted by lamplight after chores and school were completed each day. Although A. D. was left-handed, he learned to write with his right hand. The reading textbooks commonly used at that time were "McGuffy's Readers." Those many hours of evening schooling were to be A. D. McKever's only formal education.

Settling into the Dallas community, A. D. met nineteen-year-old Dora Vititow a lovely young woman from a large and happy family. Her parents were Daniel Vititow and Sarah Chinault Vititow. After a short courtship, A.

Frank Archibald McKever (Source Find a Grave)

D. and Dora married and in 1881 had their first son, Samuel O. McKever. They had another son Arthur in 1886. Sometime during this period, the family moved to Denton, Texas.

Dora became pregnant again in 1887, and McKever decided it was time to look for more profitable work to support his growing family. Stories were circulating in Texas about the new sawmills in the Oregon Territory so hoping for a new start, A. D. packed up his family and came out to Portland on the immigration train. From there the family took the riverboat to LaCamas landing on St. Patrick's Day, March 17, 1888. Throughout his life, A. D. McKever called St. Patrick's Day "The 17th of Ireland."

The Columbia River Paper Company had a boat dock that the riverboats used for loading and unloading passengers and freight. Usually, the livery wagon was there to greet the riverboat but, on this occasion, no one was in sight. The McKever's disembarked in the pouring rain and stood with their few belongings, becoming thoroughly drenched. Local lore has it that Walter Marchbank who owned the livery stable and all the other townsmen were in the town bar toasting good old St. Patrick! A. D. walked the few blocks to town and persuaded Walter to venture from the bar and out into the storm. Marchbank packed up the McKever trunks in his low wagon and took the family to the Duncan Boarding House on Clara Street close to the railroad tracks. There were three small houses for rent next to the boarding house and the McKever's were able to move into one of these dwellings. It should be noted here that before a year had passed, A. D. McKever had purchased all three homes as well as several other pieces of property in and around LaCamas.

Although A. D. originally went to work at the White Salmon sawmill up the Columbia River Gorge, he soon got a job at the LaCamas sawmill. The LaCamas Colony Company built this sawmill in 1883 near the potholes near the lake. They had also constructed a larger water tower on the property. The townsfolk nicknamed the sawmill "The Sawdust Pile" because during its' hay day, it cranked out 30,000 board feet of lumber a day, making a huge pile of sawdust. Old Timer's report that, during the early 1900's, sawdust from the mill was used to fill in the holes on the old football field. In the 1920's local grade school children attended a one-room school next to the then deserted mill and adjoining shacks. The school children were sternly told by the principal not to climb the old water tower. The one room school was later moved to Crown Park where it served as the "Boy Scout Cabin" in 1992 when this book was written.

McKever's youngest son, Jack, claimed that his father never worked at the Columbia River Paper Company, but there is an 1888 photograph that identifies McKever standing next to the newly constructed brick paper mill building. Other mill workers were identified as Charles and James Farrell, Charles Lorenz, and Henry Karnath.

On August 10, 1888, A. D. and Dora became parents of Frank who was born in the Clara Street house downtown. They had a daughter, Irene, in 1891. After Irene's birth the little Clara Street house became very crowded for the seven-member family. They made the decision to move out to the south shore of LaCamas Lake where the family could do some farming. A. D. purchased two lovely acres close to the lake, built a small frame house and moved his growing family into their new home. He rented out the three houses on Clara Street for additional income.

A short history here of the LaCamas Lake area and how it developed. The McKever's only neighbors at the south end of the lake were the Barthelemy and Lancaster families. In the late 1870's, the Barthelemy family bought several acres next to LaCamas Lake. Note: This is where the Moose Lodge was in 1992 and is currently the City of Camas LaCamas Lake Lodge. There was a small two-room cabin on the property that was built in 1871. The Barthelemy's had two children, Leonard, and Edward. When Edward married Jessie May Hannford the family needed more room, so they remodeled the cabin, raising the roof and adding a kitchen.

The Barthelemy's were a strong Catholic family and there was no real church in LaCamas. So, when they remodeled their home, they added a church building on the right side of the structure. The completed product was a very nice house decorated in gingerbread trim with the first Catholic Church in attachment. A little unusual but it worked.

Edward and Jessie May Barthelemy had a son, Edward P,. in 1898. Shortly afterwards, Edward Sr. died, and Jessie May married Godfrey Marker who worked at the mill. Leonard Barthelemy never married but had a prune dryer next to the road and his neighbors, including the McKevers, helped him pick the prunes. When Edward P. Barthelemy grew up, he married Fay Phillips, and they went into the marina business at the lake in 1935. Ed was known as the authority on LaCamas Lake, and the 1953 Columbian featured him in a long article about the lake. The Barthelemy family sold the land to the Moose Lodge in 1975.

The Lancaster family, who was also McKever's neighbors, consisted of Mr. and Mrs. Lancaster and a son called "Burt." Their property was located directly north of Barthelemy's and south of the Catholic Cemetery. Burt married Rose Nigretto daughter of Charlie Nigretto whose brother Joe had just bought the land south of the Barthelemy place. Joe Nigretto raised strawberries and hired neighbor children, among them Jack McKever, to help him harvest his crops.

In 1883, Henry Pittock and his agent, D. H. Stearns, bought 2,600 acres of land from LaCamas Lake to the Columbia River to form the LaCamas Colony Company. By the time McKever moved to the lake, Pittock's son-in-law Fred Leadbetter was busy buying up all the remaining lakeside land. Pittock-Leadbetter had taken possession of all the property surrounding the McKever farm, but had somehow let McKever's little two acres slip through their fingers. They needed those two acres so there would not be a "dent" in their vast holdings. Leadbetter approached McKever in 1892 with an unusual offer. In an even trade, McKever would receive six and a half prime acres on the east side of the road along the lake slough in exchange for his two-acre farm. McKever accepted the generous offer, and the transaction was completed.

Around the time of the land swap, McKever bought LaCamas' first water system in town for seventy-five dollars. The system had eight taps and McKever charged each of his customers fifty cents per month. Water was taken from the mill ditch and stored in a tank near the wooden Presbyterian Church. Everyone carried their drinking water from "The Spring" that was in a ravine between 5th and 6th Avenues near Columbia, later named Division Street. The ravine later became part of the mill yard, was enclosed, and filled in.

Expanding on his water system business, McKever built a water tower on his six and a half acres of land out by the lake. The tower was located where the mobile home park was in 1992. He dug wells and put in pumps that were run with gas engines. Eventually he had three gas engines, three big pumps, and a wooden water tower. In 1894 McKever ran a water line to downtown LaCamas that was six inches in diameter, wooden and had metal wire wrapped around it for reinforcement. A neighbor boy, thirteen-year-old

George Purrier helped him maintain the equipment. McKever was responsible for the first real water supply that LaCamas ever had.

In 1892, Dora Vititow McKever passed away at the age of thirty-two, leaving five young children in her husband's care. After her burial, McKever went to Texas to comfort the Vititow family and ended up marrying Dora's younger sister, twenty-five-year-old Emma Vititow. The newly marrieds returned to LaCamas and a daughter, Violet, was born in 1894. The next year, in 1895 Emma died. Her death certificate dated October 17, 1895, states she died of Galloping Consumption at the age of twenty-six, though in reality she was twenty-eight. McKever was again a widower but this time with six children to care for, the oldest was just thirteen years of age.

For eight years after Emma's death, A. D. remained unmarried. But then he took another trip to Texas, rekindled his friendship with Martha Jane Daniel who, in 1903, was thirty-three years old and unmarried. McKever was forty-six but at that time the thirteen-year difference in their ages did not matter. The couple married on June 10, 1903, in Dallas and traveled immediately by train to Portland and from there took the boat upriver to LaCamas.

When the McKever's arrived home, the youngest daughter, Violet, was seriously ill. She died on July 8, 1903, at 4:00 p.m. at the age of nine years. The cherry trees were laden with fruit that was not quite ripe. The doctor said the cause of her death was eating green cherries and drinking milk. However, Martha McKever always thought that Violet died of undiagnosed appendicitis.

In 1898 fourteen-year-old Charles McKever went to work at the LaCamas paper mill. There were eighty-seven employees at that time who worked eleven-hour days for $1.50 per day. His older brother, Samuel may have also worked at the mill. Arthur "Happy" McKever became a machine tender on the Cannon Ball. Happy moved to Dallas for a short time in 1908 but moved back to Camas when "he had spent all of his money" per the LaCamas Post January 1908 edition.

More bad news for the McKever family in 1903 when Charles was nineteen. He lost his left forearm in an industrial accident after five years of mill service. He suffered a long and painful trip by horse and buggy to the nearest hospital in Vancouver where he was treated for his injury. On May 18, 1904, John Aubrey "Jack" McKever was born to A.D. and Martha Jane. Although Martha Jane always called her new son Aubrey, A. D. called him "Jack." When McKever would arrive home from work, Jack would stand up in his highchair and clap his hands and laugh. Pleased by his son's reaction, A. D. nicknamed him "Happy Jack" and the name stuck with Jack McKever all of his life.

In late 1905, the McKever family purchased a fine family home at the lake that had been built in 1902 by Louis Tidland. Tidland died in 1905 and the Tidland family moved back into town. The McKever's loved the two-story white farm style home with its' large porch that swept across the front elevation. The porch was decorated with spindle rails and full columns.

Frank McKever (Source TRHM)

Frank McKever attended school in the early 1900's at the newly built two story wooden school building on the hill overlooking town. Although three years younger, Irene McKever shared the same classroom with her brother. After graduation Frank joined his brothers in working for the mill clearing jams on the flume that ran from the lake to the mill. Often when he worked near his home, he would cheerfully yell to his stepmother "What's for dinner tonight?"

It was hard to put A. D. McKever into a category for this book because he was so many things, a farmer, an engineer, a possible mill worker, and a businessman in Camas. In 1908, McKever built a two-story wooden store building at the southeast corner of N. E. 4th and Clark, a street now called Adams, on a property he had purchased several years before for $300.00. Two of the first businesses to occupy McKever's building were the Red Front Meat Market and Cowan's Cigar Store that was a local gathering spot for the men of the town. The upper floor of the building was used as a lodge hall and for church services.

Around 1909, Glenn Cottrell and his father ran an electric power line out to McKever's for the water pumping. McKever paid $30.00 per month for the electricity and because of this had to raise the monthly water rates for his customers. There were many complaints. He built another wooden tower, this one was thirty feet tall by the Gitting's place, near the current Hilltop Market location. Shortly afterwards he sold his water company to Pittock-Leadbetter who continued to use McKever's mode of operation for a couple of years.

In 1912, Pittock-Leadbetter developed their own facilities across the road from the lake slough, building the Butler Reservoir and installing a six-inch steel water line. They hired George Purrier, the young man who had helped McKever to manage their water operations. George later married Tillie Bauman's sister of Mrs. O. F. Johnson. The newly married Purrier's lived in the Bauman on the corner of N. E. 5th and Hayes.

Jack McKever grew up on the McKever property by the lake and attended the small school by the old sawmill close to the high school. He started school in 1910 and walked to school each day from the lake on a well-trod trail that came out at the Tietz's place. His best friends were Eddie and George Purrier Jr., who were the McKever's closest neighbors to the north, and the Cole kids, who were related to the Purrier's and visited often. In 1913, Eddie Purrier accidentally drowned in the lake from an overturned canoe. Jack McKever and George Purrier Jr. witnessed the accident, ran to get help but the cold water and rushing currents prevented his life saving rescue. Eddie was buried in the Camas Cemetery.

The July 9, 1915, Camas Post relates an account of the grand 4th of July Parade through Camas. Among the participants mentioned were Mr. and Mrs. A. D. McKever in their decorated automobile.

Charles D. McKever married Bertha Leona Smith, and they had four children, Veva Dora, Gordon Richard who later owned McKever's Service at the lake, Marjorie Leona, and young Charles D. McKever Jr. born on October 20, 1917. Charles Jr. was to die in an automobile accident in 1935 at the age of eighteen.

McKever Building, corner of 4th & Adam St, Camas 1919 (Source TRHM)

In 1920, A. D. McKever bought the office building formerly occupied by Patton & McAllister and moved it onto an empty lot he owned on N. E. 4th Avenue between Clark and Columbia Streets. The purchase was noted in September 15, 1920, Camas Post.

Arthur "Happy" McKever died at age thirty-five on November 3, 1921. He shared a plot at the Camas Cemetery with his mother, Dora, his sister Violet, his stepmother Emma, and his aunt Alice Vititow.

In 1922, the old wooden McKever building was moved to face Clark Street. Another old timer, Gus Karnath did the moving. A basement was dug at the old location and a new McKever building was erected. Citizen's State Bank moved its' headquarters into the fine two-story brick building and as noted in the September 15, 1922, Camas Post "the opening of the bank was celebrated by the passing of cigars to the men and red carnations to the ladies who called during the afternoon.

Roy Dobbs is the cashier and Mrs. Carkin is assistant cashier. A. D. McKever also put into place the first drinking fountain in town in front of his new building. He sent the first fountain back to the manufacturer because it did not have facilities for birds and dogs to drink. The "new" McKever building was still standing in 1992 although it looked a little tired and worn. It still housed many businesses located across from the paper mill's administration office at N. E. 4th and Adams.

The old wooden McKever building suffered roof damage from a fire during the 1920's, possibly in 1923 when a whole block burned down. Most old west towns were originally built with wooden buildings, and they constituted a fire hazard anytime a stray spark was set loose. McKever's old building was saved from total destruction in the fire and was purchased in the 1930's by Dr. A. E. Bird, who had it demolished in late 1958.

The City of Camas purchased McKever's water system from Pittock-Leadbetter in 1923 and still owns the water system to this day.

In the 1920's, Frank McKever moved to Portland where he became a premier plumbing and heating expert. He met his intended bride, Bella, at church, and during the Depression the couple moved back to Camas where Frank opened his own plumbing and heating business that became very successful. Irene McKever moved to California where she married Warren Ranney. They were the first directors of the Child Evangelism Fellowship of Southern California. Irene wrote many Christian books that were translated into foreign languages and sold worldwide.

Jack McKever opened a barber shop on Adams Street in 1928. At that time, he

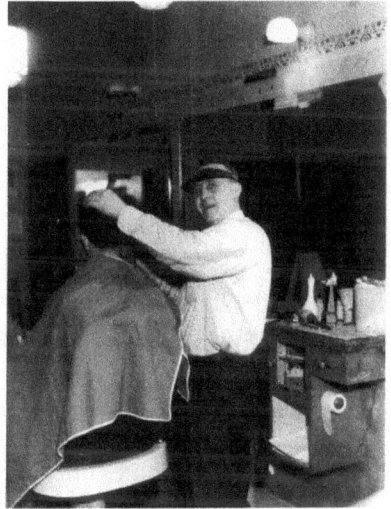

Jack McKever (Source TRHM)

was married to Clara, and in 1929 the couple welcomed a son, Dean, who unfortunately died in a plane crash in 1954 at the age of twenty-five. In the 1930, Camas High School yearbook it was noted that Charles McKever's daughter, Marjorie, graduated as a science major and her quote was, "Love me, Love my Lizzie!"

The adventurous fellow who started it all, Archibald Duncan McKever, lived a long, full life and passed away July 8, 1937, at 4:00 p.m. at the age of eighty. His beloved wife, Martha Jane and his children were at his bedside. Martha Jane exclaimed "Why he died at exactly the same time and date as Violet!" And yes, he had, thirty-three years later exactly to the minute. Frank and Jack McKever were trustees of their father's estate and sold the three downtown houses shortly thereafter.

The December 5, 1940, Camas Post announced Jack McKever's marriage to Lillian Lambert at the A.D. McKever home the previous Sunday in a quiet ceremony. I could not discover during my research on this family what happened to Clara, Jack's first wife.

In 1941, Frank McKever started building a one-story brick residence on the McKever property at the lake but died of a heart attack while working on the project. The house was completed sometime later and is called the "McKever House" today. His widow, Bertha celebrated her 100th birthday in the early 1990's when this book was written. Samuel, A. D.'s oldest son by his first wife died in 1946 at the age of sixty-five. Samuel's brother, Charles McKever became a city councilman and member of the cemetery board after retiring from the paper mill in 1949. He was the first Crown Zellerbach employee to complete fifty years of service and was honored by Chairman Louis Bloch with a fifty-year pin and a vacation trip to San Francisco.

Martha Jane McKever, A. D.'s third wife lived to be ninety, dying in 1960. After his mother's death, Jack McKever started McKever's Trailer Park on the lake slough property. In a 1987 interview, he recalled that thousands of yards of dirt had to be hauled onto the property to even out the land and make roads. Around the same time, the Camas Fire Department burned down the grand, old farmhouse where most of the McKever's had begun their journey through life.

In 1970, Jack McKever's third wife, Roberta, died at the age of fifty-six. I could find no record of what happened to his second wife, Lillian. Jack retired from his barber shop the same year and spent winters in California where he married for a fourth time. During each spring he would bring his trailer back to Camas and stay until the weather turned bad. Sort of like a "snowbird" today. His sister, Irene, lived in California throughout her life and passed away in 1984 in Pasadena at the age of ninety-three. Irene was remembered as a worldwide recognized author and as the inventor of the "flannel graph board."

After Irene's death, Jack moved back to Clark County but chose to spend his remaining years in Vancouver instead of Camas. He died in 1991 in

Vancouver. Jack Keel, who was like a son to Jack McKever, continued to run Jack's Barber Shop in Camas in 1992.

Today fifth generation McKever's are still living in Camas. They are quite proud of Archibald Duncan McKever, a man with no schooling to speak of, but a man with a sharp engineering mind and a good business head for buying and developing property. He contributed a great deal to early Camas, both downtown and the lake area. He will always be remembered by historians as a very "vital" Camas pioneer.

DREAMS OF LIFE IN A NEW LAND

THE BEGINNING OF LIFE IN A NEW TOWN

AENEAS MACMASTER

Author's Preface: There was one very special pioneer who no one dares dispute as being in the forefront of development in Camas. At age forty-four, feisty Scotsman Aeneas MacMaster left his homeland seeking new adventures across the seas. He moved his large family first to Quebec and then to LaCamas where he opened the first store in town, started a church and began a dynasty that lasted well into the 1930's. In 1884 MacMaster seized an opportunity presented by Henry Pittock and his LaCamas Colony Company. He built his business on pure faith that the paper mill would succeed, and this determination proved to be a long-term asset to what became the town of Camas.

AENEAS MACMASTER WAS born on October 15, 1830, and grew up in the hilly farming county of Inverness, Scotland. When he reached the age of seventeen, he traveled to the City of Glasgow, Scotland where he learned the trade of carpenter and joiner, and after that he went to work using his trade. This sustained Aeneas for a short time, but being a smart businessman, he decided the lumber business would be more lucrative than carpentry, and so for the next few years earned a good living dealing in lumber.

During his years in Glasgow the full-bearded Aeneas met and married the tiny but lovely Scottish lass Elizabeth McIndoe, whose birth date was September 23, 1833. The well-matched couple proceeded to have a family of thirteen children although four children died in Scotland.

The other nine were Elizabeth, Hugh, Jessie, Donald, Agnes, Violet, Isabel, Mary, and Annie. In 1874 Aeneas who was forty-four at the time decided to leave his homeland of Scotland and start anew in Quebec, Canada. This was quite an undertaking for a middle-aged married man with nine children. And, it had to be sad for him because he was leaving his beloved Scotland.

But they left with all their belongings going across the sea to Quebec arriving on May 24, 1874, Queen Victoria's birthday. They were quickly established in Ontario, then moved to Ottawa and finally settled in Compton County until 1883. Aeneas found a job as a manager for a Scottish owned real estate and lumber company.

However, Aeneas was getting itchy feet again and had heard of the opportunities for land grants in the United States of America. Off he went once more, leaving the family behind for a short while to find a better home and better times, so he hoped. He traveled first through New York, then Chicago, St. Paul and heading west all the while, finally reaching Portland in the Oregon Territory. Aeneas took a temporary job in Portland as a carpenter keeping an eye open for other, more rewarding opportunities. Like so many others, he soon heard of a small community being established across the Columbia River in east Clarke County, Washington named LaCamas. A new paper mill company called "Columbia River Paper Company" had just begun operations under the flagship LaCamas Colony Company owned by Henry Pittock. Excited, he took the riverboat upstream and upon disembarking at the little mill town, he knew he had finally found his destiny.

Quickly seizing upon the many chances of success offered by this busy, new paper mill town, Aeneas MacMaster invested in Lots One and Two in Block 21. He then built a general store and house combined on Lot two that was located close to the mill site. He called his store located at 4th and

Aeneas MacMaster General Merchandise 1883 (Source Camas Post)

Columbia, (what else?) but "Aeneas MacMaster General Merchandise." It was the very first store in LaCamas and was welcomed by not only the people who were building the paper mill but the influx of new residents and the existing Native American population.

MacMaster sold building supplies and hardware to the mill and early settlers, plus a wide variety of other items including kitchen supplies, clothing, medicine, and feed. All the goods he sold had to be shipped by boat because there were no railroads at that time. Once the MacMaster store was open for business and thriving, he sent for his family who arrived by steamboat in September of that year.

Aeneas MacMaster (Source Camas Post)

During their years living in Glasgow, Scotland, and Canada, most of the MacMaster children had grown up and received public school educations. When they reached LaCamas many were ready to begin work in their own trades, get married and begin their families. Nineteen-year-old Elizabeth MacMaster began teaching school in a one-room shack on Third Street and she had twenty-six pupils in the very first school in La-Camas.

In 1883, Aeneas was fifty-three, and with his store well established, he turned his attention to his second love, the Presbyterian Church. He felt that any decent town needed a church, so he contacted the Reverend J. R. Thompson of Olympia, Washington, who was kind enough to come to LaCamas and conduct the first services at the MacMaster residence within the store building.

On December 9, 1883, the official date of establishment of the Presbyterian Church of LaCamas, Aeneas was elected the ruling elder. Besides Aeneas, the original membership consisted of his wife Elizabeth, his daughter Elizabeth, and three other Presbyterians discovered in town. The

GRANGE BIRTHPLACE – In this homely hall, the architectural gem of LaCamas in its day, the Washington State Grange was born on Tuesday, Sept. 10, 1889. It was by far the finest building in town, 26 by 50 feet and was built just four years before. It was owned by A. MacMaster and run by Hugh MacMaster.

The MacMaster Pioneer Store in Camas proudly served as the very first Washington State Grange. Now a part of Camas mill site (Source TRHM)

seventh member of the church was to be Alan Duffin, his future son-in-law, who later married Elizabeth MacMaster.

In 1885, MacMaster built a new, larger store at Third and Columbia on the original lot he had purchased in 1883. This store, named "The Pioneer Store," remained a LaCamas landmark for many years occupying the ground floor of the building. A spacious, much needed lodge hall was built on the second floor, and this was later to be the birthplace of the Washington State Grange. The MacMaster family moved to a newly built but small home at the top of Columbia Street. Their new home overlooked the mill and MacMaster store. In 1992, the small red house with numerous additions, appearing like a little "choo-choo" train, was still at the same location.

In the meantime, the Presbyterian Church's membership was increasing rapidly, and the Elders began to plan for their first church building. It was to be located just below MacMaster's new home on the hill and was an exciting project for everyone in town because every religious denomination would be able to use the church for services on a rotating basis. While the church was being constructed services were held in the little schoolhouse. Aeneas was elected Clerk of the Session.

He was also becoming a town leader. At the annual Fourth of July celebration in 1885, he was Arrangement's chairman, meeting dignitaries and other important visitors at the steamboat landing. He was also secretary of the Domestic Water Company.

The new church building was dedicated on the first Sunday in October and was called St. John's Presbyterian Church after the new minister, the Reverend Thompson. By May of 1887, the church had fifty members and had elected five Elders. However, Aeneas was suffering from ill health and had to resign as Clerk of the Session.

During 1888, Aeneas was able to keep his store going but his health continued to fail. Not realizing the seriousness of his father's illness, his son, Hugh, decided to visit friends in Quebec during the summer. He was never to see his father alive again. Aeneas MacMaster died on September 18, 1888, at the age of fifty-eight. While still in Canada, Hugh MacMaster received a telegram from his mother and immediately returned to Camas to manage his father's store and business affairs.

Ella and Hugh MacMaster 1891 (Source TRHM)

Aeneas MacMaster, who searched and searched but did not find what he was looking for in life until his travels brought him to LaCamas at age fifty-three, had found happiness and success in his final five years of life. Although the MacMaster store no longer exists today, Aeneas will always be remembered as a man of fairness, good Christian ways, and excellent business judgment. His legacy of starting the first store in Camas, as well as organizing the first church in Camas, is one that no other man can claim. A true Camas pioneer was Aeneas MacMaster.

ALLAN DUFFIN

Author's Preface: It must have been frightening the day Allan Duffin left his homeland of Ireland bound for America, alone but carrying a letter of recommendation neatly folded in his jacket pocket. This letter was to be the key to his fortune in America and he was not disappointed. LaCamas was a long way from Ireland, but a Scotsman, Aeneas MacMaster, took him in like a son, giving him both employment and his daughter in marriage. This is the story of the Duffin family, their business, family and religious traditions, and the impact that they have had on the Camas community right up to the present time.

❦

ALLAN DUFFIN WAS born in Belfast, Ireland in 1857. His parents were of strong Presbyterian stock and moved to Larne, Ireland, when Allan was small. They became industrious and respected members of the community, providing their son with a good education and a fine religious upbringing in Reverend McMurray's congregation.

Allan worked in an office in Belfast for a short time, then as a letter carrier for the postal service. In 1872, he left Larne, Ireland, with a letter of high recommendation dated October 7, 1872, from R. P. Minister of Larne, Ireland, James R. Moody. Reverend Moody praised Allan as being a man of very great promise, strictly honest, and perfectly trustworthy.

It is said that Allan spent some time in Canada before coming to LaCamas in 1883, and the eleven-year gap between leaving Ireland and arriving in the LaCamas area would certainly support that assumption. Confident, handsome Allan, with his high credentials in hand, had no trouble landing a job with Aeneas MacMaster at the Aeneas MacMaster General Store.

MacMaster was fifty-three, fresh from the Scottish Highlands via Montreal, and had just opened the first general store in LaCamas. The small, two-story wooden building had been constructed in record time, and the early LaCamas settlers were excited at having their own store. It had been difficult for MacMaster to leave his wife and family of nine children in Canada while he was seeking his fortune in the western territory of the United States of America, but once established in the exciting new community of LaCamas, he sent for his family to join him.

There were about twenty dwellings in LaCamas in 1883 that could be described as "shacks." All goods had to be shipped up the Columbia River from Portland, Oregon, and Vancouver, located ten miles downriver. In no time at all, MacMaster's store shelves were brimming with a variety of food items, supplies, and equipment. The store area was fairly small, with living quarters to the rear of the first floor as well as on the second floor. Aeneas, who was a strong Presbyterian, felt lucky to find someone of Duffin's fine character to help him in the store, and the two worked side by side until the MacMaster family arrived in town. Allan was pleasantly surprised to discover that one of Aeneas' nine children was a lovely daughter, nineteen-year-old Elizabeth, born in Glasgow, Scotland, on February 22, 1865.

Elizabeth MacMaster-Duffin and Allan Duffin (Source TRHM)

When she arrived in LaCamas, she began teaching at a makeshift one-room school building with an old cook stove for heat. Her first class had twenty-eight pupils of all ages, including some older than Elizabeth. Five of her pupils were her younger brothers and sisters.

Because of the proximity of the MacMaster store where Allan worked and the MacMaster living quarters, Elizabeth and Allan spent a good deal of time together and their friendship soon turned to deeper feelings. In 1885, after a proper courtship and engagement and with the blessings of the MacMaster family, the two were married.

Elizabeth's parents had recently moved from the store building's living quarters to a newly built house at the top of the hill above the paper mill on

Columbia Street, which is now called Division Street. After Allan and Elizabeth married, they built a much larger home right across the street from the elder MacMaster's. The Duffin House was considered quite "grand" for those days. It was built in a Rural Gothic Vernacular style with sweeping porches on two sides. It was still standing in 1992, although, like the MacMaster Home, it had been modified throughout the years. Old photos show the two houses perched alone on the hill above the mill, with wooden sidewalks on each side of muddy Columbia Street going up the hill. Both homes had "victory" gardens as the only source of fresh vegetables because there were no local canneries.

In 1884, Allan joined the newly formed LaCamas Presbyterian Church that Aeneas MacMaster had started the year before. He was the seventh member of the congregation and was soon elected secretary of the Building Committee. His first assignment was to secure funding for a new church building because the services were currently being held in MacMaster's store.

There were many new members interested in joining the congregation, so there was a need for a decent church. The planned site for the church was below Aeneas MacMaster's home, where the PUD Station was located in 1992. With diligent efforts, Allan and others raised money to begin construction and, in October 1886, St. John's Presbyterian Church was dedicated. Mary Elizabeth "Leila" Duffin, the daughter of Allan and Elizabeth, was born February 8, 1886, and was the first infant baptized in the new church. A year after Leila Duffin's birth, the Duffins welcomed their first son, Charles G. Duffin.

Allan became Clerk of Session for the church in 1888 and remained in that post for twenty-seven years. Elizabeth Duffin was also active in the church as the recording secretary of the women's group. In 1889, the Duffins had a third child, Marjorie MacMaster Duffin. Five years later, on July 21, 1904, the baby of the family, Ella Maye "Maysie" Duffin, was born.

The patriarch of the family, Aeneas MacMaster, passed away in 1888, and his son, Hugh, returned from Canada to take over management of the MacMaster General Store that had moved in 1885 to larger quarters at 3rd and Columbia. After the move, Aeneas MacMaster renamed his store the

"Pioneer Store." Realizing the value to the firm of long-time employee and brother-in-law Allan Duffin, Hugh offered Allan a partnership in July 1890. The two decided to call their new business MacMaster and Company, and sales flourished as never before.

Around this time, Baby Maysie Duffin contracted tuberculosis and because it infected her spine, she had to wear a brace that was fitted in Portland. That meant the Duffins had to travel a full day by steamboat for Maysie's medical care. It also meant she couldn't play with other children.

In the early 1900's, the two oldest Duffin children, Leila and Charles, attended school with other pioneer children, including Nora Self, Harry Farrell, the McKever children, Claude Knapp, and Alice Asher. In 1901, Leila was a member of the first eighth grade class to graduate from LaCamas.

Graduation was a gala day with exercise held in a pavilion. Leila and the other girls wore white dresses with big white bows in their hair. After Leila graduated from high school in 1904, she taught school in Ellsworth and directed church school cantatas. Charles graduated in 1911, and his class included Vera Harrington, a young lady who would later marry Charles Duffin. In 1914, Marjorie MacMaster Duffin graduated from Camas Grammar School and entered Camas High School with a scientific major.

A new Duffin family home was built in 1913 on Spruce Street, with the current address being 1306 N. E. Birch. The house was just across from St. John's parsonage, where the present St. John's church is today. The new home was a Bungalow-style with horizontal emphasis, exposed rafters, and stout porch posts expressing structural purloins and braces with a gabled dormer. The home, still in its' original condition, was sold by the Duffin heirs in 1992.

In 1915, a tragedy befell the Duffins. Allan Duffin was shepherding a barge load of church children and teachers to a picnic on Lady's Island. A riverboat bore down on the barge and would have rammed it if Duffin had not intervened. In the struggle to push it away from the riverboat, he fell into the swift, cold currents of the Columbia River and gave his life for those on-board, including members of his own family. Although he was a good swimmer, it was assumed that his head hit the boat because he was never seen again. Allan Duffin was dead at the age of fifty-eight. His tombstone reads, "Here lies a Woodsman of the World."

Being a woman of strong faith helped sustain Elizabeth in dealing with the unexpected loss of her husband. The next year was a difficult one, with two small children in school and having the responsibility of providing for her family plus keeping her household going. She made the decision to assume her husband's partnership at MacMaster and Company, and as the company continued to grow, her financial affairs improved. In 1916 the partners decided to erect a new, modern two-story concrete reinforced building at 4th and Clark. It was superbly designed with many windows, and the store carried a full line of general merchandise. They hired numerous clerks to wait on the everexpanding trade from all the surrounding communities.

Marjorie Duffin graduated from high school in 1918 after being an active participant in the glee club and several plays. "Great feelings hath she of her own" was her quote in the 1918 Camas High School yearbook. Marjorie married Harold Blake in 1920, who was the son of early pioneer and feed store owner, A. M. Blake. They had two children, Betty Rose and Glenn "Skeeter" Blake. Harold started Columbia River Trucking and with its' success, built a lovely home on the Columbia River. Betty Rose married Wally Matthews, and Skeeter married Alice Blake. Both couples settled close to Marjorie and Harold Blake.

Despite a difficult childhood disease, Maysie Duffin graduated high school in 1922 as president of her class and a standout in music, both piano and glee club. "Her hair is curly, but she is straight in every other way," was the caption beneath her school photo.

Leila Duffin married Kent Chappell, who became a partner in MacMaster and Company. Kent was responsible for starting the first Boy Scout troop in town and was elected Ward Captain for Camas Heights in 1924. The Chappell's moved into the old Cowan House on N. E. 14th Avenue, one of the oldest houses in Camas. The couple had a son, Allan Chappell, and a daughter, Katherine Anne "Kay" Chappell. When grandmother Elizabeth Duffin came to visit the Chappell's on winter days, young Allan would give her a lift home on his sled. He recalls Grandma Duffin hollering, "Slow down, Allan, slow down!"

A popular vacation spot for many living in Clark County was the Washington coast, where the Pacific Ocean roared onto sandy beaches. A news item in the June 24, 1927, Camas Post notes, "A local group is leaving Wednesday for a season at the beach including Mrs. Elizabeth Duffin, Mrs. Harold Blake and children, Ella Maye Duffin and Mae Borigo. They will occupy a cottage at Ocean Park, a Washington beach resort."

Prematurely gray, Charles Duffin married Vera Harrington, daughter of the town's first mayor, J. J. Harrington. When the new Camas-Washougal Golf Club was formed in 1932, Charles was elected to represent the club in the Oregon Public Golf Association.

In 1932, Elizabeth Duffin was named one of the first women Elders of St. John's Church. She was also active in the Missionary Society and the Women's Christian Temperance Union. On February 24, 1944, Elizabeth was interviewed by the Camas Post on the occasion of her seventy-ninth birthday. She was bright and witty and related many humorous stories of early Camas and her family. However, she died a scant year later, in 1945, after a bad fall at the age of eighty. She had spent two weeks in the hospital trying to recover, but to no avail. Her tombstone read, "I have fought the good fight, I have finished the course, I have kept the faith."

Indeed, Elizabeth MacMaster Duffin had kept faith from being the first schoolmarm in Camas, to her many years of service to St. John's Church and her contributions to the MacMaster business legacy. One hour after her death, Elizabeth's first great-grandchild was born to Lt. Kenneth Powell and Katharine A. Chappell Powell in Roswell, New Mexico.

Allan Chappell served his country in World War II, married Beverly, a young woman from Iowa, and became a doctor, moving to Portland. Kay Chappell married Lt. Kenneth Powell and lived for a time in New Mexico, where they had Elizabeth Duffin's first great-grandchild one hour after she passed away. The Powell's returned to Camas for the rest of their lives. In Katherine's later years, she became St. John's Clerk of Session, a major accomplishment for a woman. She was the first woman in the MacMaster-Duffin family to follow the heritage of Aeneas MacMaster, Clerk of Session, in 1883, and Allan Duffin, Clerk of Session, in 1887. It took one hundred years for this to happen.

Leila Duffin Chappell died on November 30, 1937; Charles Duffin passed away on June 19, 1957; Vera Harrington Duffin on March 20, 1969; and Marjorie Duffin Blake on December 29, 1987.

The baby of the Allan and Elizabeth Duffin family, Ella Maye "Maysie" Duffin, followed in her mother's footsteps with active participation at St. John's that included being the unpaid church organist for over thirty years. She also started the first Camp Fire Girls group in town. Maysie, blessed with a good financial head, served as Camas City Treasurer for twenty years.

She was named the "Who's Who No. Six" personality in the October 1, 1959, edition of the Camas Post, and that was considered a big honor. When the Trailblazers came to Portland, Maysie became an avid basketball fan. As she grew older, she continued to be involved in community affairs, including the Camas Washougal Historical Society.

Being the eldest living Duffin, Maysie lovingly fussed over all of her nieces and nephews, worrying about each one, deeply touching their lives. She continued to live in the family home on Birch Street until 1991, when she became ill and was hospitalized. At the hospital, her room was crowded with Duffin family members who kept a loving vigil over her bedside until she passed away on August 18, 1991. She was survived by her two nieces Betty Rose Matthews and Kay Chappell Powell of Camas, both deceased as of this writing, and her two nephews, Glenn Blake of Camas and Dr. Allan Chappell of Portland, plus their children and grandchildren.

There were still many descendants of the Duffin family living in Camas in 1992. Those fine people are carrying on the Duffin tradition of being a vital part of the Camas community.

RICHARD T. COWAN &
JOHN A. COWAN

Author's Preface: Once in a while, in this life of ours, we discover someone who possesses so many qualities of leadership and strength that you can only feel awe and admiration for what they are able to accomplish. When you add these qualities with the handicaps of living in the mid to late 1800's, you can only conclude that if that person lived today, he would probably be a senator, governor, or maybe even the president of the United States. Richard Tankersley Cowan fought in the Civil War, owned his own business, and sired eight children. Then he came to LaCamas. In the next decade, he became a legislator, successful businessman, real estate developer, postmaster and county commissioner. We will relate here the amazing story of Richard Cowan, but are unable to explain why his life ended in disappointment. Also, in this story we included his son, John Cowan, who was a community leader in his own right, and John Ginder, who began the town's first newspaper in 1887.

❦

RICHARD TANKERSLEY COWAN was born January 15, 1834, in Lawrence County, Missouri, the fourth of ten children born to Campbell Cowan and Elizabeth Tankersley of Tennessee. When Richard was twenty-four, he married Margaret Corrilla Eidson in Barry County, Missouri. Margaret, the daughter of Henry Eidson and Mary Buford, was born October 19, 1835, also in Missouri.

Following their marriage on February 11, 1858, Richard served as a 1st Lieutenant during the Civil War, fighting for the Confederate Army. His unit was Company G, 8th Missouri Infantry "Mitchell's," and he served from 1862 through 1865.

The family moved around a bit until Richard became the owner of a general merchandise store in Ritchey, Missouri. During those years, Richard and Margaret had eight children, three that died as infants, and another, James H. Cowan, who died when he was thirteen in 1875.

The surviving children were John Alexander Cowan, born May 17, 1866, in Iron Mountain, Missouri; Florence who was born April 9, 1868, also in Iron Mountain; Martha Ann, born April 2, 1870, in Belleview, Missouri; and Clara, who was born in Ritchey, Missouri December 11, 1874. John Alexander suffered from polio as a child.

In 1884, Richard and Margaret decided to sell their business in Ritchey and join with many others who were seeking their fortunes in the west. They traveled on the old OWR&N Railroad on the Oregon side of the Columbia River. When they arrived in Portland, they took the boat upstream to the new paper mill town of LaCamas on the Washington side of the river. When the family arrived in LaCamas, John Alexander was eighteen years of age, Florence was sixteen, Martha, was fourteen and Clara was ten.

Arriving in June that same year was Aeneas MacMaster, who had bought land and built the first general store in town. He opened for business in September 1884. Following the pattern of MacMaster, Richard Cowan, who had operated a

Richard Cowan (Source Post Record)

successful mercantile business in Ritchey, Missouri, opened a similar store in the center of LaCamas. The business was named "Cowan & Knapp's" with his partner, one of the Knapp family. Richard was a smart businessman and soon realized the value of forested land on the north ridges above the LaCamas community. He wisely bought fifty acres of timbered land that became known as "Cowan's Addition."

Cowan's Addition contained 29 blocks on the first bench above town and had been surveyed in August 1884. The Addition boasted 57 inhabitants.

In 1885, the Cowan's built their Classical Revival style family home "out in the country" in the middle of the Cowan Addition at 137 N. E. 14th Avenue. That house, if it still stands in 2011, is considered "in town" today. It was built with two stories with four rooms on each floor, as well as a bath and storage areas. The Cowan House and the MacMaster House on what is now Division Street were built the same year, and as far as I could determine they are the oldest homes that were still standing in Camas in 1992. Horace Belding built his home on N. E. 2nd in 1887, and that home, although modified, was also still standing in 1992 when this book was written.

The street running north south along the side of the Cowan House was originally named Cowan Avenue. Today, it is called Ash Street. Two other streets in the area were named after his daughters, Florence and Martha. The street names were later changed, but the Cowan girls' names still appear on the curbstones. One of the main streets downtown was named Clara after the wife of D.H. Stearns, the LaCamas Colony Company's first manager, so Clara Cowan was not able to have a street named after her.

In the late 1880's, a movement was underway to build a church in the new Cowan's Addition. Services for the Presbyterian Church had previously been held at MacMaster's store. Richard Cowan became a member of the building committee for the soon-to-be St. John's Presbyterian Church, just below MacMaster's house on Columbia, now called Division. Richard had previously been an elder in the Cumberland Presbyterian faith back in Missouri and transferred to St. John's, where he was a very active member.

On December 11, 1887, there was a very grand and special event in LaCamas; nineteen-year-old Florence Edna Cowan became the bride of thirty-year-old John H. Ginder at Cowan's spacious new home on 14th Avenue. John Ginder was an experienced newspaperman, having worked for the Columbia Churchman and Vancouver Independent as a typesetter. He was from strong pioneer stock, born in 1857 on William Ginder's Donation Land Claim at the mouth of the Lewis River. He was one of six children born to Wiliam and Louisa Powers, who was his second wife. William was a farmer but later became a judge in Vancouver, and the family attained quite a prominent status. John Ginder and Florence Cowan met and fell in love while on a river boat excursion up the Columbia River.

After their marriage, John and Florence decided to settle in LaCamas, where John started the first newspaper in town that he named The LaCamas News. In the 1889 Portland City Directory there was an advertisement for

Ginder's newspaper that he called "the official newspaper of Clarke County." In the same directory, there was an ad for R. T. Cowan's establishment offering goods, groceries, and general merchandise, and five and ten acre lots in Forest Home. Even with his widespread advertising the LaCamas News was not to be a success for John Ginder. He had been plagued with ill health and could not publish the paper on a regular basis. The LaCamas News went out of business in 1892, and the Ginder's moved to Stevenson. A year later, Cowan's daughter, Martha, married F. J. Vandemarr in 1893, and the couple moved to Portland.

Richard Cowan was appointed LaCamas Postmaster in 1888, three years after arriving in town. There is a Postmaster General's Draft signed by Hugh MacMaster to R. T. Cowan dated November 1890. Enjoying his political appointment, he became a member of the Board of County Commissioners and was elected to the third Washington State Legislature in 1893. In the resume Richard wrote for the Legislative Manual of Washington, Richard leaves the years 1862-1865 blank. Those were the years he served in the Confederate Army. When he ran for office, his opposition made note of Richard's Confederate service. Cowan's photo still hangs with other early legislators at the Capital Building in Olympia.

Although Richard Cowan was tremendously successful as a politician, he went through a period of hard times financially, suffering great losses in his business. Others had the same problem during the depression years of 1893-1895 but had the stamina and means to recover. Although he had been one of the most successful community leaders and business owners in LaCamas, Richard became discouraged with the hard life of Clarke County and returned home to Missouri alone, leaving his family behind. By that time, the children were grown, and it was supposed to be a temporary arrangement. In Barry County, Missouri, he joined a partnership with another general merchandise store. In 1898, three years after leaving LaCamas, Richard Cowan died alone at Bowers Mill, Missouri. He had never returned to the west. When Margaret Cowan made the decision to stay in LaCamas instead of leaving with her husband, she did not realize it would be a final parting for the two.

Margaret sold the home on 14th Avenue shortly after Richard returned to Missouri. She must have had a feeling he would never return. The new owners of the Cowan House were Walter and Julia Marchbank. Walter was a successful businessman who owned the livery stable and delivery service in town. He went on to become a county commissioner. Sometime around 1910 the Marchbank's had a portico added to the front elevation of their Camas home and also added a new porch with large two-story columns and a foundation made of "Roffler Rock."

John and Clara accompanied their mother, Margaret Cowan, to her new home on N. E. 5th Avenue. It was very painful for her to move from the home Richard had built with so many promises and the home she loved so deeply. Her feelings were expressed in a letter to a cousin written by Margaret on July 4, 1897. She writes, "I was up the hill to church today. I don't get up there often, it is such a climb for me, though it seems good to get on the hill occasionally. I have been up to see Mrs. Mitchell once since you left, that is. The closest I've been to the old house. I don't care to see it; it makes me feel lonely."

Back row: John Cowan, Clara Cowan Sampson, Front row: Margaret Cowan Vandemarr, Margaret Cowan, Florence Cowan Grinder. circa 1900 (Source Camas Post)

The Cowan's new home on the north side of N. E. 5th Avenue was a Western Style Farmhouse with a continuing porch on the front and side elevations. Today, Margaret's 5th Avenue home is no longer there. Some say it was not demolished but moved to another location. If so, it would be interesting to discover where. Margaret Cowan died on June 11, 1908, at the age of seventy-two. She is buried in the Camas Cemetery.

The baby of the family, Clara Cowan, remained single until she was thirty-four. She had grown up an adventuresome girl and traveled to Alaska

J.A. Cowan Store, circa 1920 (Source TRHM)

in the early 1900's to open a bake shop. She loved books, especially poetry. One of her favorite poets was Tennyson. While still in her twenties, she worked at Rose Roffler Farrell's hat shop with Anna Roffler Eddy. On November 5, 1908, five months after her mother's death, Clara married Thomas Sanford Sampson. Sampson owned the shoe shop to the left of Cowan's Cigar Store. Just as a footnote, their only son, Willard "Bill" Sampson, followed in his Uncle John's footsteps by becoming Mayor of Camas in 1966. Bill served in that post for many years and was responsible for the new city hall, among other achievements.

But this story continues with John A. Cowan. He had been educated in Missouri, and his 1884 report card showed he had excellent grades even though he had very low attendance. When the Cowan family arrived in LaCamas, John had no trouble getting employment with the paper mill. He also had connections with the lumber business, and from 1888 to 1895, he invested financially and shared in the profits of the company store. In 1895, he was appointed postmaster by the Cleveland Administration and ran a cigar and confectionery store. Then, for some reason, he became a steward on the Columbia River boat, Ione, for about a year. In 1899, tired of the boating life, he established "The Old Pioneer Cigar Store" in the old McKever Building at 4th and Adams, with a billiard room and fruit store in connection.

In 1904, John became a member of the IOOF. In 1908, he was elected treasurer of the LaCamas Sluggers baseball team. In 1909, he bought a lot and constructed a new store at 216 N. E. 4th.

The store was a favorite hangout for the men of the town. It featured a bar with a brass rail, pool tables, the finest of cigars, two large round candy jars by the front door for kids waiting for their dads, and an outdoor privy just beyond the back door.

John Cowan became the second mayor of Camas from 1909 to 1911, and that was considered a big honor. He had the pleasure of seeing the first street graded during his administration. He also had the interior of his store "tastefully redecorated" in Columbia River scenery, in 1912. You could see Rooster Rock, Cape Horn, Bridal Veil Falls and other familiar scenes painted in vivid colors on his walls. Vincent Ast, as a young boy of ten, remembers riding with his dad in a horse and buggy to Cowan's Saloon in 1924. He recalls going up to the bar and ordering a "near-beer" that was a juiced-up soda pop. Going into Cowan's Saloon made him feel like a big guy!

John Ginder, Cowan's great nephew, recalls Cowan's penny dish in the store that the children were able to rummage through to find Indian Head coins.

In 1917, at the age of fifty-one, John Cowan married for the first time. His bride was his childhood sweetheart Lulu Sanders of Missouri, who had a daughter by a previous marriage, named Lena Privet, later Mrs. Andrew Moore. John built a new home in 1919, at the foot of Oneonta Street, now Garfield Street, next to the railroad. As construction progressed, John took photos of the new home where he and Lulu were to settle down as a married couple in Camas.

Lulu was a traveler and often took exciting trips away from Camas with encouragement from John to travel at will. He had to stay home to run his store while Lulu visited Berkeley, California, and Los Angeles, then on to Missouri by way of train. A news item in the June 24, 1927, Camas Post relates that a letter was received by John from Lulu, relating all her wonderful travels.

The years went by and the Ginder children fondly recall John and Lulu's visits at family gatherings. Lulu would play beautiful tunes on the piano in the living room without using sheet music. In fact she was so talented that the manager of the Camas Opera House hired her to play for his silent movies. John Cowan would bring bricks of ice cream from his store that would be cut into slices for the children who considered it a real treat.

A Camas Post item on April 1, 1932, reported that Cowan's store had been broken into by someone who smashed a back window. The bandit stole two hundred nickels from a slot machine after breaking the glass with a hammer.

John Cowan continued to be active in his business and the community until his sudden death in 1934. He had been a member of the Knights of Pythias, The Modern Woodmen of America, and the Elks Club in Vancouver. John was remembered by his many friends as being "genial and friendly with excellent personal qualities." On September 14, 1934, the Camas Post listed a Notice to Creditors of John Cowan's estate, and J. D. Currie as attorney and administrator. John Cowan died without ever having children, leaving no direct heirs. After John's death, a bereaved Lulu sold the home that John had so lovingly built at the foot of Garfield, then left Camas to live with her daughter Lena in Missouri. She did return occasionally to visit family and friends, but her final resting place was Baxter Spring, Kansas when she died in 1952.

John's sister, Martha Ann Cowan Vandemarr, passed away on May 18, 1940, in Portland, where she lived after her marriage. On February 24, 1948, baby sister Clara Cowan Sampson died in Stevenson, Washington.

John and Florence Ginder followed another path throughout their lives. After the failure of The LaCamas News back in the early 1890's, they moved to Stevenson, Washington, with their three sons, Ralph, William Eugene "Gene," and Richard, and their daughter Bernice. While in Stevenson, Inez and Arthur were born. Their daughter, Vera, was born in Vancouver. John had the opportunity to purchase the White Salmon newspaper called The White Salmon Enterprise in 1903, so the Ginder's moved, with their seven children, to White Salmon. Ruth Ginder was born during their time there.

John ran the Enterprise for six years, and in 1909, he moved with Florence and his eight children back to Stevenson where he became owner and editor of the Skamania County Pioneer. They moved into a nice home in Stevenson on Vancouver Street, but never owned a horse and buggy or an automobile, because the family walked everywhere. John ran the newspaper in Stevenson until 1922, using his children as "printer's devils." At sixty-five, his eyes were failing, so he sold the paper and moved back to Camas. He died in 1937, at the age of seventy-nine and was buried at the I.O.O.F. cemetery in Stevenson. Florence followed her husband in death in 1942 and was buried next to her husband and two sons in the family plot.

Their son, Gene Ginder, married Arlie Woods in 1909, and settled down in Camas, going to work for the paper mill. They lived in Camas with their children throughout their lives. At one time Arlie was a typesetter for the Camas Post. Their home was featured in the 1938 Industrial Edition of the Post as one of the finest homes in the city. Gene retired from the paper mill in 1953, and was featured for his "woodcutting" abilities in the 1959 Camas Post. At that time, Gene and Arlie lived on N. E. 4th Avenue.

In 1910, Florence and John's oldest son, Ralph, was tragically killed in a hunting accident at the age of twenty-two. Another son, Richard, passed away in 1929 at the age of thirty-eight.

All the surviving Ginder children were married at the time of Florence Ginder's death and living away from home. Bernice had married Walter Attwell in 1916, at Stevenson. In 1918, Arthur married Dorothy Milner and ended up in La Jolla, California. Vera moved to Wheeler, Oregon, where she worked as an assistant on the local newspaper. She met and married Clive Troy in 1924 and was able to attend her 70th class reunion at Stevenson High School in 1990. At the time of this writing in 1992, she was ninety-years old and still living in Shelton. Ruth Ginder married James Freeman in 1928, and in 1992, was still an active Camas citizen. Inez Ginder also married in 1928, a New Englander, Austin Spear, who was teaching at the time in Hempstead, New York, where they made their home after their wedding in Port Townsend, Washington.

In 1970, seventy-nine-year-old Gene Ginder passed away in Camas. His wife Arlie died ten years later, in 1980. They were the only two Ginders buried in the Camas Cemetery as of 1992. Their daughter Florence Ginder Virts, who married Charlie Girts in 1944, is also interred in the Camas Cemetery. In 1992 their son, Bill Ginder, was living with his wife in Fern Prairie. Cowan's Cigar Store continued to operate for many years after John Cowan's death. An ad in the May 14, 1953, Camas Post states, "Cowan's Cigar Store, the quickest lunch in town. Tobacco, candy, pool. 212 N. E. 4th Camas, Phone 531." So, even without the colorful John Cowan, the great tradition of his store carried on.

Both Richard T. Cowan and John Cowan will long be remembered by the citizens of Camas for their many contributions to the town's beginnings. The one hundred plus year old Cowan House on N. W. 14th was still standing in 1992. During the 1920's, Kent Chappell and Leila Duffin Chappell, occupied the home. Since then, there has been a series of owners. In 1992, the house was being seriously considered for the Local Register of Historic Places.

HUGH MACMASTER

Author's Preface: The man described in this chapter put aside his own personal happiness to carry on the tradition of his famous father, Aeneas MacMaster. Hugh MacMaster was in Quebec in 1888 ready to marry and settle down when the news came of his father's death. He returned to LaCamas, took up the reins of running the general store and it was three years later before he could marry the woman he loved, the very patient Ella Patten. In the following years, the MacMaster's were active participants in all aspects of the town's growth. They were both strong role models for those who came later. Because of his huge contributions to the beginnings of business in downtown LaCamas, I felt that Hugh MacMaster deserved his own chapter in this book.

❮❮❯

HUGH MACMASTER WAS born August 31, 1865, in Glasgow, Scotland, the son of Aeneas and Elizabeth McIndoe MacMaster. He was one of thirteen children born to the Scottish carpenter and his wife. Nine of the children survived the rigors of childhood, and together with their parents, they left Scotland in 1874, destined for Quebec, Canada. Hugh was nine years old.

During the next nine years in Canada, the family moved three times and it took a diligent effort on Hugh's part to complete his public-school education. He graduated from high school at the age of seventeen and went to work for a wholesale dry goods house in Montreal. When a restless Aeneas MacMaster went seeking new opportunities in the United States, the family including Hugh stayed behind. His father began his search on the east coast, and then headed west toward the Pacific Coast, because he had heard of a possible new paper mill town on the north side of the Columbia River. He arrived in LaCamas and built the first store in town, a two-story wooden building with living quarters attached, and hired himself a helper, Allan Duffin. Aeneas then sent for his family, who quickly followed, first by an exhaustive train ride, then by river boat up the Columbia River from Portland. When Hugh arrived at the LaCamas Landing with the rest of his family, the river boat dropped anchor in the middle of the river where a small rowboat brought them to shore. After living in cosmopolitan Canada, Hugh was surprised at how primitive the LaCamas settlement was. The town site of LaCamas was laid out on September 10, 1883, the same month the MacMaster family arrived.

Seventy-nine-year-old Elizabeth MacMaster Duffin, was interviewed on February 24, 1944, by the Camas Post and described the following about the MacMaster family's arrival, "The only store in the area was the one our father had built and most of the houses were small wooden, one room affairs. There were no schools or churches to be seen, only dense forests of trees and the beginnings of a mill ditch. Even though it was last summer, there had been heavy rainfall making the streets mud, mud and mud, the wettest mud I've ever seen with nary a plank to walk on. Settlers, Indians and animals of all types and kinds gingerly negotiated the mucky streets." Hugh MacMaster was able to get work at the newly formed LaCamas Colony Company's paper mill. The Columbia River Paper Company was not incorporated until March of 1884.

Hugh MacMaster (Source TRHM)

His first job was to help them clear the large stand of trees on the current mill site. Several trees had been uprooted by a severe windstorm in 1876, so Hugh was put to work bucking up the wood and burning tree stumps and roots. For this hard labor, he was paid fifty-nine cents for a ten-hour day.

On December 31, 1883, a large force that was mostly Chinese, began work of connecting LaCamas Lake by tunnel with the LaCamas waterfront project. The work was scheduled to be completed by May 1, 1884, and sure enough, as reported in the Portland Standard's May 8, 1884, newspaper edition "A complete sawmill having the capacity of 30,000 feet is in running order and supplies present demand."

In the five years between 1883 and 1888, the Aeneas MacMaster General Store grew by leaps and bounds. The store sold nails, shingles, and other materials to the builders of the new mill and offered a wide variety of goods to the early settlers and Native American Indians who still lived in the area. MacMaster accepted traded goods, as well as coins, in payment. The store outgrew the small wooden building and in 1885, a larger two-story structure sprang up at 3rd and Columbia, now Division Street. The new "Pioneer Store, " offered the upper story for use as the communities' lodge hall. In 1889, the Washington State Grange held its' first convention in the lodge hall.

The MacMaster's built a new little house on Columbia Street up on the hill above the paper mill, and Hugh and the family moved there. Hugh took time off from the mill in 1888 to travel to Montreal, Canada, to visit his many friends, including Ella Patton, a former school mate. Ella was born December 11, 1868, in Bury, Ontario, Canada, and had met Hugh during high school, where the two became very close. After Hugh graduated high school and left with the family for LaCamas, he was forced to leave a very good job and, also the companionship of Ella Patton, who he admired greatly. In 1888, he was determined to renew that "friendship" with Ella and begin the courting process, so he lingered in Canada until September.

An emergency wire from his mother changed all of Hugh's plans, because he was summoned quickly home. His father, Aeneas, had died suddenly on September 18 and being the oldest son, Hugh had the responsibility to return immediately to see to his father's funeral and business affairs. One of his new responsibilities was the management of his father's store. Genes run strong in the MacMaster family, and like his father, Hugh MacMaster proved to be an able and progressive businessman. The community continued to grow, and the general store flourished, and although Hugh had the help of Allan Duffin, his father's employee, he needed to share the responsibility of management. So, Hugh brought Allan in as a partner, and they renamed the store MacMaster & Company. An early advertisement for the newly named store listed H. MacMaster and Allan Duffin as owners. The ad went on to say, "The largest and best stock of general merchandise in Clarke County. We sell everything you use, eat or wear, the house where quality counts."

In a story told by another pioneer descendant, Vincent Ast, relates, "A farmer came to buy rope from Hugh MacMaster and because Hugh was the only one on duty that day, he measured rope in the usual way by sliding the rope through his hands until his arms were extended and that would measure three feet. Hugh measured out 200 feet that the farmer had asked for and then went into the back to get his rope cutting knife. Before he left, he asked the farmer to hold his hand on the 200-foot mark. While Hugh was away the farmer quickly measured out several more feet of rope and when MacMaster returned he cut the rope at the point of the farmer's hand and sealed off the end. Hugh then said to the farmer, 'okay, let's carry this rope over to the scale and give it a weigh.' It seems that Hugh was selling the rope by the pound and not by the foot. It appears the farmer had been foiled."

In 1891, with his new partner Duffin firmly established in the business, Hugh MacMaster returned to Canada to propose to Ella Patton. They returned to LaCamas and were married October 28, 1891, with the following item appearing in the November 6, 1891, LaCamas Post, "A very pleasant affair took place on the evening of the 28th of October at the residence of Mrs. Aeneas MacMaster being the marriage of her son, Hugh, to Miss Ella Patton a very estimable young lady from Montreal, Canada. A little after 8 o'clock the bride and groom made their appearance while a wedding march was being played by Mrs. Elizabeth Duffin. The bride was attired in a very becoming suit of slate while the groom wore conventional black. The solemn and impressive ceremony was performed by S. S. Meyer of the Presbyterian Church. Among the presents were some very costly and very useful." It must be noted that there were twenty-five guests present in that very small house of Aeneas MacMaster up on the hill and that was before all the little additions.

The Hugh MacMasters settled down in Camas, and became active participants in St. John's Presbyterian Church, the church Aeneas had founded. Hugh became a ruling Elder, following in his father's footsteps. When postal service first came to LaCamas, the logical place for the first post office was at the "Pioneer Store" with Aaron Mills as first postmaster. In the mid 1890's, Hugh served a term as postmaster, and some say he was responsible for the U. S. Postal Department dropping the "La" from LaCamas on October 1, 1894. The business continued to grow, making it necessary to add an additional story to the MacMaster & Company store at 3rd and Columbia. The owners decided, in 1893, to give Hugh's younger brother, Donald, an interest in the business. Donald went to work at the store, but when he married Julia Webster in 1895, he decided to study for a law degree in his spare time.

For the next three years, Donald combined work at the store with his legal studies, and in 1898, he received his legal degree and was admitted to the bar. At that time, he left Camas and moved to Vancouver to practice law. Donald went on to enjoy a very profitable legal career and become a county judge.

In July of 1898, he and Julia had a son they called "Hugh," after Donald's older brother, who he greatly admired. Unfortunately, the baby died of premature birth when he was only six hours old. Donald and Julia did have five daughters, Mildred, Dorothy, Jessie, Francis, and Margaret. Donald and Julia built a beautiful large wooden-shingled home in Vancouver, that is now on the Clark County Historical Register called "The McMaster House." Donald had dropped the first "A" out of MacMaster after moving to Vancouver. In the February 2, 1911, Vancouver newspaper, it notes that Judge Donald McMaster of the Superior Court was ill and unable to hold court in Kalama. In later years, the Donald McMasters, and Hugh MacMasters seldom socialized for reasons unknown.

After Donald left MacMaster & Company, his interest in the store was assumed by his sister, Violet MacMaster. When Violet married David Burham and moved to Long Beach, Washington, George Self bought Violet's interest. The year was 1902.

On December 15, 1905, Elizabeth B. MacMaster, mother of Hugh and the other surviving children, died at age seventy-two. She had outlived her husband, Aeneas, by more than seventeen years. They are buried side by side in the Camas Cemetery.

As a city councilman, Hugh became interested in promoting Camas to outside business, and in doing so wrote letters to interested parties in the eastern and midwestern parts of the United States expounding the virtues of Camas. One of his letters was reproduced in the 1909 Coast Magazine. His activities probably were responsible for the beginnings of the Camas Chamber of Commerce. Hugh also served as chair of the "Good Road's Committee" in Camas, when it first came into existence. This committee was a prelude to the "North Bank Highway Committee," later formed to develop plans for the Vancouver to Camas link of the Columbia River Highway.

The Camas Post of January 19, 1912, mentioned, "Mrs. H. MacMaster was a passenger to Portland yesterday." It is assumed she traveled by train because that was the popular mode of transportation to Portland at that time.

A.C. Allen, of Ridgefield, was admitted as a partner to the MacMaster and Company firm in April of 1915, and became secretary and treasurer. A few months later in September 1915, Allan Duffin met an untimely death, and his wife Elizabeth MacMaster Duffin took over his partnership, becoming a full member. Kent L. Chappell entered the firm in 1916 and became vice president with Hugh MacMaster remaining as president.

Ella MacMaster (Source TRHM)

In 1915, MacMaster was elected mayor of Camas and served in that capacity for two years. In the meantime, MacMaster & Company had grown to such proportions; plans were formulated for another larger building. In an exchange of property, Lots One and Two with the paper mill company, MacMaster & Company secured two large lots, Lots Five and Six, on the southwest corner of 4th and Clarke Streets.

Then began an immense amount of time in which MacMaster & Company inspected buildings in Washington and Oregon for those features and ideas that should be incorporated into a public service building that would prove beneficial to all the people and a mark of distinction for the town and community. In 1916, a large two-story building of reinforced concrete was erected. The first floor, that was to be the store area, boasted many glass windows and a light, airy interior. In addition, it was departmentalized to make the work of serving the public so easy that it would be a pleasure to transact business there. There were broad aisles, glass floor cases and snow-white walls to insure absolute sanitary conditions. A large lady's restroom was also provided, something that had been needed for a long time. The new restroom included rockers, couches, tables, toilet, and lavatory facilities that were available for all the ladies, regardless of whether you were a patron or not. The building's second floor was equally fine with twenty modern offices and apartments. The new building also had a full basement for storage.

MacMaster & Company hired additional clerks to handle the full line of extensive merchandise, and folks came from a wide radius surrounding Camas to shop and trade there. Hugh MacMaster, by that time short and bald, was often seen bustling here and there overseeing transactions. It was said that he was a difficult taskmaster, watchful and thrifty, and totally in control of his store's operations and staff. But his hardness as an employer dissolved when it came to serving his customers. He absolutely loved his customers and was very understanding of the paper mill's financial ups and downs, allowing folks to charge their goods until the end of the month. When

MacMaster Building, Camas 1920, current site of mill administration building on Adam Street. (Source Post Record)

they paid their bill, he would give them a free bag of candy as a thank you for doing business in his store.

Upstairs in the new building, doctors and other professionals quickly rented out the new, modern office space, and the apartments were filled up almost immediately. The corner of 4th and Clarke Streets soon became the "hub" of the town, with the new Urie "First National Bank" building being constructed on the northeast corner, and the equally new McKever Building going up on the southeast corner.

After his term as mayor, MacMaster became president of the Farmer's Cooperative Creamery Company, and a director of the Citizen's Bank of Camas. He served as president of the Camas Cemetery Association and was a member of the Masonic Fraternity and Kiwanis Club. He remained active in his business but still took time to "smell the roses." An article in the May 1, 1925, Camas Post notes. "Hugh MacMaster stepped into the post office Thursday with a fine specimen of the first rose of the season, the "Empress of China" grown at his home on the hill."

Through all their many activities, Hugh and Ella's greatest love was St. John's Presbyterian Church. Hugh was a Ruling Elder for thirty-eight years, and along with Ella, worked with the children of the parish. Ella MacMaster had a good influence on many of the young women who attended St. John's, and she started a Camp Fire Girl's group in town. She was thought of with great affection by all the young people in town and was actively involved in the Women's Christian Temperance Union.

On June 24, 1927, the Camas Post noted that Hugh MacMaster had motored to Seattle to meet his sister, Mrs. John Scott, and a contingent of his family circle from Canada. They were making an extended visit among relatives in the northwest. Another news clip, in September of 1934, reported that, "Mrs. Hugh MacMaster, Mrs. E. C. Duncan and Mrs. J. H. Roffler attended a meeting of the Columbia River Presbyterian Association in Kelso as representatives of St. John's Presbyterian Church."

In September of 1934, MacMaster aspired to become the Republican candidate for County Treasurer but was defeated by Fred Strickling 2,087 votes to 1,395 votes. Although there was heavy local voting for MacMaster in east Clarke County, he was unable to get enough votes to carry the whole county.

Of interest to MacMaster was an October 9, 1931, editorial in the Camas Post-Washougal Record regarding the Perfection Twine Company operation of the Crown Willamette Paper Mill. The editors expressed concern that having outgrown the Old Opera House building site, Perfection Twine might relocate to another city taking the payroll with them. The editorial concluded, "It is up to the businessmen and civic organizations if they want to keep the Twine Company and its' growing payroll in Camas. Certainly, it is worth a big effort."

By 1935, the height of the Great Depression was upon the country. MacMaster & Company had struggled to stay alive during the past few years because people were out of work, and those folks working had just enough money to barely survive. There was just no money for extras. At one time, MacMaster had his whole back room filled with potatoes that were brought in by people trading them for groceries. MacMaster hated potatoes and his business was declining at a sharp pace. He was a sprightly seventy years old, but he decided that it was time for him to retire. MacMaster & Company ceased operations forever, thereby closing a significant chapter of Camas history.

Although the first floor of the MacMaster Building was vacant for some time, there were still doctors and other professionals plus apartment dwellers, on the second floor. One of those who rented an apartment was, newly married Vincent, Ast who grew up in the town, and went on to become a great source for background information on Camas' history.

In 1938, seven years after the Camas Post editorial, Crown Willamette purchased the MacMaster Building to house their ever expanding Perfection Twine Company. The building, henceforth became known as "The Perfection Twine Building," and was featured in the 1938 Industrial Edition of the Camas Post. Crown Willamette, and later Crown Zellerbach, conducted operations there until 1966, when the building was demolished to make room for new administrative offices. The demolition of this historic old building was recorded by photographs in an edition of the 1966 Camas Post.

As the Post article begins, "Another chapter in the history of Camas came to an end last week." And truly, what Aeneas MacMaster had begun so many years before was now gone forever.

Hugh MacMaster, who had served as City Clerk in Camas from January of 1935 to December of 1944, fortunately did not live to see his fine building demolished. He died at a hospital in Vancouver on April 24, 1948, at the age of eighty-two. Ella, his loving wife of fifty-seven years passed away a few months later on January 18, 1949, at a nursing home in Battle Ground. They were both interred in the Camas Cemetery.

The MacMaster's were an energetic community and church minded couple who loved Camas, helping in any way they could to promote its' business and civic growth. In History of the Columbia River Valley, Hugh is described as follows, "A man of sterling character and upright principles, an able and progressive businessman and an enterprising and public-spirited citizen, he has long commanded to a marked degree the unqualified confidence and respect of his fellow man and has well merited the prosperity that has come to him."

Although there were no MacMaster children, there were many nieces and nephews in future generations who continued to live in Camas and were proud of their famous "Mac and Auntie Mac", Hugh and Ella MacMaster, early Camas pioneers.

The MacMaster's beautiful Birch Street home still stood in the same location in 1992, halfway through a loving restoration by the current owners. Throughout the years, many families lived in the spacious gentile home including the MacMaster family's own descendants, Wally and Betty Rose Blake Matthews, who owned the home for sixteen years from 1952 until 1968. They purchased the home in 1952 for $8,500 and sold it in 1968 for $13,500.

The large, elegant Hugh MacMaster House and the smaller original Aeneas MacMaster house were the only physical evidence in Camas in 1992 of the MacMaster legacy. Hopefully the two MacMaster chapters in this book plus the Duffin chapter will renew interest and bring to light once again how much this wonderful family did for Camas.

STATEHOOD AND THE GOOD LIFE

BUILDING A COMMUNITY

CHARLES FARRELL &
JAMES FARRELL

Author's Preface: Say the name "Farrell" in Camas today and most everyone fondly remembers long-time civic and community leader, Charles E. Farrell. Indeed, he was a major player in the development of Camas. However, this is the story of two brothers, James, who was the oldest of the Farrell sons, and younger brother, Charles. Both were early workers at the paper mill, both contributed in many ways to community service, and both were elected to civic positions. The Farrell brothers together helped steer a growing Camas in the right direction, to the prosperity, pride and dignity the city now enjoys.

※

JAMES AND CHARLES Farrell were the sons of Martin Farrell, who was born to Catholic parents in Ireland in 1829, and Irish Catholic Mary Mulligan, born in 1830. Martin immigrated to the United States, settled in Massachusetts, and became naturalized citizens in 1856. He was a Democrat in politics, and although he took an active interest in public affairs throughout his life, he was never elected to office. Martin and Mary met and married during the final years of the Civil War. Little did they suspect, on their wedding day, that God would bless their union with fourteen children, nine sons and five daughters.

First born was Kathrin in 1851, then James, born on September 25, 1852, in Lowell, Massachusetts. Two other Farrell sons with births recorded in Lowell, were Michael in 1854 and young Martin in 1859. Around 1860, the family moved to Oxford, a college town in Southern Ohio, about thirty-five miles from Cincinnati. It was there that Eva was born in 1861 and Anna Ella, no known date of birth, William E. in 1868, and Juliet in 1875. Charles E. Farrell was born in Oxford four years after the Civil War had ended, on November 24, 1869. Five other children were also born to the Farrell's, but names and birth dates were not found during my research.

While the family resided in Ohio, a horrible diphtheria epidemic struck the area, with six of the Farrell children coming down with the dreaded disease. Three of the "unknown" Farrell children died because of the epidemic and were buried in Oxford.

During the years in Oxford, the older Farrell children completed their education and became adults. The oldest son James married Nora, who was three years younger than him. They had six children, R. Henry, Frank, Catherine (Yettech), Harriet (Klum), Estella (Hill) and Terese "Tessie" (Wallace). The younger Martin Farrell wed Margaret, and the two became the parents of George, Edward and Gertrude.

After the diphtheria epidemic, a discouraged and saddened Farrell family, including all the married children and grandchildren, left Oxford and moved to Abilene, Kansas, to try their luck at farming. When they arrived in Abilene, the elder Martin Farrell was hired at the local

Charles Farrell (Source Farrell Family)

sorghum mill making sorghum syrup and was soon elevated to head man. With the help of his sons, he also raised corn and for a few years life went very well. One of the Farrell's farming neighbors was Mr. Eisenhower, who was the grandfather of Dwight D. Eisenhower who, as we all know, went on to become president of the United States.

During the time he was growing up in Oxford, Charles Farrell had completed most of his formal education, and although he had chores to do on his farm, he was able to finish his schooling in Kansas. But no amount of schooling could prepare Charles and the rest of his family for the years of terrible drought that befell the farmers of Kansas. The sorghum and corn fields withered and dried up, and crops turned to dust. This resulted in extremely hard financial times for everyone involved.

In 1888, James and Will Farrell, together with their friend Will Durham, left their families and made a scouting trip to Oregon. They were full of determination that a better life awaited them out west. Their hard overland trip ended in Portland, in the Oregon Territory, where they heard of a new paper mill that had opened on the Washington side of the Columbia River, ten miles east of Portland. The trio took the riverboat to the new, but bustling, community of LaCamas and were successful in obtaining jobs at the mill.

Joyous at their good fortune, James and Will returned to still bleak Kansas to move their families to what they described as a wonderful, fertile land of opportunity. The James Farrell family arrived on the Sternwheeler Ione in 1890. Nora and the children's first view from the dock was a small town with muddy streets, board sidewalks and tiny stores. Farm animals, both large and small roamed the streets trying to keep out of the way of the many pedestrians, horses and buggies. A dense forest surrounded the downtown area.

James, Nora, and their family stayed for several weeks at the wood frame Mountain House Hotel on 4th and Clara Streets. The hotel charged $1.00 per night for a room and twenty-five cents for a meal. They found a little house and lived there until one of the town's leaders, Horace Belding, died in 1895. He had owned a lovely two-story home at the corner of 2nd and Burton that he built in 1887 after selling Henry Pittock 600 acres of prime downtown real estate for Pittock's paper mill. At the time the Farrell's moved into the house it was considered "out in the woods." There was a trail that led through the woods to whatever downtown there was at that point. After dark, the Farrells found it necessary to take a lantern along so no one would step in a hole or trip over a root or a cow lying in the path.

In the meantime, the rest of the Farrell family, including twenty-two-year-old Charles E. Farrell and the elder Martin Farrell, gradually trickled westward toward LaCamas. When Charles and his parents arrived in 1891, they found most of the early settlers in the area were either farmers or paper mill workers. Several of the farmers had homesteaded in Grass Valley or Fern Prairie, but some had staked their claims on the wooded north hills that rose above the small community. There were heavy stands of timber and beautiful lakes, but no real clearings for raising crops and building a home.

The elder Martin Farrell bought property on Woodburn Hill northeast of town and began clearing his fifteen acres of trees to create a farm. Charles and one of his brothers helped their father clear the land, selling the wood to the Columbia River Paper Company for use at the mill. After the land was cleared, Charles went to work at the mill where his older brother, James, was employed. The first position he held was that of "Beater Man." The paper mill, at that time, was run entirely on waterpower supplied by LaCamas Lake. When the water level was down low in the summertime, the grinders had to be shut down.

In the 1890's, the Columbia River Paper Company went through some hard times financially due to low water and the flood of 1894. The company often missed paydays, and when times got tough the single workers got laid off first. The men were paid in gold and silver, and it was company policy that unless all the men were paid, no one would be paid. With the company close to bankruptcy, Henry Pittock's son-in-law, Fred Leadbetter took over control of the business and soon had the paper mill moving forward again. Charles ended up with the job of paymaster, a position he held for over twelve years.

While Charles was getting established, his brother James was becoming a community leader as well as a manager at the mill. When the city was founded, James helped lay out the plans and later became the City Planner. He took an active part in the construction of the railroad to the west, and was a strong leader in civic affairs. James' family was growing up, with the children attending a small three-room schoolhouse in the area. Tessie Farrell graduated from the eighth grade in 1901, along with Lylia Duffin and Herbert Coffey, children from two other pioneer families. High school was taught by one teacher in a room separate from the grade school classes. After graduation Tessie married Charles Wallace and had a son Merle. James's son, Frank "Biddy" Farrell, went to work at the mill.

In 1901, with a decent job and a steady income, tall handsome Charles Farrell's thoughts turned to marriage and the enchanting Miss Ursula "Rose" Roffler, who he had met upon arriving in Camas, occupied his thoughts nonstop. Rose, who worked full time in the paper mill, was born February 9, 1871, in Wisconsin. In 1889, two years before Charles arrived in town, the

Roffler family had traveled the overland trail from Wisconsin and arrived in LaCamas after a long, hard trip. Rose's family included her mother, Katherina, her sister Anna, and her brothers John and Ulrich. They homesteaded out by LaCamas Lake, cleared the land, and built a fine farmhouse. By the time the Martin Farrell family had settled on Woodburn Hill, the Roffler family's roots were firmly established on their own LaCamas Lake property and the Roffler's were an integral part of the budding community.

After a suitable courtship period, Rose and Charles were united in matrimony on November 30, 1901, by Reverend Father Moens who was then "Rector of LaCamas." The townsfolk remarked at what a marvelous pair they were, attractive, intelligent, and determined to make their mark in Camas.

Sometime in the early 1900's, a house was built at 4th and Clark that was referred to as the "Farrell Bungalow" or "Charlie Farrell's House." When the Urie Building was constructed at that location in 1914, the house was moved to 924 N. E. 5th Avenue where it still stood in 1992.

Charles really liked his job at the mill and made many friends but being a man of "enterprising and progressive methods" he decided, in 1903, to take a chance on a new career. After talking it over with Rose, and against words of advice from his

Ursula "Rose" Roffler Farrell (Source Farrell Family)

superintendent, Charles Farrell bought the G. N. Ranck General Store located at 4th and Clara Streets. Mr. Ranck had conducted a very successful business in the two-story wood frame building since 1888. The ground floor contained a grocery and general merchandise business, and the upper floor was living quarters.

His customers included logging cooks and towns people. Mr. Ranck's friendly competitor was Scotsman, Hugh MacMaster who had taken over the business started by his father, Aeneas MacMaster when Aeneas died in 1888.

It took no time for Charles Farrell to be regarded by the Camas community as an earnest and determined businessman who, according to a local quote, was held in high esteem for, "his sound judgment in all affairs." Working side by side, Farrell's grocery and general merchandise store, flourished and grew. Charles and Rose moved into the living quarters on the second floor of the wooden building, and in 1907, their first son, Glenn, was delivered in their home by the noted local physician, Dr. Louisa Wright. A second son, Clayton, was born April 7, 1910.

In the meantime, James Farrell continued with his civic good deeds, becoming a member of the first city council, in 1906, when Jack Harrington was mayor. James later became the City Marshal. A photo was taken around 1906 of the James Farrell family gathered all dressed up in front of their home on 2nd Street. In the photo are James and Nora, Charles and Merle, Frank and Harry Farrell, Stella Farrell Hill, Harriet Farrell Klum, Pete and Catherine Farrell Yettech, and Marilyn Bruce. The tidy Western Farm Style home was surrounded by a white picket fence.

As the years went by, Charles and Rose Farrell's store not only prospered, but became more diversified, handling a wide range of goods. Rose became a real asset to the business because she was a woman who greatly appreciated all the finer things in life. She was determined to bring items of high quality into the store that included the finest lace, china, beautiful yardage, fashions from the east and elegant hats. Rose loved to create millinery of the highest style, and her frothy hat creations were not only sold locally, but also in Vancouver and Oregon City. Her lovely younger sister, Anna Eddy, soon got involved in the business and took over management of the Oregon City stores' millinery department.

Charlie kept his team of horses and delivery wagon at an old barn he owned next to where the Dairy Queen was located in 1992. He hired a grocery manager, Will Fletcher, who phoned customers for their orders. Will would then hitch up the team and off he would go on a delivery round traveling the whole Camas, Fisher, Grass Valley and Fern Prairie area. If a customer did not have money, Charlie would trade him needed goods for wood, storing the wood until winter on the lot where the library is located. Then when winter came, he would sell the wood to the local townsfolk.

By 1911, Charles Farrell was well known as a town leader actively involved in the welfare of the community, serving for several years on the Town Council among many other activities. The May 1911 Camas Post listed C. E. Farrell as one of the top citizens, giving him credit for his excellent business know-how and work on the Town Council.

The Camas Post March 15, 1912, edition notes that twenty-five-year-old George Farrell, a well-known farmer in the area had died. He was the brother of James and Charles and left behind a young wife, Elizabeth. George was buried in the Catholic Cemetery at LaCamas Lake. On October 16, 1914, Charles' father, Martin Farrell died. Martin's wife and Charles's mother, Mary Mulligan Farrell, lived another two years and passed away on February 24, 1916. The passing of the elder Farrells left oldest son, James Farrell, the head of the Farrell clan in Camas.

In 1915, Charles and Rose Farrell contracted John Roffler, Rose's brother and early Camas home builder, to build them a new home on the outskirts of town. Rose had received a postcard from the east coast with a photo of a large, stately mansion on it. She showed the photo to her brother saying, "I want a house just like this one." So, without benefit of blueprints and just working from the image on the photo, John Roffler constructed a magnificent home for the Farrell's with huge columns and porticoes. The home and surrounding gardens took in a whole city block and is still located today at N. E. 4th and Ione Streets. A very excited Farrell family moved into their new

"Charlie Farrell's House" - Home built in 1915 *by John Roffler for Charles Farrell and Ursula Rose Roffler-Farrell at 416 Ione.* **Photo 2005.** *(Source TRHM)*

Farrell Building 1924 – 305 NE 4th Ave (Source TRHM)

home in 1916, and this beautiful house continues to be the most spectacular in Camas with its' location of "almost" downtown.

In 1923, a terrible fire swept through most of the block of wooden buildings between Birth and Cedar Streets on N. E. 4th Avenue. Fire units from Camas, Vancouver and Portland came to battle the huge blaze. Luckily the Farrell Store was spared, but it got Charles to think that it might be just a matter of time before his wooden building went up in smoke. So, he demolished his thirty-five-year-old frame Farrell Building in 1923, and had John Roffler build him a large cement block building of two stories and a basement at the same location. The new building was in the Commercial Style, a modest two-story Classical Organization American Store Front design with Roffler cast stone or "Roffler Rock" as it got to be known.

Before the building neared completion, it was leased to J. C. Penney, a national retailer of clothing and general merchandise. Penney's conducted business in the Farrell Building for eleven years until 1935 when early businessman, Robert Stoller built a fine new building immediately across the street on the corner. Seizing the opportunity for newer quarters, Penney's moved into the Stoller Building.

During the time that Penney's occupied the Farrell Building, Charlie Farrell was busy constructing a new theater next door on 4th Street. T. S. Woolson's old theater building on Adams Street had been gone for several years to make way for the paper mill's expansion. Camas needed a theatre and Charlie was determined to give them the best one he could. The building was designed in the Mission-Mediterranean/Spanish Colonial Style, two story stucco and round headed. Construction of the new Granada Theater was completed in 1927 and when it opened it was considered one of the most modern and well-equipped theaters between Vancouver, in western Washington, and Goldendale in eastern Washington.

In the meantime, Rose had been operating her thriving millinery business out of her home at 4th and Ione. When the Granada Theater opened in 1927, she moved her expanded business into a little shop that was part of the theater building. She called her new store "The Fashionette," because it supplied the ladies of Camas with the very latest fashion as well as hats.

When Penney's moved to the Stoller Building in 1935, "The Fashionette" moved into the Farrell Building where Rose was able to expand even further. Rose and her sister, Anna Eddy, operated their successful business at this location well into their eighties. In 1955, the building was updated, but the modifications did not mar its' historic integrity. As of 1993 when this book was being written, "Farrell and Eddy's" was still in business at that location. Nevertheless, the location began in 1888 as Glen Ranck General Store and continued for one hundred and five years, making it one of the oldest businesses in Clark County as of 1993.

Glenn Farrell, oldest son of Charles and Rose, graduated from Camas High School in 1926 after being active in sports and school activities and vice president of his class. He is described in the 1926 yearbook, as being "Quiet, Modest, Useful." During his school years, he met Helen Drewfs who had moved with her family from Portland to Camas when she was a child. Helen also attended Camas High School where she was active with drama and vaudeville, graduating in 1927. Glenn and Helen both attended and graduated from the University of Washington. After graduation, Glenn found a position at First National Bank in Portland and Helen began teaching German and music in Camas. The couple married in 1934 with a lovely ceremony at St. James Cathedral in Seattle. Shortly after their marriage, Helen gave up teaching because during those times, no woman could be married and teach in the educational field. In 1936, Glenn left the bank in 1936 and went to work in his parents' store. Glenn and Helen moved into a new house on the north side of the Farrell estate and had a family of five children.

James Farrell died August 11, 1930, after an illness. His obituary in the August 15 Camas Post lauds him as a Camas pioneer and the man who helped plan the City of Camas. Five years later on July 2, 1935, Nora Farrell died and was interred next to her husband, James in the Camas Cemetery. What happened to the James Farrell children is not known to this writer.

Throughout his life, Charles Farrell continued to be active in business and civic affairs. He was a member of St. Thomas Catholic Church and the Modern Woodmen of America. In his later years he was considered "Camas Foremost Senior Citizen," spry and alert into his nineties.

Ursula Rose Roffler Farrell died Christmas Day 1957, at the age of eighty-six. Grief stricken, Charles closed the large old family home and moved into his son's house. He lived another ten years and was ninety-eight when he passed away on November 12, 1967. Two years later his son, Clayton, died at fifty-seven years of age. Glenn Farrell lived another twenty years, passing away on May 23, 1989. Glenn's wife Helen was still living in her family home at the corner of the Farrell property in 1992. Glenn and Helen's son, Chuck, and his wife Nita Farrell, were living in the large old family home in 1992, and were restoring the home to the grand and glorious residence it once was. The home had been closed up for over ten years and had deteriorated to a great extent during that time.

As of 1992, another of Glenn's sons had taken over the management of the Farrell-owned properties with all the skill, determination, and vision that Charles Farrell once demonstrated.

Margaret McCoy lived on the property that her grandfather, Martin Farrell, once owned on Woodburn Hill. The old house, built in 1895, that sits next to the Woodburn School Building is now remodeled and owned by others. The James Farrell/Horace Belding house, built in 1887, was still standing as a monument to the past at the corner of 2nd and Cedar Streets in 1992. There were some changes, but they were still easily recognizable.

All the Farrell's who have passed on would be proud that their grandchildren and great-grandchildren are carrying on the fine traditions of the pioneer Farrell Family.

J. T. SELF & NORA E. SELF

Author's Preface: A father and a daughter. One an early pioneer who worked at the paper mill and served his town well, and the other so dedicated to the educational needs of the community that she devoted her whole life to her students. These were two strong, caring people from the same family, James T. Self and Nora E. Self, both leaders in their own way. For over fifty years they made the impact of their efforts felt in Camas, and when they were gone there was a void that no one else could even begin to fill.

◈◈◈

JAMES THOMAS SELF was born on February 15, 1863, in Jacksonville, Illinois, the son of Irish-German and Scotch-Irish parents. His father was Thomas M. Self, who was born in Illinois in 1840 to James H. Self and Sarah Abrams Self, both from Kentucky. James Self's mother was Sarah Snelling Self, born June 1839, in Frankfort, Kentucky. As a young boy of six, James traveled with his family to Nebraska by covered wagon. He had one brother, George, and a sister, Edith Self (Whitman).

As James grew into manhood, he was of tall and slender build with a friendly and outgoing personality. He loved history and this was to evolve into the rare historic collections he acquired in his later life. On February 16, 1886, James Thomas Self married Mary Agnes Hallacy in Kansas. Mary was petite in stature, but cheerful and goodhearted in nature. She was born in Listowel, Ontario, Canada, on August 14, 1862, one of nine children. Her parents were Timothy Hallacy and Mary Gaynor Hallacy both of 100% Irish stock, with Timothy born in Ireland in 1823, and Mary Gaynor Irish born in 1835.

Throughout their lives together, Jim Self fondly referred to his bride as "Molly" instead of her given name of Mary. The James Selfs settled in Brock, Nebraska, and that is where their first child, Nora, was born on May 20, 1888.

The family later moved to Gerrard, Kansas and celebrated the birth of a son, Edward James "Ned" Self on August 9, 1890.

Like so many others who lived in the east and Midwest during the mid to late 1800's, James and Molly gathered all their belongings in 1891 and ventured westward where they hoped to enjoy new opportunities. Joining them on the trip west were Nora, who was three, one year old Ned, Grandmother Sarah Self and brother George Self.

James Self's first employment in the west was helping to construct the first Harney School in Vancouver, Washington. When that job was completed, he went to work for the paper mill in Camas. The family moved to Camas around 1892, and it was in that young, rapidly growing town that Mae Self was born on February 12, 1892, and Elizabeth Irene "Betty" Self, on October 19, 1893.

The Self family, except for George, became members of St. Thomas Catholic Church that was located on the south shore of LaCamas Lake. Molly would walk from town to the monthly services, pushing her baby buggy as best she could over the bumpy, one-mile-long dirt road. The other children would tag along at their mother's side. On other Sundays of the month, the children would attend Sunday School at the Presbyterian Church where their father, James, sang in the choir. It was not unusual for churchgoers in town to take part in any religious events that were held regardless of which church they belonged to. Neighbors helping neighbors and just getting together meant good times. George Self joined St. John's Presbyterian Church as a full member serving on the Board of Trustees, in 1897.

In the years that followed, James Self became quite active in community affairs and was acting "Postmaster" for nine months in 1899. He then became the new town's "police judge" otherwise known as "Justice of the Peace." After working with MacMaster in his store, Jim Self started a real estate business with T. H. Gavin in conjunction with a second-hand store, and that was an interesting combination of marketing. Their motto was "We sell you a home and everything in it." Self's next adventure was to go into a business with F. B. Barnes that involved real estate, loans, insurance, and nursery stock. Barnes served as the town's notary public, while Self was Justice of the Peace.

Record has it that around 1904, Jim Self went back to work for the paper mill becoming a long-time employee. At the same time, he became a keen student of local history and started his collection of American Indian artifacts and old guns.

George Self was elected City Clerk in 1907. According to a 1908 Camas Post, both James and George Self were re-elected to their town posts at a lively City Council meeting. In a 1911 edition of the Post, J. T. Self was listed as being a distinguished Camas citizen. While James Self was establishing himself as a pillar of the community, the Self girls and brother Ned, were growing up. Nora Self attended a local grade school between 1895 and 1903. After graduation from grade school, she traveled by boat to Vancouver to attend high school, staying in Vancouver during the week and coming home on weekends. At that time there was no high school, in East Clarke County. After high school Nora attended summer school at the College of Puget Sound and taught her first school at Ellsworth-Image in 1907-1908. Between 1908 and 1911, she taught in Washougal.

Nora Self resumed her schooling in San Jose, California, and when she graduated from college, she began to teach at St. Mary's Academy, a Catholic girl's school in Portland, Oregon. After attending summer sessions at Oregon State University, where she was a Phi Beta Kappa Key and the University of Washington, Nora was hired in 1916 to teach Home Economics at Camas

Camas 7th grade class 1911 with Nora Self as teacher. (Source TRHM)

High School. At that time the high school was a large white wooden building that perched at the top of Garfield Street overlooking the town. In 1992, the old high school was used by the Garfield Performing Arts Center.

Nora's photo can be found in all the old high school yearbooks from the late teens into the 1920's and early 1930's. In the 1922, LaCamas Yearbook, under "Faculty," she is described as teaching Domestic Economy and Algebra. Her education is listed as San Jose, California Normal and Oregon Agricultural College. Mr. William Painter was listed as principal of the school. Meanwhile, sister Betty Self married B. J. Pillette and they had a son, Jim, who in 1992 was still living in Camas. Mae Self married Leo Jerman, and moved into a house built by John Roffler at N. W. 12th and Ash Streets in Camas. This was the Jermann home for many years. Although five children were born to Mae and Leo, three of the five succumbed to fatal childhood illnesses. The two surviving children were Betty Jean and Mary Claire.

Nora Self (Source TRHM)

Edward "Ned" Self married Anna Mary Snyder in Escanaba, Michigan, and they became the parents of five children including daughters Betty, Barbara, and Lenore (Lee) Rodgers. Their two sons were Edward and Robert. The Self children's grandmother, Sarah died January 14, 1926, in Portland, Oregon and was buried in the Camas Cemetery.

Approximately 1928 to 1929, James and Molly Self hired Fred Mickelson, who was a manual training teacher at the high school, to build them a new home at 1623 N. E. Division. The home was designed in the Dutch Colonial Revival or Southern Colonial Style and originally featured Hidden Brick and many other fine details. The Self's lovely new residence was featured in the 1938 Industrial Edition of the Camas Post. Although James and Molly lived in this home for the rest of their lives, the house is referred to as the "Nora Self House." Nora never married and lived with her parents until their deaths.

There was a notice in the 1925 Camas Post that "Miss Self" supervised a Washington State College extension course in sewing at the high school. Working with her on this project was Mrs. Robert Stoller. Nora eventually became Dean of Girls and finally, Camas High School Principal for many, many years, retiring in 1949 after serving her last two years as a guidance counselor.

During the war, Nora was a community activist, doing Red Cross and Blood Bank work, and she became a member of the Community Fund Committee. After the war was over, Nora helped many Camas GI's who returned from the war effort finish high school and get their diplomas. She assisted other students in obtaining scholarships, encouraging them in their future work, always keeping track of the graduates as they scattered throughout the world.

In 1930, Nora Self was the first president and prime mover in organizing the Camas branch of the Business and Professional Women's Association. There were fifty charter members. The group honored her in 1938 by building a Tudor Revival English Style Manor house at 1313 N. E. Garfield and calling it "Nora Self Hall." Although originally used as a clubhouse for BPWA, it later became a place for community gatherings and meetings and was also used as a cafeteria for the school children. A few years later, the BPWA presented Nora with their first "Woman of Achievement" award.

Nora worked to abolish obscene magazines in Camas in 1933. She was president of the American Association of University Women, a charter member of the Camas-Washougal Soroptimist Club and organizer and first president of the American Legion Auxiliary. Other groups she belonged to through the years were Washington Federation of Garden Clubs, the Cemetery Board, the first woman member of the City Planning Commission and the National Retired Teachers Association.

Washington State University honored Nora Self for her work in community welfare, a much-deserved award. Of special interest to Nora was the Clark County Guidance Clinic. She was an active member of St. Thomas

Catholic Church, a member of the Altar Society and an early organist at the church. She collected Madonna's and Hummel's and was an expert at weaving.

Nora Self was fondly remembered by Merle Rich when I interviewed her for this book. Merle's husband, Howard, managed the former Copeland Lumber store on N. E. 3rd Street for many years. Merle describes Nora as being a very tall, strong woman who came into the store and carried out her own roofing supplies to put in her small coupe. When Merle and Howard first came to town and were looking around for houses to buy, their three favorites were the Self House, the Farrell House and the Oak Park John Roffler IV House. At that time none of the homes were for sale and Merle had no idea that someday she would become owner of the Self House.

The Selfs were mentioned in several news items throughout the years. The October 9, 1931, edition of the Camas Post notes that Miss Nora Self and her parents, Mr. and Mrs. J. T. Self drove to Salem, Oregon on Sunday to visit with friends. In the December 7, 1934, Post, J. T. Self is listed as receiving his thirty-year pin from the Camas Paper Mill along with many others.

The February 18, 1936, edition of the Washougal newspaper had a picture story of the Selfs celebrating their fiftieth wedding anniversary. Scores of friends stopped by an open house at the Self residence on Division Street. The house was filled with flowers and Mrs. Hugh MacMaster was one of the hostesses for the afternoon. It was a joyous occasion with Mary Self declaring, "I've lived fifty years with Mr. Self, and I'm perfectly satisfied." She also said that the secret to marital success was never to have the first quarrel. Saturday evening, the family celebrated the Golden Wedding Anniversary with a special dinner. All three daughters and their families were present, as well as George Self and his family from Salem, Oregon. Son Edward Self who was living in Ontario, Canada, was unable to attend.

The Self's made the newspaper again in 1941, celebrating fifty-five years of happiness. A large, captioned photo appeared in the Camas Post. A family dinner was held at Leo Jermann's residence. Two celebrations took place in 1942 for the fifty-sixth anniversary of the Selfs. Breakfast at Jermann's and a dinner at the Self's Division Street home. George Self Sr. of Salem, and Mr.

and Mrs. George Self, Jr. of Portland, were the out-of-town guests. And finally, sixty years. On February 15, 1946, an open house was held for their many friends to join the Self's in this momentous occasion.

In his later years, James Self's early Native American and pioneer collection of artifacts became the subject for several articles in the local newspapers. Historians in Clark County came to visit his collection that contained rare specimens of old guns and other weapons and tools, plus many Native American artifacts. Self was also an avid photographer and had a great collection of early Camas photos.

On June 25, 1948, Mary Agnes "Molly" Self, died at the age of eighty-six. Her adoring husband for so many years, James Thomas Self passed away on January 31, 1951, when he was 88. The couple had experienced so many changes in Camas through the years and had been an integral and important part of the town's history.

As written earlier, Nora Self remained single her whole life and her joy in life was teaching and helping others including her own parents in their final days. As an example of how Nora's students felt about her, a 1948 article in the Camas Post reported that, "Eldon Johnson a Camas

Self family - left to right: Mae, Mary, James, Nora and Bessie (Source Post Record)

High School senior and athlete has sculptured a bust out of clay of his favorite teacher, Nora Self. It is a good likeness of the high school principal."

For many years, Nora owned a choice piece of land high above Camas and the Columbia River. It was on this lovely property that she had envisioned building her dream home someday. Unfortunately, that dream was never realized. In 1957, being in ill health, Nora moved into a small knotty pine cottage she constructed on the property adjoining her family home at 16th and Division. She lived there for one year until her death on January 21, 1958, at the age of seventy.

In August 1966, Howard and Merle Rich purchased the Self House and restored many of its' original exterior features. Howard had served as Mayor of Camas for a few years. After Howard died Merle lived in the house alone tending to the beautiful gardens. In 1991, she sold the home and moved to a smaller residence in Camas. The Self House was voted to the Local Register of Historic Places while this book was being written.

Nora Self Hall has long been the property of the Tidland Corporation and used as a church building in the years leading up to the writing of this book in 1992. The condition of this historic building had deteriorated, and one can only hope that restoration work was undertaken since this book was written. Nora Self Hall is a fine example of English Tudor design and should be recognized on historic registers.

Memories of Nora Self who contributed so much to her community and her fellow human beings will be with the people of Camas forever. She was a lovely woman who spoke clearly, almost poetically we are told, regardless of the subject or location. It can only be assumed that from all her years of teaching she mastered the art of communication as few others do. It was the wish of many in this vicinity in 1992, that someday the Camas School District will give Nora Self a fitting memorial, a school building named in her honor. Rewriting this chapter in 2011, I sincerely hope that this has been done. If not, why not?

ROBERT STOLLER &
FRED STOLLER

Author's Preface: It was just a boat trip, upriver but when Robert Stoller stepped onto the dock in LaCamas he was hooked for life. First an innkeeper, then a builder of wooden buildings, followed by construction of brick buildings that are standing strong and tall today in downtown Camas. Automobile dealer, bank officer, hotel and restaurant owner, you name it, Robert Stoller did it. Then his cousin Fred Stoller came to town and went into the furniture and funeral business. Everywhere you went, it was Stoller this and Stoller that. Who said the Swiss didn't know how to do business?

❧

ROBERT STOLLER WAS born May 17, 1870, in Kaunderground, Frutigen, Switzerland. Robert was blessed with an excellent education, and in 1891 he came to the United States with his brother Christian and their families. The Stoller's had been lured to America by their uncle, the father of Fred Stoller, who was one of the first settlers in Trout Lake, Washington, around Mt. Adams. His uncle had written marvelous stories back to the old country, telling of the great opportunities in the Pacific Northwest part of the United States.

Before leaving Switzerland, Robert married lovely Swiss-miss, Lizzie Wampfler, who was born October 18, 1876. She shared his passion to seek new adventures across the seas.

When they arrived in America, the Stoller brothers migrated west with their families, originally spending time in Trout Lake, Washington, visiting with their uncle and cousins. However, the two brothers ended up in Vancouver, Washington, where they started the first match factory in the area. With the great flood of 1894, the business was washed away, and the brothers were forced to begin anew. Discouraged, Christian returned to

Switzerland with his family. Robert was left to dispose of the machinery they had managed to save and look for other work. He soon found employment at the Vancouver Brewery.

On August 16, 1896, a daughter, Liddy, was born to Robert and Lizzie, but the baby died twenty-seven days later of infant diarrhea. Robert and Lizzie were devastated but did become parents of two other children, Olga Stoller (Brown) born in 1899 and George Stoller, born in 1902.

In 1903, Robert Stoller booked passage on the Jessie Harkins riverboat captained by Captain Hosford and navigated up the Columbia River to Camas. When the steamboat arrived in the darkness of the evening, they were met at the river landing by the current proprietor of the Mountain House Hotel, the leading hotel in Camas. The proprietor escorted his guests by Kerosene lantern to the hotel gingerly, sidestepping the boulders that lay in the muddy streets. The single-story wooden Mountain House, located on the southeast corner of 4th and Clara Streets, was originally opened in July of 1884 by Grant Short of Vancouver in partnership with J. W. Wright. There were twelve rooms, and the rates were one dollar per day with family style meals served for twenty-five cents. In 1887, Mr. Westfall installed a bathroom for the accommodation of the hotel's patrons indicating that he was the current owner. In the 1890's, Fred Fallman owned the hotel and spruced it up, making it more comfortable. There was a lamp fire in one of the rooms during the 1890's that caused damage to the room and the guest.

Although Camas was still in its early growing stages in 1903, Robert and Lizzie Stoller liked the hustle and bustle of the paper mill town. The paper mill itself was housed in a red barnlike building not much larger than a modern skating rink. Robert had no desire to work at the mill, so he looked around for other possibilities. Lo and behold, the owner of the Mountain House was interested in selling the hotel and before he knew it, Robert Stoller was the new owner and "Innkeeper" of the Mountain House.

Citizens of Camas and guests at the hotel soon called Robert "the host with the most." He set out to make improvements, turning the Mountain House into a thirty-six-room hotel by adding a second story and an ell. He also modernized the restaurant, serving only the very finest of foods. He called his remodeled hotel "The Camas Hotel and Restaurant." The inn soon became a mecca for traveling salesmen called "Drummers" in those days. They used the hotel as their base of operations for selling to the surrounding territory.

On June 22, 1907, Lizzie Stoller passed away at the age of thirty-one and was buried in the Camas Cemetery. Robert was a widower with two small children, and to compensate for his loneliness he threw himself into making Camas a better place to live and work. Three years later, in 1910, Robert married a young woman named Mary D. who was born May 7, 1886, in Schleswig-Holstein, Germany. A photo in the 1910 Camas Post shows Robert and Mary Stoller, eight-year-old George and eleven-year-old Olga dressed in their finery. The Stollers built a new home at the site of the current Riverview Savings building.

The May 11, 1911, Camas Post lists Robert Stoller as one of its' leading citizens stating, "Robert Stoller has lived in this section for the last eight years and during that time has been almost continually in the hotel business. At the present time he owns and runs the Camas Hotel and Camas Restaurant. Both the hotel and restaurant are modern and up to date in every respect. They deserve to be and are well patronized."

According to the Camas Post, in 1912 Robert Stoller presented a request to the City Council that Clara Street be opened to the railroad, as the company officials has expressed a willingness to rededicate the portion of the street owned by the railroad. Also in 1912, George Stoller, who was ten at the time, played on the baseball team with Merle Wallace, William Karnath, Roy Van Buskirk, and a lad named "Tuffy." Although the team had other players, there were only six uniforms that everyone had to share.

By 1914, when automobiles were becoming popular thanks to Henry Ford, Robert Stoller bought the town's Ford Agency from Harry S. Parker. "Parkers" was housed in an old wooden building located at the corner of 3rd and Clara, next to the Camas Hotel. After completing the purchase, Stoller rebuilt the structure using "Roffler Rock" or cast cement blocks in its' construction. He renamed the Ford agency "Stoller Motor's" and his new business operated on that corner until 1944, when Weslie Motor's took over.

In 1915, the Crown Willamette Company was interested in building a large inn on the site of Stoller's house on 3rd Street. Not one to hamper progress, Stoller sold his lot to Crown Willamette and had his home moved from that site to a permanent location up the hill at the northeast corner of 6th and Birch. It took a team of horses a week to move the house up the hill and the Stollers continued to live in it during their home's transit. Once the Stoller house was settled in its new location, Robert and Mary lived there for the rest of their lives.

Olga Stoller graduated from Camas High School in 1917 as an English major. She had been very active in drama and music, as well as being president of the H. H. Club. Her motto, as written in the Lackamas yearbook was "My eyes just won't behave."

At about the same time, W. C. Mansfield, Roy Dobbs, Robert Stoller and others felt Camas had grown enough to support another bank. On September 19, 1919, the group formed "Citizen's State Bank" with Stoller as president and Roy Dobbs as cashier. A year later, Edna Blake Carkin joined the bank as an assistant cashier. The town's first banker was O.F. Johnson, who started Camas State Bank with his father-in-law, Emil Bauman in 1908. In 1915, Camas State Bank moved into the new Urie Building at 4th and Clark and was renamed "First National Bank." Citizen's State Bank took over the building vacated by Camas State Bank at 4th and Burton, renting the space from O. F. Johnson.

George Stoller graduated from Camas High School in 1921, after being very active in football, basketball, president of his sophomore class, manager of the yearbook, class plays and operettas, yell leader and student body treasurer. Sometime later, George married a young woman named "Marie" from Idaho, and they lost a newborn infant in June of 1930, and another child aged one day in June of 1931. Another son, Alan, was born to them in August of 1938, with the birth announcement appearing in the Camas Post. George and Marie Stoller owned and operated the "Sweet Shoppe" in the 1930's, with Marie being the "chocolate dipper." The occupant in 1992 was the Chamber of Commerce. After the Sweet Shoppe they owned and operated the High

Spot Restaurant and Liberty Theater in downtown Camas and the Auto View Drive-in Theater on Prune Hill.

In 1922, the new McKever building on the southeast corner of 4th and Clark, was completed and ready for occupancy. Citizens State Bank moved into the ground floor space that was directly across from Johnson's First National Bank in the Urie Building. Friendly competition then prevailed. The old Johnson bank building was turned into a meat market.

Mary Stoller and well-known teacher, Nora Self, led an extension course in sewing at the high school that was sponsored by Washington State College in 1925. The Camas Post noted in their May 1, 1925, edition that Robert Stoller had won the attendance prize, as usual, for the Camas Kiwanis Club. Much merriment was demonstrated at the announcement, according to the newspaper.

With the success of Stoller Motor's and the Camas Hotel, other ideas were forming in Robert Stoller's head. He now had the means to fulfill his dream of building his own commercial buildings in town. By 1929, a fine brick building was constructed on the northwest corner of 4th and Clara

Robert Stoller, circa 1950 (Source Alan Stoller)

Streets. The lower floor was used for retail business with apartments for rent on the second floor. Hunter's Hardware occupied the store space for many years. In 1992, "Al's Record Hut" was one of the current occupants.

In 1933, Stoller moved his bank once again from the McKever Building to the ground floor of the Urie Building across the street. H. S. Clark was president of Citizen's State Bank in 1934, with Robert Stoller as vice president. Roy Dobbs continued as cashier.

In 1934, Stoller demolished his beloved Camas Hotel. He knew that the old wooden structure had seen its' day, and Stoller thought that a fine new brick building on the site would be more appropriate. So, construction began and the one and a half story building was completed by 1935. J. C. Penney's quickly signed a lease for all the space, moving from their location in the Farrell Building that was right across the street. Penney's remained in Stoller's building until the 1980's, when they closed their Camas store and left the area. John's Western Store then took over, but in 1992 the space was occupied by a restaurant.

The May 1938 Industrial Edition of the Camas Post lauded the success of nineteen-year-old Citizen's National Bank, reporting that the bank's resources were over one million dollars. The bank's directors were Dr. Andresen, James Duvall, W. E. Ginder, Karl Laux, and Sam McKever.

An article in the October 13, 1938, Camas Post reported that the Robert Stollers, George Stollers and others from Camas attended a meeting of the Eastern Star in Vancouver on Saturday night to meet the Worthy Grand Matron. This was followed by a visit to Camas on Monday by the Worthy Grand Matron, where Mary Stoller was one of the hostesses.

Stoller constructed his third downtown building in 1940 just to the west of Swank Home Furnishings. Several businesses have occupied the one-story space through the years, and in 1992, Crown Home Furnishings was using it for their appliance sales. While Robert was busy constructing buildings, Mary Stoller was active in "White Shrine," as were many other women in town. She was also a member of St. John's Missionary Society and was president of the Fidelis Club of the Eastern Star.

By 1944, Robert Stoller was seventy-four and felt it was time to retire. He sold Stoller Motors to Weslie Motors, ending thirty years of operating his automobile business in Camas. Eleven years later, on October 22, 1955, Robert passed away in Vancouver, at the age of eighty-five. In 1957 his wife, seventy-one-year-old Mary joined her husband in death.

As of 1992, it had been nearly forty years since Robert Stoller died, but the buildings he so lovingly constructed still stood as monuments to his memory and many years of dedication to his town. The Stoller family continued to live in the community their ancestor helped to build.

In 1959, Robert's grandson, Alan Stoller married Gwen Beauchamp the daughter of Lawrence Beauchamp, Camas' first paid fire chief. Alan and

Gwen raised their family in Camas as have numerous cousins and other descendants of the Stoller's.

And, now to the other Stollers headlined in this chapter, Frederick "Edward" Stoller, cousin of Robert and Edward's son Fred Jr., who were also important in the development of Camas. Edward was born in 1863, also in Switzerland. His family immigrated to the United States when he was eighteen and originally settled in Illinois. Edward had two sisters, Lizzie and Mary, and one brother, Kelian. Early on, Edward became a naturalized citizen loving the natural resources and land of opportunity that America offered. The family followed the Oregon Trail to the Oregon Territory ending up in Trout Lake, Washington. Edward became engaged in dairying and farming and joined the Washington State Grange when it was formed.

It was in Trout Lake that Edward met beautiful Lydia. She was born in Iowa, on March 7, 1869, and came west with her family in 1878, as the first settlers in the Trout Lake area. Edward and Lydia were married in 1893, when Edward was thirty and Lydia was twenty-four. They raised two sons, Fred Jr. and Gilbert, and a daughter, Edith.

Fred Stoller Jr. (Source Steve Stoller)

When the children were grown, Gilbert decided to stay in Trout Lake with his parents. Daughter, Edith, married Frank Wallace and moved to California. Fred Jr. fell in love with Laura Pennell who was born in Forest Grove, Oregon, in 1899. She went to Canby High School and after graduating in 1919, she went to work for First National Bank in Canby. Laura and Fred married in 1922, and a year later moved to Camas where Fred Jr. purchased a furniture business from William Baz at 231 N. E. 4th Avenue. The store that Fred named "Stoller Furniture" was housed in an old wooden building like most of the businesses in Camas at that time. The Stollers became involved in the Camas community and soon had a wide circle of friends. They had one son, Dale F. Stoller.

The elder Stollers, Edward and Lydia, moved to Camas in 1928 to be closer to their son, Fred Jr. and other relatives including Edward's cousin, Robert Stoller. Edward and Lydia became active in the local grange, and in 1930, they moved to Washougal. They also took time out to visit friends in Trout Lake according to a news item in the September 14, 1934, Post Record. The same year his parents moved to Camas Fred Jr. constructed a new brick building at 415 N. E. 4th Street to accommodate his expanding furniture business. That building was still standing in 1992 and had been used for many different businesses including the Camas Vision Center.

In 1932, Fred Jr. had another gracious building constructed that he called "Stoller Memorial Chapel." It was located on the northeast corner of 4th and Beesan Streets, now called Dallas Street. His funeral business was immediately successful because of the care and dedication demonstrated by Fred and Laura in carrying out the duties of their sensitive profession. Little did Fred know when he opened his funeral chapel, that he would be holding services there for his own wife, Laura, who died unexpectedly in 1935 after an operation at Clark General Hospital. She was only thirty-five years old, and at the time of her death she was president of the Business and Professional Women's Club, past Matron of the Eastern Star, and a member of the Library Board, plus being active in White Shrine.

In 1940, Fredrick "Edward" Stoller, Sr. died at his home in Washougal, at the age of seventy-seven, after suffering from heart problems. Lydia followed him in death three years later in 1943. She was staying with her daughter in California at the time, but services were held at the Stoller Chapel in Camas with interment in Portland.

Fred Jr.'s son, Dale grew up in Camas and became a funeral director at his father's funeral chapel. He married Phyllis Hart from Walla Walla, and they had three sons, Steve, Jeff and Lloyd. After his father sold the funeral home to the Brown family in the 1960's, Dale went to work for Wilhelm Trucking in Portland. Fred built Brown's Funeral Home's new building for the chapel on Garfield, and the old funeral home was converted into a store building for

Camas Furniture Company. In 1992, it was the site of Coast-to-Coast Hardware. Dale passed away in the early 1990's.

Dale's son, Steven Stoller, married Linda Lorenz, who was the great-granddaughter of another pioneer, Henry Lorenz. In 1992, they lived in the old Lorenz home on 17th Street in Camas. Fred Stoller, Jr. left his mark on Camas with his two buildings. Although the first building looked pretty much the same in 1992, the other building was greatly remodeled after its funeral chapel days and is barely recognizable.

WILMER SWANK

Author's Preface: The first man in Camas to combine furniture and funerals was Wilmer Swank. Somehow the two trades seemed to go together when Swank set up business in Camas in 1905. Of course, that meant attending and graduating from embalming school but that was okay with Wilmer. But that did not stop this industrious man from other activities. When he wasn't busy with his furniture store and taking care of the deceased, he served as city clerk, city treasurer, on the city council and several terms as mayor of Camas. In his "spare time" he organized the fire department and raised money for its operation. Somehow all this activity by Wilmer Swank fit into the style of early Camas quite nicely. Give much of yourself and you shall reap the benefits and joys of life in Camas, a beautiful community nestled by the mighty Columbia River.

❧

WILMER SWANK WAS born November 2, 1884, in Fruit Valley, Clarke County, Washington Territory. His parents were twice-married Absalom Swank and thrice-married Mary M. Firestone who married on March 10, 1872, in Missouri. Absalom came into the world on January 11, 1840, in Montgomery County, Ohio the son of Jacob and Ellen Swank. His first wife was Barbara E. Heffleman and the couple had four children, the last born on Christmas Day 1869. Mary Firestone was Virginia born to Michael and Rebecca Firestone. Mary married John Paynter in 1858 and had three sons, two who were twins. After being widowed in 1865, Mary was wed to Young Thompson and became a widow once again in 1869, one year after her first daughter was born.

When Absalom Swank took Mary Firestone as his second wife in 1872, they each had four children by previous marriages. Absalom had been serving in the Civil War and after discharge, was farming his land in Missouri. The couple's first child together was Michael born December of 1872. Hiram arrived in 1875 and Jemima in 1879.

Missouri was the stepping off place for those folks who decided to migrate across the Oregon Trail to the west. In 1880 Absalom and Mary also felt the beckoning call of the newly explored western territory and with their eleven children joined a wagon train of three hundred covered wagons. Their wagon was drawn by oxen and although the journey was rigorous to say the least, they finally arrived in Baker, Oregon. In July of 1881 their twelfth child, Altha Swank, was born in Washington County. Late in 1881 Absalom and Mary moved their large family to Clarke County, W.T. in the community of Fruit Valley, close to Vancouver. They had finally found their permanent home, and welcomed their thirteenth and final child, Wilmer Swank in 1884.

Once in Fruit Valley, Absalom bought a tract of land that he turned into a ranch that he farmed until just before his death in 1915. As the baby of the family, Wilmer grew up on the ranch and helped his dad with the heavier farm chores. By doing the hard labor that was required of farm workers, he developed a physical strength that was to sustain him his whole life. However, a good education was also important to the Swank family, so Wilmer attended public schools in Vancouver, then a business college in Portland, Oregon across the Columbia River. He aspired to be a dentist but had to give up that dream for financial reasons. After graduation he

Hannah Laver-Swank 1909 (Source Post-Record)

worked for a time in Brush Prairie, and then went into business with his brother, Hiram, in Vancouver. Their new hardware business was aptly named "Swank and Company."

In August of 1905, Wilmer married nineteen-year-old Hannah Jane Laver, daughter of immigrants from England. Hannah's father was Charles W. Laver who along with his sister, Fanny, was born in Somesetshire, England. At age twelve Charles went to work as a cabin boy on a ship and after several years as a seasoned sailor, he was promoted to first mate. The ship headed for America and a few months later docked in Portland, Oregon. Charles was a grown man by this time and left the ship to settle in the Mill Plain District three miles north of Fisher's Landing on the Washington side of the Columbia River. He soon met Missouri born Keziah "Kissie" D. Gillihan and they married February 27, 1878. The couple had seven children, Charles, Roy, Edward, George Gidion, Hannah Jane, Robert Sigel, Lucy Alma, and Clyde Frank.

The Laver's built a nice, big house and had beautiful furniture shipped to them from England. Some of that furniture remained with the Laver family when they were interviewed in 1992 for this book.

Charles's sister, Fanny Laver married William Bartlett and left their home in Liverpool, England by ocean liner in 1884 with their two children, Elizabeth Ann and William Frank. William worked for a while in a Pennsylvania coal mine before moving his family west to Portland, Oregon.

They took a steamboat named Calliope to Fisher's Landing on March 14, 1885. Fisher's Landing at that time was a central point between Portland and Washougal for receiving and shipping hundreds of tons of dried prunes and farm produce. Owner, Solomon Fisher also sold cord wood for fueling the many boats plying trade on the Columbia River.

The Bartlett's were met at Fisher's Landing by Charles Laver. They stayed with the Laver's for a few weeks before settling on Government Island where they rented a farm from Solomon Fisher. William Bartlett later became Fisher's dock agent living just up from Fisher's Landing in an old house that still stood in 1992 when this chapter was written.

Wilmer Swank's new bride, Hannah Jane Laver, was born January 25, 1886, the year after the Bartlett family settled on Government Island. She grew up on the family farm and attended Mill Plain School located at Fisher Road and Mill Plain. After she graduated from high school Hannah went to Willamette University in Salem and studied music. Hannah met Wilmer at a 1903 family wedding when she was eighteen and was immediately attracted to Wilmer's vitality and charm. During the wedding of Hannah's brother Ira to Wilmer's sister Altha, Wilmer could not keep his eyes off the attractive and regal Hannah. Their romance quickly turned to love and they married in 1905 when Wilmer was twenty one and Hannah was twenty.

On a Sunday morning, shortly after Wilmer and Hannah's marriage, Wilmer and his brother, Hiram gathered all their personal belongings in a goose-necked truck and started out for Camas from Fruit Valley. When they neared Camas, they got stuck in the mud and had to be hauled out by a team of horses. After they arrived in town, Wilmer and Hiram became partners in a business dealing with furniture and hardware. Although the brothers had limited capital, they opened their store in the Camas Hotel building. Wilmer soon became known for his common sense and good judgment, and this helped make the new business successful. Three years later Wilmer bought out his brother and named his store "W. Swank & Company." He was on his own and on his way.

When the newly married couple first arrived in Camas, Hannah was responsible for setting up the household. Wilmer gave her as much money as he could afford, and off Hannah went to shop in Portland for furniture, pots and pans and other items. When she first arrived at the Portland store, her eyes were drawn to a beautiful piano sitting in one corner. With her love of music and her talent for playing the piano, Hannah just could not resist. When Wilmer arrived home that evening, proudly displayed in the living room was Hannah's prize. No new furniture, no pots and pans, just a lovely new piano.

Hannah gave birth to baby Evaline in 1906. The tiny infant died three days later and was buried in the Camas Cemetery. The town's physician at that time was Doctor Don Carlos Urie. He became a good friend of the Swank's and helped them deal with their loss. Their friendship was to last throughout all their lifetimes.

Swank concentrated on his expanding business and, by late 1906, had moved from the Camas Hotel to the frame IOOF Hall down the street. There was much ado when the cornerstone was laid in 1890 complete with a time capsule, but construction of the building was not completed until 1905. In 1906 Swank's business covered the whole first floor of the building selling furniture, stoves, ranges, dry goods, paint, and all kinds of hardware.

The townspeople were very impressed with young Swank, who was respected for his goodwill and kind heart. Each morning would find Wilmer outside sweeping his sidewalk or washing the windows of his store. The sidewalk really did not need sweeping nor did the windows need washing, Wilmer just wanted to meet and greet his friends and neighbors as they strolled by. It was no surprise when he was elected city clerk and city treasurer at the time Camas was incorporated in 1906.

In 1908, a downtown volunteer fire department was organized with Wilmer elected secretary. He was an instrumental force in establishing the volunteer firemen, a tradition that still existed in 1992. One of the lead stories in the February 2, 1908, LaCamas Post noted that Wilmer Swank was sworn in as a new city councilman. There was another news item in the January 25, 1908, LaCamas Post that W. Swank & Company had consolidated with the firm of Laver & Company. One can assume that it was his brother-in-law Ira Laver's business. Wilmer's company now offers shoes, hats, mattresses, garden seeds and even poppy flour made in Athena, Oregon.

On March 5, 1909, Hannah gave birth to a son, Roy Laver Swank. Partly because of the influence of Dr. Urie, Roy grew up to become a well-known and respected doctor.

The May 11, 1911, LaCamas Post listed among their prominent citizens, W. Swank.

Wilmer Swank (Source TRHM)

The article stated that Swank conducted one of the largest furniture and hardware establishments in this section of the state, and that he served as a member of the Camas Town Council and the Board of Education. Also, in 1911 the IOOF Hall and Swank store underwent a remodeling. At that time the capsule was removed from the cornerstone and new items from 1911 were placed inside. The capsule was then returned to the cornerstone for a few more years.

In 1912, Swank entered the undertaking business that he ran as an entirely separate organization under the name "W. Swank Undertake and Embalmer." He purchased the business of Mr. Stone who had provided undertaking services in the old Farr Building. Swank's banker, O.F. Johnson suggested that Wilmer attend embalming school in Cincinnati, Ohio. Wilmer went without a qualm, graduating with honors. Once his new business was set up he owned a well-equipped funeral parlor and had the distinction of being the only undertaker between Vancouver and Goldendale, Washington.

Around 1915, Wilmer contracted with a local contractor, John Roffler, to build him a house and funeral parlor on the corner of N. E. 3rd and Burton Street. It was in this house that Roy Swank grew up. I was fortunate to interview Roy extensively for this chapter and he remembered swimming with the other children in the ditch that was dug by the Chinese for the paper mill.

As a schoolboy he would often help his father do the undertaking duties. When Wilmer was away, Roy would pick up the bodies of those who had passed away. On one occasion, in 1921, he was asked to pick up a body of a very poor man who lived on Prune Hill. His friend, Elmo Scobba, accompanied him by horse and buggy to the man's hovel. Sure enough, he was dead, but his pocketbook bulged with $17,000 in cash. Just as Roy and Elmo discovered the fortune the Chief of Police arrived on the scene and looked in the window. It was later revealed that the "poor man" who had lived so frugally all his life also had a huge bank account. Roy never forgot that experience.

Hannah Swank continued to enjoy her piano. She not only played at church but also at school events and shows. Roy Swank played the sax and mother and son would often entertain with duets.

The years went by, and by 1922, W. Swank & Company had outgrown the frame IOOF Building. The building was torn down and the time capsule in the cornerstone resurrected once again. A beautiful new Mission Mediterranean/Spanish Colonial style two-story building was constructed on the same site. New items were added to the time capsule, and it was laid in the cornerstone for the third time. During the construction process, Wilmer temporarily moved his business across the street into a vacant livery stable without missing a beat or a sale in the process.

In 1992, the Carmack Building was situated where the livery stable was in 1922. Once the new building was completed W. Swank & Company occupied both floors and the basement. He incorporated the business in 1923 personally taking ownership of most of the stock. The store was now simply called "Swank & Co." Tragedy struck on November 15, 1923, when a $50,000 blaze wiped out most of the Camas business district that was mostly comprised of wooden frame buildings. Swank's stucco building was miraculously saved. After the fire, Wilmer was a motivating force in convincing store owners to not give up but to rebuild using brick and mortar instead of wood.

In 1924, a proud Camas organized a real fire department with Wilmer Swank conducting the meeting at city hall. The city was divided into four wards with a siren designating in which part of town an alarm is sent in from. Ed Reed was appointed the first fire chief. Another article appeared in the January 18, 1924, Camas Post reporting "there is a swell fire truck, a thousand feet of new hose and a new fire hall in which to house the truck and paraphernalia with a sleeping room for the night truck driver." In another article "W. Swank among others were taking part in a big minstrel show to raise funds for the new fire department. Everyone sang and danced including Mayor Swank."

Two of Swank's best friends were Roy and Myrtle Young. Roy was superintendent at the mill and the Young family lived in the designated "Mill Manager's House" at N. E. 5th and Garfield. The Youngs had three daughters, and the two families went to Gearhart, Oregon each year on vacation, renting a house on the beach. Wilmer Swank served two terms as mayor and during his tenure, Camas built its' first city hall and bought its' water system. Being mayor meant there was much entertaining to be done at the Swank home on Burton Street. As Camas' first lady, Hannah was a gracious hostess and in 1992, Roy Swank fondly remembered how popular his mother was with his friends. After school the Swank home was the usual meeting place with Hannah serving root beer and fruit, then playing the piano for the enjoyment of all.

Roy Swank graduated from Camas High School in 1926, and then attended University of Washington, graduating in 1930. He took his postgraduate classes at the N. W. Medical School, and then spent four months working with Dr. Urie in Camas before leaving for Boston to do research work. During this time Roy married Eulalia Snively, and they had three children, Robert, Susan, and Stephen.

Swank & Co. continued to flourish even through the Depression years and Wilmer was fortunate and proud of his good help in the store. Harry Clapp oversaw the Hardware Department and "Prince" Albert took care of the furniture side of the business. Albert's wife kept the books early on, and then Tillie Bauman was the very able bookkeeper for years. Swank Funeral Chapel built a new facility in 1932 that was Spanish in design and quite beautiful to behold. That chapel still stood in 1992 at 3rd and Cedar in Camas but had been recently remodeled and no longer had the Spanish style.

In 1933, Mayor Swank led the column of celebrants at the "Wild Spree of '33" parade that attracted ten thousand visitors to Camas. He was still mayor in 1934 when the fire

Roy Swank (Source Swank Family)

department completed major remodeling on their facilities at city hall. In 1937 Wilmer was responsible for organizing the Camas-Washougal Port District and served as chairman until his death. He was a member of the Camas School Board, the Mason's, the Odd Fellows, the Elks, and the Kiwanis Club.

Throughout all this time, Swank was immensely proud of his son, Dr. Roy Swank who was renowned for his work in MS research. In 1949, Roy went to Europe to see how the war had affected MS research and invited his father along. It was a wonderful experience for them both, taking a boat to Oslo, Norway in April and spending three months traveling Europe. Everywhere they traveled, Wilmer made friends, standing on street corners, and talking to people of all ages in his easygoing manner. On one occasion after meeting

new friends, Wilmer went to Italy for three weeks, rejoining Roy in Switzerland. After their trip, Dr. Roy Swank did research work at the Montreal Neurological Institute. He worked on projects involving neuroanatomy, vitamin deficiencies, multiple sclerosis, and other fields. When Wilmer began to have dizzy spells, Roy brought him to the institute for evaluation.

Wilmer Swank never returned to Camas except for his funeral. On February 25, 1952, he died at the age of sixty-seven. The town deeply mourned the death of a person who had given so much of his life to the community. Hannah Swank moved to a home on N. E. 4th Avenue following Wilmer's death. She sold the store and mortuary and felt sadness at having to do so. She lived for another twenty-two years until December 3,, 1974 when she passed away at a nursing home at the age of eighty-nine years. She was buried next to Wilmer in the Camas Cemetery.

In 1959, Dr. Roy Swank authored a book "Low Fat Diet" that became a best seller. He continued doing research work at Oregon Health Science University inventing a filter for MS Research that is used all over the world. When I last interviewed Dr. Swank in 1993, he was eighty-four years old and still raising large sums of money for his MS research projects. We met for lunch in Portland several times during the interview process and I was amazed at his brilliance and quiet dignity. However, his focus was a need to share the story of his wonderful father and mother and their contributions to Camas.

There is one final note to this chapter. On July 4, 1993, a terrible fire raged through the old IOOF/Swank Building, and it was destroyed. The cleanup crews found the old-time capsule still intact. Inside the time capsule were items from 1890, 1911, and 1923. At that time the new owner stated he would rebuild and replace the time capsule in the cornerstone of the new building. I spoke to the new owner about placing this chapter in the time capsule so that Wilmer Swank's life and what he accomplished for Camas would be there for all to see the next time the time capsule was resurrected. However, my book was not published at that time, so this chapter was not included. Hopefully, what Wilmer Swank did for Camas will never be forgotten.

O. F. JOHNSON

Author's Preface: Many of Camas' early pioneers were well educated people who were doing well in the midwest and the east but felt they could lead even better lives out west. O. F. Johnson was a bank employee of the highest caliber who dreamed of owning his own bank. What it took was moving out west to Camas, convincing his new father-in-law who had "start-up" money to also move west, having a supportive wife who was a hard worker, and faith in his fellow man. With all these ingredients Johnson's new Camas Bank took off like a shot and O. F. Johnson never looked back.

※

OSCAR FRANKLIN JOHNSON was born June 6, 1880, in Sherburn, Minnesota, the son of Perry Gustav Johnson and Anna Christina Johnson. The older Johnsons were from Sweden, Perry born in 1843 in Gothenburg, and Anna in 1842 in Grolanda. Perry was a farmer, a small, slender quiet man with a mustache. Anna was fair and petite in stature. In 1867 while still newly married the couple decided to leave Sweden and try their luck in America. They picked Minnesota because it was a good state for farming, and they were able to homestead property there. Perry built a small sod house with one door and two windows, and he and Anna started to raise a family. O. F. Johnson was born in this modest, little house.

The Perry Johnsons did well on their farm and were soon able to move to Dunnell, Minnesota where they built a large, beautiful home on six hundred and forty acres. That house still stood in 1992. Perry and Anna were of the Lutheran religion and became so successful on their new farm that they were able to donate land for the new Lutheran church at Dunnell. Perry Johnson was considered a "gentleman farmer" by everyone in the community.

Unfortunately, when Oscar was five years old his mother died six days after giving birth to her fifth child. Anna was only forty-three. This left Perry who lived to be ninety-one, with a family of five young children, including four sons. At this point the whole family had to pitch in and help with the farm work and that meant arising at dawn's first light and working until dinnertime out in the fields. Oscar learned to hate farm labor and vowed never to follow that profession. After dinner there was no television to watch, nor any movies and not even electricity. Families in those times had quiet evenings reading by candlelight or lanterns.

O.F. Johnson (Source TRHM)

When he wasn't working on the farm Oscar went to school in Sherburn, graduating from Sherburn High School. Although he loved music and wanted to learn all about music, he was not allowed to because it was considered a "sissy's subject."

After each of his four sons graduated from high school, Perry Johnson offered them each one quarter of his farmland if they would stay home and farm the land. Much to his disappointment there were no takers on his proposition and all four left home to follow other career paths, including Oscar who was determined to become a banker.

To prepare for his banking career, Oscar spent four years attending Highland Park College in Des Moines, Iowa and Tolland's Business College at Fairmont, Minnesota taking specialized courses in financial matters. Armed with his college credentials Oscar got a job as a cashier at a bank in Ceylon, Minnesota. Although his starting salary was a mere twenty-five dollars per month the bank job provided an unexpected bonus. There was a piano tucked away in the back room next to the vault. Oscar would stay after work teaching himself how to play the piano, composing little tunes of his own.

Another bonus was Amelia Beatrice Bauman, another teller at the bank. Amelia preferred to be called "Beatrice" and she was known by that name all of her life. She was a lovely young lady of German heritage from Nebraska, twenty-four years old and shared Oscar's love of music.

Beatrice had graduated from Cedar Falls College in Iowa and taught school in Ceylon where she became principal of the Ceylon, Minnesota School District. When she went to work at the bank, she resigned her position with the school district because employment in the banking industry was considered a "broader life experience" and one with much higher pay.

Beatrice played an accomplished piano and sang with a lilting voice endearing her to Oscar. Before he knew it Oscar was completely enamored by the fair and talented Beatrice, and they soon became engaged. Any dating that the pair did was by horse and buggy because there were no automobiles at that time. However, in 1904 Oscar saw his first automobile in Ceylon and dreamed of the day he would own one of these dazzling metal creatures. Most folks laughed at the car thinking it as a plaything, but Oscar knew that someday it would take the place of the horse, even though at that time it could only go twenty miles per hour.

Oscar and Beatrice Johnson 1907 (Source TRHM)

Beatrice's parents were Emil Bauman, born 1847 in Germany and Katherine Rozenkranz Bauman, born in Germany in 1850. They had also immigrated to the United States where Emil became a successful lumberman with a strong financial background and was well respected for all his endeavors. Emil and Katherine approved of the ambitious young Oscar Johnson who was seriously courting their daughter and had so many dreams for the future.

Oscar had another friend at the bank named Robert "Bob" Carmack, who grew tired of Minnesota living and left the bank moving out west to Kent, Washington, a small town a few miles from Seattle. Bob sunk his money into a general store and did so well that he wrote a long letter to Oscar extolling the virtues of living in the west. Unable to resist his friend's offer of adventure and greater wealth, Oscar took a leave of absence from the bank and travelled to Seattle. Upon arrival he contacted an employment agency and soon found employment at the Chehalis County Bank in Aberdeen, Washington. He was to begin his new job at the prestigious sum of one hundred dollars per month, double what he was making by that time in Ceylon, Minnesota. His work would be dealing in gold and silver only, not paper money. Folks in the west did not trust paper money in the early years of west coast banking.

It was 1906 when Oscar moved permanently to Aberdeen, a booming lumbering village, to firmly establish himself before sending for Beatrice. By 1907 Oscar felt settled enough to be married and a wedding announcement in the Aberdeen paper stated "His fiancée immediately came to him like a sensible girl, and they were married in the Hoquiam home of Beatrice's old schoolmate Mrs. L. A. Benedict. The Rev. L. A. Benedict performed the ceremony." Apparently, Beatrice was unable to make it in time for an originally scheduled wedding date because her train was delayed by a blizzard in Montana. She finally arrived but her beautiful white lace wedding dress did not. It seems that all the trunks containing her clothing were snow-bound in Haverill, Montana.

O.F. Johnson home 1911 - 526 NE Hayes Street
(Source TRHM)

The young married couple set up housekeeping in a small home at F and 3rd Street in Aberdeen where they paid twenty dollars per month rent. This "large" rent amount was offset somewhat because their bachelor friend, Bob Carmack, rented a room from them for ten dollars per month. Their new home was beautifully furnished with classic furniture of the era including a dark wooden secretary that was still being used by their daughter, Winston in 1992. In the Johnson's living room hung a stunning framed floral painting by Beatrice's sister, Clara. That painting also remained within the Johnson family when this chapter was written in 1992.

Although Oscar enjoyed his cashier's work in Aberdeen, he was smart enough to realize the potential of "owning" one's own bank in the new western territory. So, the ambitious Oscar began investigating twenty towns in Washington and Oregon to find the best possibility for starting his own bank. It was lucky for Camas that the small, bustling paper mill town was Oscar's final choice as the opportune place to set up his banking business.

In January 1908, when both Oscar and Beatrice were twenty-eight, they arrived by riverboat at what was to become their lifetime hometown, Camas, Washington. The pilot of the riverboat said to O. F. Johnson "I think you're making a big mistake in starting a bank in Camas because Washougal has a bank that is plenty for the surrounding country." One of their fellow passengers on the riverboat was Roy Dobbs who later became a business associate and lifetime friend of the Johnson's. In future years, both were bankers and Dobbs served as mayor while Johnson was treasurer for the city of Camas.

When the Johnson's first arrived in Camas there was no railroad locally because the Golden Spike for the railroad was not driven until March 1908, and the railroad was not completed until later that year. There were also no electric lights, graded streets or sidewalks in town. At nighttime oil lamps and lanterns were the norm. The Johnson's stayed for a short time at the new Commercial Hotel, later called the Camas Hotel, but because Beatrice was pregnant, they decided to rent a new, five-room house at 4th and Oneonta, now Garfield Street, for ten dollars per month. The owner worked at the

O.F. Johnson and his Imperial 1914 (Source TRHM)

paper mill. The address today of that little house is 713 N. E. 4th Avenue and when I viewed it in 1992 it was still there, slightly remodeled just one short block from the library building. An old photo showed forests of trees to the east of the house. In 1992 there were blocks of homes to the east where forests once were.

Johnson immediately organized and began to build the first bank in Camas, with financial help from his father-in-law Emil Bauman. Emil invested five thousand dollars, a goodly sum in those days and Oscar put in one thousand dollars to get the operation started. First Johnson bought the

First National Bank, 4ᵗʰ and Dallas
O.F. Johnson and W.C. Anderson 1914 (Source TRHM)

lot at the northwest corner of 4th and Burton Streets, and then construction began on a fine brick building that faced the corner. It was the first brick building to be constructed in Camas and caused quite a stir among locals as it was taking shape. An article in the January 25, 1908, LaCamas Post notes the "Johnson's arrival in town and that work on the new bank building was progressing rapidly." In the same article the editor announces that "construction had begun on an opera house being built by T. S. Woolson at the corner of 3rd and Clarke Street."

In record time by modern standards, a mere eleven months after arriving in town, O. F. Johnson proudly opened the doors of his new Camas State Bank. The date was November 2, 1908, and what a big day it was for Camas. The April 1909 Coast Magazine reported that the bank was "modern in all respects, supplied with the best fixtures, and has one of the strongest solid concrete fireproof vaults in the state." H. H. Rosenberg was named first president of the bank, J. H. Rosenberg was vice president, and O.F. Johnson became head cashier. Emil Bauman was listed as a large stockholder. The Coast Magazine called the officers of the bank "practical up-to-date men who have had wide banking and business experience."

As head cashier, Oscar paid himself one hundred dollars a month plus dividends earned from the new bank. Beatrice worked with her husband as an assistant cashier. Although Oscar was still a young man in his twenties, he was an excellent judge of character and would make loans to farmers without collateral. He said that he knew the men were honest and would pay back the loans. His personal creed was "any man can succeed if he works hard and keeps honest."

When Johnson went into the banking business his vow was never to smoke, drink or swear. One evening in 1908, the local Methodist minister knocked on the door of the Johnson's 4th Street home and found Oscar and Beatrice playing cards. In those days you either played Flinch or 500. The minister proceeded to give the Johnson's a lecture about the evils of playing cards and claimed that the two of them would go to hell. After the minister departed, Oscar proclaimed that, "he would never, ever join that church." And he didn't even though he took on the job as church treasurer for over eighteen years. Years later, a new minister came to town and said to Oscar, "I can't find your name on our membership rolls," Johnson replied "You won't! I'm not a member." The new minister had him join immediately.

Early in 1909, the Johnson's first baby was born. What began as a joyful day turned into a tragic day for the couple. The doctor, who had newly arrived in town, was apparently drunk and accidentally suffocated the tiny baby as it was born. The sad parents buried their "Baby Johnson" in the Camas Cemetery. In the next few months Beatrice got pregnant again and taking no chances the Johnson's imported a doctor from Aberdeen to deliver the child. Winston Eleanor Johnson arrived in 1910 and was described as a beautiful, precious daughter by the Johnsons. She was to be their only child and was a delight in the town. In fact, a 1911 news clip in the local paper reported "Baby Johnson has two brand new teeth."

In 1910, electricity came to Camas to everyone's joy. Store owners and wealthier residents no longer needed lanterns and candles to supply light. Oscar built an addition on the Cedar Street side of the Camas State Bank, renting the new space out to the Camas Post. The newspaper listed O. F. Johnson as one of the town's leading citizens in 1911, because he was not only an astute businessman, but was also town treasurer and treasurer of the Commercial Club, a forerunner to the Chamber of Commerce. The Post stated "As a banker Mr. Johnson has been very successful." Around the same time, Beatrice won a prize of five dollars from the Commercial Club for submitting the winning design for their window card. It had a large star and bore the inscription "Camas, Star of the Columbia."

O. F. Johnson was so impressed with his good fortune in Camas that he talked his friend Robert "Bob" Carmack into the new adventure of moving from the Seattle area to Camas. The past few years had been good and bad for Carmack. The good part was marrying Johnson's niece from Minnesota. Oscar had introduced the pair while still living in Ceylon. Carmack sold his Kent store and property making a good profit and bought a larger store in Christopher, Washington, moving there with his new wife and baby son. The Carmack's did very well at their new general store, telegraph office and Northern Pacific railroad stop, but the bad part was that the marriage did not work out and the Carmack's divorced. With an unsuccessful marriage, Bob was in need of a positive change in his life so accepted Johnson's offer of a move to Camas. He sold his Christopher store and headed south.

Carmack's first action when arriving in the paper mill town was to purchase the "Camas Grocery Company" located in the Johnson bank building. He changed the name to "Carmack's Camas Grocery" and was soon one of the town's leading businessmen. A few months later he rekindled an old friendship with Daisy Wilhite of Tacoma, and they were soon married and happily settled in Camas. Carmack and Johnson remained friends, business neighbors, and fellow golfers until Carmack's death in 1938.

All his life Oscar was proud of his golfing ability. In the 1920's while still president of the First National Bank he was written up in the paper for scoring a "hole in one" at Clark County's Country Club's golf course. He later became a member of Orchard Hills Country Club.

In 1912, with a growing daughter on their hands and the financial means to do so, the Johnson's decided to leave the small rental house and build their own home. They had discovered a photo in the Portland Oregonian that was the "home of their dreams." Oscar contacted local builder, John Roffler, showed him the photo and asked him to make it a reality. John was able to copy the design and build the Johnson's their dream home "way out in the woods" at 526 Whitman Street, now called Hayes Street. The original lumber bill for construction of the home dated December 1, 1911, was from Larch Mountain Lumber Company and made out to John Roffler for a total of $762.12. This bill was still in the Johnson family records in 1992. Total construction cost was $3,500. The new home was Bungalow Style with broad, sloping gable roofs. A porch on the west façade echoed these lines as did two smaller gables on the south elevation. A higher gable above the main roof at the east or rear of the home was later added.

The one and a half story wood frame building was shingled and did not have a basement. At about the same time, Beatrice's parents, Emil and Katherine Bauman who had moved to Camas, built a large frame home at the corner of 5th and Whitman right next door to the Johnson's. The home was of Colonial Bungalow style with a pediment above the entrance and caps porch posts. In 1992 both homes remained unchanged or modified and stood at their original locations between 5th and 6th Street on Hayes.

Income tax came into being in 1913, but Johnson did not have to pay any because he made just one hundred fifty dollars per month as president of his bank and a mere ten dollars a month as town and city treasurer, a post he held for sixteen years.

Always entranced with automobiles, Johnson posed in 1914 for a photo showing him proudly behind the wheel of his 1912 spanking new "Imperial." It was the second automobile in Camas, the first was owned by Bob Stoller, the Ford dealer. To have a place to park his car, Johnson had to cut down a section of the forest behind his house. In the background of the photo is the Johnson home sitting by itself in an open field. The home is now part of a downtown city block surrounded by homes and huge trees that almost obscure the house. The Johnson house was placed on the local historic register with a plaque on the front porch designating it as a historic home.

In 1915, Emil Bauman, father-in-law and business partner of O. F Johnson passed away. He had lived to see his initial investment in the Camas bank grow to momentous proportions. The Camas State Bank was so

O.F. Johnson Building 225 & 227 NE 4th Street in downtown Camas 1924. (Source TRHM)

successful it went "national" becoming the First National Bank of Camas. The bank purchased the corner lot at 4th and Clark, now Adams, for one thousand dollars, a hefty price for a lot in those days, and the new Urie Building was constructed. In 1919 First National Bank moved into the ground floor of the Urie Building and Citizens State Bank owned by Roy Dobbs rented the old bank building at 4th and Birch from Johnson. Citizens State Bank remained at that location until 1922 when they moved to the new McKever Building across the street from the Urie Building at 4th and Clark.

Part of the problem of travelling the ten miles between Camas and Vancouver was the road conditions. O. F. Johnson and Bob Carmack helped form the North Bank Highway Committee in 1921 responsible for planning a new section of highway between the two cities. Johnson promptly bought his second car, a "Franklin" that was air-cooled and went fifty miles per hour. On trips to the mountains, he would sail past stranded motorists whose engines had boiled over.

The notorious 1923 fire swept through the block of wooden stores between Clara and Burton Street, also burning to the ground Johnson's 1908 brick bank building. Fire units responded from Camas, Vancouver, and Portland. Although a tragic turn of events for Camas, Johnson rallied his forces and immediately began construction of a much larger two-story building on the northeast corner of 4th and Burton. The "Johnson Building" as it was called was completed within two months with another new building next to it called the "Burton Building." The Johnson Building originally housed "Dungan's Clothing and Shoes" and the Burton Building was occupied by "Terminal Haberdashery," "R. W. Carmack's Real Estate," and "Home Laundry."

An article in the 1925 edition of the Camas Post reported that the concrete walk in front of the "Johnson Block" was being repaired adjacent to the stage depot. It appears that water had been seeping into the basement of the Dungan store that occupied the corner building. By 1932 Sprouse Reitz occupied the Dungan store on 4th Street and the "Bus Depot and Confectionery" and the city library occupied the Cedar Street side. In 1992 Sprouse Reitz was still there with Camas Meats on the Cedar Street side.

Winston Johnson graduated from Camas High School in 1927 with honors. With the help of high school principal, Nora Self, who was another early pioneer, Winston entered the highly recommended Mills College in Oakland, California where she attained at BA in music at the age of twenty. The chairman of admissions at Mills later wrote Nora Self praising the caliber of students such as Winston Johnson who excelled in their music program. Because of Winston's many talents, Mills College offered further scholarships to Camas High School graduates.

O. F. Johnson retired from the presidency of the First National Bank in 1928, after being in the banking business for thirty years. He sold his bank for one hundred fifty thousand dollars and that was pretty good for a guy who started out at one hundred dollars per month. Johnson's bank was the only bank in Clark County to withstand the "Crash of '29." He was asked to become the president of the Vancouver National Bank but did not accept. Oscar chose retirement instead.

Winston Johnson married Evert Ezra Ellis in 1931, at the Westminster Presbyterian Church in Portland, Oregon. Ellis was a YMCA secretary who later became a Methodist minister and was appointed vice president of the Southern California School of Theology at Claremont, California. This necessitated a move to California for the newly married couple. Shortly after the wedding Winston's grandmother, Katherine Bauman passed away at her home at 506 N. E. Hayes. She was buried next to her husband Emil in the Camas Cemetery.

In 1932, with the absence of their only daughter and the lure of living in sunny, warm California instead of rainy Washington, the retired O. F. Johnsons moved southward to Los Angeles, saying goodbye to their many Camas friends. Two years later the Johnsons became grandparents when Winston and Ezra had a son, Donald Johnson Ellis. They later welcomed two daughters, Winston Katherine (Kay) in 1938 and Susan Beatrice in 1943.

Oscar's father, Perry Johnson died in 1934 at Dunnell, Minnesota at the age of ninety-one. The Swedish "gentleman farmer" who had done so well in America was gone.

After spending three years in Los Angeles and missing friends and associates plus the town they loved so dearly, the Johnsons returned to Camas in 1935. It was a wonderful homecoming with all of Camas welcoming two of their favorite citizens back with open arms.

Oscar came out of retirement the same year, building a uniquely designed brick store front building at 225 N. E. 4th Street. He opened a real estate, loan and insurance business there and became quite successful at this location. His old friend Bob Carmack had been in the real estate and insurance business for many years and had done so well that Oscar thought he would give Carmack some competition. Roy L. Storms joined Johnson's agency as an assistant in 1936 and throughout the years to come Johnson rented out half of the 4th Street building to various pharmacies including Rexall and Economy Drugs. At one time Camas Columbia Market and Safeway Stores were located next door. In 1992 Camas Sport Shop occupied the building.

In 1938, the real estate business in Camas was handling the development of many properties including Russell Acres and Pederson Acres in Washougal. These were small home sites and tracts that Johnson personally platted and sold. In honor of his daughter, Oscar named two streets "Winston" and "Ellis", but years later, the names were changed. He was also responsible for selling several farms and older homes in Camas.

R. W. Carmack died suddenly of a heart attack in 1938, after two years of failing health. It was with great sadness that Oscar Johnson said goodbye for the final time to his old friend. As he laid his friend to rest, Johnson reflected that knowing Carmack "he would no doubt be sending Johnson an invitation to join him in some new 'heavenly' adventure before too long."

Oscar continued to be active in the Camas community and club affairs as a member of Kiwanis, IOOF, Scottish Rite, Shriners and many other local groups including the Republican party. He was also trustee in the Camas Methodist Church, where Beatrice played the piano and sang solos. Beatrice also sang in the choir and one Christmas they were putting on a "Cantata." The day before the "Cantata", she came down with laryngitis and since there was no one else to sing her part she bravely went ahead and performed but lost her voice and could never sing again.

The years were kind to the Johnsons. Their business interests flourished, they had plenty of time to play golf with Oscar belonging to the notorious four-member "70-year Golf Club," and to enjoy their many friendships. Their grandson Don Ellis realized his grandfather's musical career dream and went on to become a composer, trumpeter, and big band leader of international fame. Their granddaughter, Winston Kay, became the owner of a computer business, and their granddaughter, Susan, followed a career as a respiratory therapist.

In 1963, Amelia "Beatrice" Johnson died of heart failure at the age of eighty-three. Although alone, but still active, Oscar chose not to live at his home on N. E. Hayes. He moved to Quaker Gardens, a retirement community in Stanton, California. Although eighty-three years of age, he enjoyed the warm weather, played golf and bridge and even played the piano occasionally.

On Christmas Day, December 25, 1971, Don Ellis wrote and dedicated a special piano number for his grandfather entitled "For G.D." Oscar, whose love of music had never dimed, was very touched by his grandson's musical tribute. At the age of ninety-one he did his best to attend every one of his grandson's band concerts in Los Angeles.

O. F. Johnson lived twelve years after his beloved Beatrice and passed away in 1975 at the age of ninety-five. The two are buried side by side in the Camas Cemetery. The couple was survived by one daughter, one grandson, two granddaughters, and four great-grandchildren in 1992. At the time of his death, Oscar owned the Johnson and Bauman homes, Sprouse Reitz building, Runyan's Jewelry Store building and the drug store that in 1992 was the Sport's Center.

Winston and Ezra Ellis lived in the old family home on N. E. Hayes Street for a few years and retained all the downtown buildings that Johnson had so fondly and energetically built. In 1978 their son Don Ellis died at age forty-four. Eventually the Ellis family followed the same pattern as the Johnson's and moved back to California to be near their daughters. Winston sold the old real estate and drug store building to Camas Sport Shop and the Runyan's Jewelry store building to Paul Runyan. In 1992 she still owned the Sprouse Reitz building.

There is an old photograph of Ann Fletcher who was the great granddaughter of Beatrice Johnson trying on the 1907 wedding dress of Beatrice and it fit perfectly. Blonde, beautiful Ann Fletcher bears a striking resemblance to the lovely petite Beatrice Amelia Bauman whose photo was taken when she graduated from college.

My interviews and so much more with Winston Eleanor Johnson Ellis were absolutely invaluable in writing this chapter about her father and mother and I will never forget her dedication in helping me with the research. She was a true inspiration. We hoped to get this chapter, and my complete book, published in 1992 when she was still a vital force, but it did not come to pass.

However, she wanted all to know that her father, O. F. Johnson, will always be remembered by Camas citizens as a man of tremendous vision and determination. Challenges and goals did not bother this man, they inspired him! O. F. and Beatrice Johnson were true Camas pioneers and will never be forgotten in the annals of Camas history.

ALBERT M. BLAKE

Author's Preface: A farmer came to Camas in 1908 determined not to work in the paper mill. Instead, he took his savings and built a feed store to serve the farmers of the area. The store became a landmark and Albert M. Blake gained local fame as a business and community leader. With the same entrepreneurial spirit, Blake's children continued the tradition, owning and operating many new businesses in Camas, plus serving their city and community. Driving past the old Blake house up on the hill in Camas reminds us of times past and you can almost see those Blake boys playing football out on the large, grassy lawn.

⊗∾◎

ALBERT M. BLAKE was born in 1862 to William Pearce Blake and Rebecca Margaret McGinnis in Jo Daviess County, Illinois. Orphaned at an early age, William Pearce Blake had traveled to the United States from Devonshire, England in 1857, when he was eighteen years old after spending his birthday on the high seas in a sailing vessel enroute to America. William was a man of slight physical stature, and this trait was passed on to future generations. His older brother, Tom, had chosen to find his fortune in Australia, and his dearly loved sister Mary Ann opted to remain in England with other family members including some very tall uncles. The three orphaned Blake children had been in the care of one of the uncles who was a drinking man, unkind to them and who had squandered most of the money meant to care for the children. For that reason, William Pearce Blake was glad to have gone from England.

Upon arrival in his new country, William heard of the rich land recently made available for white settlers in Illinois. There were many Native Americans who did not want to give up their lands, but the pioneer settlers pushed them westward and set up their farms in the northwest corner of Illinois where there was an abundance of fruit, berries, wild game and turkey. In 1859 William met and married Rebecca McGinnis who was the daughter of a neighbor. Rebecca was a large, overweight girl who walked with her head held high. She had large, soulful eyes and her manner was dignified and quietly poised. Rebecca's mother had died leaving Rebecca in charge of the family along with her widower father, Francis McGinnis. After their marriage William and Rebecca continued to live with the McGinnis family in Jo Daviess County.

Two of the McGinnis boys served and died in the Civil War and that prompted William to enlist in the Illinois Troops. He returned home safely except for a severe case of sunstroke suffered while on a forced march.

A daughter, Sarah, was born to William and Rebecca in 1860, then a son Albert M. on September 4, 1862. Five more children were born between 1862 and 1878. They were Mary Ann named after William's sister in England, Thomas Arthur, Ada Jane, Alfred Enoch, and William Robert Andrew. By the time William Robert Andrew arrived in 1878, the family had moved from Jo Daviess County to Loran, Stephanson County, Illinois, moved back to Jo Daviess County, then to Dickenson County Kansas in 1877.

It is reported that William Pearce Blake was a very kind father to his children instilling in them the value of "right" and the joy of a job well done. He spent a lot of time with his family conducting spelling bees and helping the younger ones with their schoolwork. Both Albert M. Blake and his brother Tom inherited this placid disposition and love for all mankind. From the McGinnis side of the family the children learned the happiness of dancing and music. Albert and his sister Ada were taught the Irish Jig at an early age. At every family gathering the Irish Jig was the finale and was called "The McGinnis Irish Jig."

Being a farmer in those days meant hard times because when the land became barren and overused, the family would move on to a new farm. The Blake family was no exception, moving first to Waverly in Coffey County, Kansas in 1881, then to Barber County, Kansas in 1884, then to Piedmont in Greenwood County, Kansas in 1888. William's final address was Eureka in Greenwood County, Kansas where he moved in 1896 to retire and receive a medical pension from Civil War disabilities because of sunstroke.

Albert M. Blake took after his father with his medium height and build and a full head of light brown hair. He never grew a beard, a custom that was popular in those days but remained smooth shaven his entire life. As a young man growing up Albert moved with his family to the various farms they occupied working hard to help. On one of those farms Albert got his arm caught in a farm machine pulley, breaking it in several places. Because of this accident Albert did not have full use of his arm and hand for the rest of his life.

On December 31, 1885, Albert married beautiful eighteen-year-old Rozina Hill. Born in 1867 in Marietta, Ohio, Rozina was the daughter of Samuel B. Hill and Melvina Ross and the granddaughter of John Hill from Pennsylvania and Rozina Bartlett of Ohio. The Hill family lived in Burlington a scant twenty miles from the Blake family in Coffey County, Illinois. It is thought that Albert and Rozina met during a wheat harvest event.

The newly married couple lived in Kansas for several years until bad times forced them to move to Oklahoma in 1894 seeking a better life. During their years in Kansas and Oklahoma they had seven children. Ralph M. was born in 1887, Edna May in 1889, Frank Ross in 1891, Maude Ann in 1893, Albert Lester in 1895, Harold H. in 1901, and Rozina E. in 1905.

The oldest son, Ralph, learned early the value of hard work. While living on the Sandhill Farm in Oklahoma, his father took a job in town and depended heavily on Ralph to run the farm with his brother Frank's help. It is said that one day Ralph was chasing rabbits for dinner, came over a dune and startled two outlaws who went for their handguns. Ralph quickly retreated and later reported that he had never run so fast in his life. As the boys grew up, Ralph and Frank played football at Northwestern Normal School in Oklahoma, gaining quite a reputation for their football skills.

The family again faced a difficult decision in 1909. Should they stay in Oklahoma where it was more and more difficult to eke out a living, or travel westward to the new state of Washington where they heard the opportunities were much better? Rather than move the whole family to an unknown future, Albert and his wife's brother John "Jack" Hill decided to explore the Washington Territory alone. They set out on a scouting trip and Albert ended up in the paper mill town of Camas where he realized the need for a feed store. Jack Hill wanted to be a farmer and felt that Kennewick, Washington was the best place to farm the land. He attended Seattle's Alaska/Yukon/Pacific Exposition, and then bought a farm in Kennewick.

After hearing the good news from Washington, the Blake family accompanied by Albert's brother Tom and Jack Hill's fiancé, Sarah Hutchinson, packed up all their belongings, boarded a train and headed towards what they hoped was another new start in life. On the way, the group stopped in Kennewick to witness Jack and Sarah's wedding. The Blake family left the newlyweds and continued their journey to what was now a very vibrant town of Camas. Their journey was completed with a long train ride on the new SP&S Railway which had just begun operations through Camas in 1908.

Albert Blake was a thrifty man and although times had been rough in Oklahoma, he had still managed to save some money to invest in his new feed store in Camas. He erected a new building at the corner of N. E. 3rd and Clark, now called Adams, and named his new business "A.M. Blake's Feed and Fuel Company." Blake's customers were the many farmers of the area who not only sold their dairy products but raised livestock and a variety of crops. Blake sold these farmers equipment, baby chicks and other farm needs. The store also carried cement that was badly needed for the muddy streets of town because the only paved street at that time was 3rd Street.

The Blake boys were quite handsome and were warmly welcomed in town by the young ladies of the area. In 1909 Ralph and Frank organized a football team with high school principal/coach/professor A. E. Heaton who had played football in a teacher's college and possessed quite a knowledge of the game. Although Ralph Blake was twenty-two years old, he became the quarterback of the team. Eighteen-year-old Frank was the halfback and team captain. The first Camas High School football team won one game and lost one game that year. Both games were against Vancouver High School with one game played at Louis Bloch Park in Camas. One hundred interested fans watched the game.

After the feed business opened and began to show a profit Ralph was hired to help his father in the store. This extra help gave Albert and Rozina time to be active in school and community affairs. They became stalwarts in the First Christian Church and attended services throughout the years with the Asher family, Frank Blake's family, and Albert L. Blake's family.

Shortly after arriving in Camas, Edna May Blake began teaching school at the Grass Valley School, the oldest school in east Clark County. Many of the young, educated women in the area taught at the school located west of Camas in the early years.

The May 11, 1911, LaCamas Post wrote that A. M. Blake was one of the town's leading citizens. The article stated "A. M. Blake arrived in Camas two years ago from Oklahoma. He is a member of the Camas Feed and Fuel Company, dealers in hay, grain, feed and coal. He is also a member of the Camas Contracting Company that has the contract for grading 3rd Street. Mr. Blake is constructing one of the most modern homes in the city."

And indeed, the Blake's new home was a sight to behold. With their fortunes increasing at a rapid pace, Albert and Rozina proceeded to construct one of the most beautiful homes in Camas on half a city block at 535 Martha Street, now

A.M. Blake Home 1329 NW Benton 1910 (Source TRHM)

1329 N. W. Benton. This large, six-bedroom home was built in the Craftsman style with horizontal emphasis also called American Four Square. It had a hip roof and exposed rafters, a rectangular bay on the side elevation and a full columned portico. When completed the house was the talk of the town, providing a perfect home for the Blake's and their seven growing children.

The oldest son, Ralph, purchased twenty-five acres of land two blocks west of the elder Blake's new home. This land had several springs and a creek running through it. Ralph engineered and built two concrete reservoirs and piped water from the springs and creek into them. From the reservoirs he piped water to not only his father's home but also to several neighbors. After city water was brought to that area, Ralph's water was used only for irrigation.

Maude Ann Blake was on the Camas High School's basketball team in 1911 as was her best friend, Alice Asher. The two friends were part of the first six students to graduate from Camas High School. Maude received a teacher's certificate, originally teaching at Mt. Vernon, Washington and later had a long career at Virginia Mason Hospital in Seattle. She married Hans Peter Meyer, and the couple had one daughter, Lou Ann Meyer Gallaner.

After leaving high school, Frank Blake was a teamster with a sturdy team of horses and a stout wagon. Several early Camas pioneers including A. M. and Rozina Blake had purchased stock in the Idaho Gold and Ruby Mine in Leonia. Frank was hired to transport supplies at the mine with his team and wagon. His friend Gert Karnath also worked at the mine. While in Camas, Frank had been dating Alice Asher and was quite serious about her. It was difficult for them to be apart when he was in Idaho. Gert was having the same problem with a young woman named Bess.

So, Frank, Gert and two other mine workers proposed marriage to their four girlfriends inviting them to Idaho. When the girls arrived, the group went to Coeur d'Alene, Idaho where the four couples were married in a joint ceremony on June 20, 1912. Shortly afterwards Frank and Alice returned to Camas and Frank went to work in his father's store.

Frank's bride, Alice Asher Blake, was born on a farm in the Woodburn area in 1890 to parents who were also early Camas pioneers. Her brothers were responsible for constructing the First Christian Church. When the newly married Blake's returned from Idaho they settled down in Camas and began to raise a family. First to arrive was Madge Rozina Blake in 1914, then Frank Leighton Blake on March 3, 1917, Alice Grace Blake Snoey in 1919 and in 1922 the baby of the family, Janet Nan Blake Slater was born. Madge Rozina Blake died of tuberculosis in 1930 at the age of sixteen.

Albert M. Blake's third son, Albert Lester, had inherited his father and grandfather's easy-going nature. He had a great love of family unity and was able to handle any misunderstandings between the siblings. Like his brothers he played football all four years of his Camas High School days and played on the basketball team. He graduated in 1916 and with his older brother, Ralph, enlisted in the U. S. Navy during World War I, with both brothers serving aboard the U.S.S. Wyoming.

Harold, the Blake's youngest son, was the liveliest and loudest according to his family. They said you could hear him laugh two blocks away. He had many interests including football and played the sport in 1916, 1917 and 1918. By that time Camas High School played six football games per season with their opponents being Gresham, Hood River, Estacada, and Vancouver. The star of the football team was Harold and the legacy of "Blake" football in Camas was to continue for many generations to come. The high school cancelled the 1919 football season during Harold's senior year due to a flu epidemic. After graduation Harold also went to work in his dad's store.

Ralph Blake returned from the Navy in 1919 and went into partnership with his brother Frank to lease their father's feed store. Albert M. Blake was ready to retire after so many

Left to right: William Robert Blake, Thomas Arthur Blake, Mary Ann Blake Johnston, William Piere Blake, Ada Jane Blake Grimes, Albert M. Blake. Circa 1922 (Source Meakia Blake)

years of running the business. Prunes were the big commodity in Camas during that time so as a sideline to the feed business the Blake brothers shipped nine hundred tons of prunes each year to Portland.

After Albert Lester Blake returned from the Navy in 1919, he and his brother Harold jointly enrolled at Washington State College in 1920 with Albert majoring in electrical engineering. He went on to become a real expert in that field throughout his life. Also enrolled at the college was Harold's high school sweetheart, Marjorie Duffin, the daughter of Elizabeth MacMaster and Allan Duffin. Harold and Marjorie renewed their courtship and were married in 1920. They returned to Camas and built a home on the southwest corner of the elder Blake's home site next to Ralph Blake's home facing Couch Street. They buried their stillborn infant son in 1921 in the Duffin-

MacMaster plot of the Camas Cemetery. The couple had two other children, Glenn "Skeeter" Blake and Betty Rose Blake Matthews. The whole family was active in St. John's Presbyterian Church.

Meanwhile, Albert Lester fell in love with Eula Mildred Trosper of Pullman, Washington and they married in May of 1921. The pair decided to stay in the college town for a few years and later moved to Torrance, California. But the lure of Camas and family drew them back to the paper mill town and they built a home on the corner of 14th and Birch Streets. They had one daughter, Janrose Blake Hetler.

Edna May Blake, the oldest daughter of A. M. and Rozina Blake left her teaching job at Grass Valley School and married Jack Carkin who operated a men's clothing store in Camas in the early 1920's. They purchased a home on the N. E. corner of 14th and Division just a few blocks from the elder Blake's property. No one could doubt that the Blake family was close knit and enjoyed living near each other. In 1920 Edna May Blake took a job as assistant cashier at Citizens State Bank. The newly organized bank was managed by Roy Dobbs who was also head cashier. Years later when the bank was sold, Edna went to work in the Roy Dobbs Insurance Agency and when Roy finally retired in 1963, so did she.

Albert M. Blake, who had built up his feed business from a small store to a much larger, highly profitable enterprise, sold the business to R. J. Blair in 1921. Although Frank continued to work for Blair during the next four years, Ralph decided to take a job with the Crown Willamette Paper Company, and he worked there until his retirement. He married Kathleen Lamourieux from New York, and they had one daughter, Mildred Rozina Blake Benedict. They too built a home close to Albert's parents, directly behind the Blake barn on the southeast corner of N. W. 14th and Couch Streets.

After selling his business, A. M. Blake became one of the stockholders of LaCamas Creamery, a company that made Bead Island Butter and Cheese. The Bead Island products were named after a small island that the Native Americans used to occupy in LaCamas Creek, with the creamery location close by. The creamery was renamed "Farmer's Cooperative Creamery" in the 1930's. Albert M. also served on the Camas School Board for a few years.

The elder Blake's youngest daughter, Rozina E. "Rose" Blake graduated from Camas High School in 1921 and was featured in the LaCamas yearbook for being on the yearbook staff, Chrestomathean and Operetta in 1918, 1920 and 1921. Rose was the baby of the family so was much adored by all of the Blake clan. She learned to shoot a rifle and could usually beat her brothers in target shooting. Once she was chased by the family's pet goat and had to climb a tree to get away with her brothers, all laughing merrily at her predicament. Rose went to Oregon State College, graduated with a teacher's certificate in 1928 and took a teaching job in Buckeye, Arizona for a year. A. M. and Rozina stayed with Rose during that school year because Albert's brother Tom Blake lived close by, making it a good reunion time for them all.

While at Oregon State College, Rose became engaged to Verne Owen and after her return to the northwest they married and settled In Klamath Falls where they helped establish Oregon Technical Institute. A building on the campus bears the name "Owen Hall." Rose and Verne had two children, Jim Blake Owen, and Rozina Jean Owen Heller.

In 1922, Frank and Alice Blake purchased the Grimes house on the northwest corner of 14th and Couch Streets kitty-corner across the street from Ralph's home. Frank's home was originally built by Will Grimes, husband of A. M. Blake's sister, Ada Jane. The Grimes moved to Camas shortly after the Blake family and were the owners of the town's lumberyard. Grimes house was located just two houses below Roy Dobb's lofty home that was built by John Roffler and had a wide, sweeping porch overlooking the town.

The Blake brothers, Harold and Frank purchased a Mack chain-drive truck with hard rubber tires and began a freight hauling business in 1925 they called "Columbia River Truck Company."

Their new business was located close to the feed store at 3rd and Clark. Harold also started a delivery service called "Merchant's Delivery" that delivered meats and groceries from the stores on regular routes throughout the area. Harold was blessed with a good business head like his father and the trucking company grew and prospered. Although Columbia River Truck

Company started with local delivery, they were soon able to deliver to Vancouver and Portland.

In 1927, Albert L. Blake, who had recently returned from California, got together with his brother Frank and bought the feed business back from Blair. The two brothers renamed the store "Blake Brothers" adding a grinder and mixer to the business so that feed could be prepared in their own Camas plant. They sold "scratch feed and egg mash" for chickens and "dairy feed" for cows to retail and wholesale customers. Although the brothers owned the store building, A. M. Blake continued to own the real property through all the years. Harold Blake was elected as an initial director of the new Camas-Washougal Golf Club in 1932 because he enjoyed playing golf in his spare time. The club was later renamed Orchard Hills Country Club. His other love was bird hunting, and he kept several German Shorthair bird dogs running them in field trials. It was related that when "bird season" arrived in the area, the whole town closed so that all could accompany Harold on his bird hunting expeditions.

The patriarch of the family, Albert M. Blake, passed away in 1933 at the age of seventy. He had gone into the basement to get an armload of wood for the stove and did not return. His loving wife Rozina found him dead of a heart attack. Albert had been bothered by heart problems for some time as the outgrowth of rheumatism but was in apparent good health before his death.

All their lives, Albert and Rozina had been excellent parents, stern with their children but always showing them love and kindness. Rozina was well known for her affectionate ways and good-natured personality to one and all. As a widow she became closer to her children who all lived within proximity. Alice Asher Blake would bring Rozina fresh bread and Rozina would go to Frank and Alice's each Sunday for a chicken and noodle dinner.

In 1934, Frank sold his interest in Columbia River Truck Company to Harold and Harold promptly added a standard fuel oil delivery service. He also purchased the Roosevelt Hotel complete with cabaret at North Bonneville just after the repeal of prohibition, and became part owner of a sawmill in Lewiston, Idaho. In addition, he owned logging trucks in the late

1930's and was well known for his diversified business interests. On December 7, 1934, Harold's company placed an advertisement in the local paper "congratulating the Crown Willamette Paper Company in appreciation for the service they had rendered Columbia River Truck Company for the past seven years." The company's slogan was "We feature fast freight, fuel and diesel oil."

Harold Blake purchased a large parcel of Columbia River property directly south of Oak Park in 1937. He built a new brick home close to the river and next to the port dock that was featured in the 1938 Industrial Edition of the Camas Post. Harold loved boating and won many trophies throughout the years for his boating expertise. He owned two boats, one a small cruiser that he ran up and down the Columbia, and the other was a Crist Craft named "Betty Rose" after his daughter that he used for boating on LaCamas Lake. In addition to building his new home, Harold built a barn and other outbuildings on his property. During World War II he bought some Standard Bred harness horses that he raced all over the country, primarily California.

Harold and Marjorie would often leave Camas to attend the season of harness racing in California and did so until his death in 1962. He developed a large oval-shaped trotting horse track on his property for training sessions and called his stable "Green Acres." When Highway 14 was put through at a later date, his trotting horse track became a thing of the past. However, in 1992 the old Blake house still stood next to the Columbia River although it was sold after Marjorie Blake's death in 1987.

In March 1937, the Camas Post published a humorous account of three women who served without pay on the school election board. The three ladies, Mrs. Grant Salisbury, Mrs. Ralph Blake, and Mrs. Hugh Gitting's were on duty for the balloting in the science room. They removed the top from the science aquarium and unknowingly five gentlemen placed their hats on the open top while casting their votes. It was reported that the gentlemen fished out their hats, shook them off and made "appropriate masculine remarks." In the same Post edition, it was news that "Blake Brother's Feed Store has installed a new Haines feed mixing machine that will mix a ton of feed of any kind in five minutes. The ingredients are poured in at the bottom where an auger carries them up through a tube in the bin. The old mixer has been converted to a grinder bin. Other improvements in the business include a 13 x 16 concrete basement under the mixer and elevator."

The success of Blake Brothers Feed Store was proclaimed in another article published in the 1938 Industrial Edition of the Post. The headline was "Blake Brother's Serves 250 Farmers in Eastern Clark County." The article goes on to say, "Besides all types of dairy and poultry feeds, Blake Bros. handles Aberdeen coal, Gasco briquettes and the Iron Fireman coal stoker, an automatic stoker." Blake's slogan at this time was "Blake's quality feeds mean extra profits."

A news item in the October 13, 1938, Camas Post is captioned "Mrs. Blake Improving" and reports "Mrs. A. M. Blake who has been ill with pneumonia was reported this morning to be improving rapidly." However, seventy-one-year-old Rozina Blake, who outlived her husband by five years passed away on November 26, 1938, with complications from pneumonia.

During the 1930's, Ralph Blake served as a Camas City councilman from the Third Ward. Ralph and young Albert were both charter members of the Bennett-Barnett Post No. 27 of the American Legion. And Ralph, Albert and

1940 Camas elected officials – Front Row R-L: Earl Lambert, Ralph Blake, Jay Woodworth, Oliver Hansen, Hugh McMaster. Back Row L-R: Bijah Smith, Al Paris, Odmund Egans, Belvel Dailey, John D. Currie, Wm Knauff, Ben Reed, Marvin Lewis (Source TRHM)

Harold were members of the Clarke Chapter of the Masonic Lodge. The women in the family were active in Eastern Star. Frank Blake was also involved in community affairs serving on the city council and a leader in 4-H among other activities. Alice Blake served her community in the PTA and Girl Scouts. In 1938 their son Leighton became a "Little All-American Football Player" at Willamette University in Salem, Oregon. Leighton married Betty Ann Faxon and their sons became third generation football players at Camas High School. In later years Leighton's family bought back the old Grimes house and lived there for some time.

In 1943, the Blake Brothers sold their feed store to H. R. Ward. Frank and Alice put the Grimes house up for sale and moved to a Fern Prairie farm where they became active in the Fern Prairie Grange. Both Frank and Alice held offices in the grange during that time. The old family home of A. M. and Rozina Blake at 1329 N. W. Benton was sold to the John Gant family in 1944. In 1992 the elder Gants were no longer living but a descendant of the Gants was restoring the house to its original elegant condition of 1911 when it was first constructed by A. M. Blake for his big family.

Harold and Marjorie's son Glenn married Alice Anderson, and they had five children. The Glenn Blake's built a home on the Harold Blake property. Harold and Marjorie's daughter, Betty Rose married Wallace H. Matthews in 1946, and their family lived for sixteen years in the historic MacMaster House at 12th and Adams before building a home in 1968 on Marjorie's parent's property close to the Columbia River.

In the 1950's, Edna Blake's husband, Jack Carkin, served on the Camas City Council. Seven members of the first Camas High School football team reunited in Camas for the dedication of the new football field in 1958. The event was organized by Frank Blake's son Leighton and was attended by both Frank and Albert Lester Blake.

In 1961, the old Blake owned feed store building, then called the H. R. Ward Company, was demolished to accommodate an expanding paper mill operation. The feed store had served the farmers of East Clark County for fifty-two years and it was with great sadness that the townsfolk watched the building go down. However, the building materials from the demolished building were donated for construction of a 4-H building at the Clark County Fairgrounds and that building still stood in 1992 as a fitting memorial to Frank Blake's 4-H efforts. In 1962 Frank and Alice Blake celebrated their fiftieth wedding anniversary. This was noted with a photograph and story in the Camas Post.

Harold Blake died in 1964 after a very productive and busy life. After his death, son Glenn took over management of Columbia River Trucking with four of his five children helping out in the business. Marjorie Duffin Blake followed her husband in death three years later at the age of eighty-eight. Alice M. Blake died April 20, 1968, in Fern Prairie where she and Frank had settled so many years before. Her husband, Frank Ross Blake, died five months later on September 20, 1968, after suffering a stroke. Reflecting on their courting days, it was always hard for the two of them to be apart.

On May 19, 1971, Albert Lester and Eula Blake celebrated their Golden Wedding anniversary with the occasion written up in the Camas Post. There was a tradition of long marriages in the Blake family. Albert died in 1977 at the age of eighty-two and in 1992 when this account was written, Eula was in her nineties and continued to live in the brick house that she and Lester had built at 14th and Birch so many years before.

A 1990 article in the Post-Record reported that sixty-five-year old Glenn Blake was retiring after fifty-two years in the trucking business. In 1992, the little company that Harold Blake began in 1925 as a local grocery delivery business had seventeen trucks, many trailers and other equipment and was approved to operate in forty-eight states.

It is clear that when A. M. Blake came to Camas in 1909, he started a dynasty of successful business and community leaders that continues to this day. Special thanks to Glenn Blake, Eula Blake, Mildred Benedict, Grace Snoey, and Frank Leighton Blake who provided so much information for this chapter.

ROBERT N. "BOB" GAINES

Author's Preface: Talk about entrepreneurship and you are speaking about Robert N. "Bob" Gaines. Here was a risk taker, a man who had no fear of failure. When he did not succeed in certain projects, he would simply redirect his energy to something new. From mailman to pool hall operator to gas station owner, Gaines added that special quality to every job making many friends in the process. He certainly possessed that spark that was so important in the formulative years of building the Camas community.

☙

BORN DECEMBER 2, 1882, in Bates City, Missouri, Bob Gaines came to Camas in 1909 at the age of twenty-seven with his family. He was hired at the paper mill where he worked on and off, and then he took a job at John Cowan's Cigar Store.

In 1918, Gaines began delivering mail by horseback to Prune Hill and because that work only took him three hours a day, he moonlighted by working in a pool hall. Bob saved up five hundred dollars from the two jobs and bought a card room at 4th and Clara Street, now Adams in Camas. He built up his business and sold out at a profit and that enabled him to start a new business that he called "Palace of Sweets" located between Birch and Adams on 4th Street. This too was successful and two years later he sold the business for another big profit. With his financial gains, Gaines bought two pool halls, one in Camas and one in Portland. That turned out to be his first business mistake. He went broke shortly afterwards.

During his idle time, Bob became a charter member of Clarke Lodge No. 203 F&AM of Camas and joined the York Rite Bodies of Vancouver.

In 1926, Bob Gaines had once again saved enough money to go into business. He built and operated one of Camas' first gas stations at 3rd and Adams that he aptly named "Gaines Service Station." With all the new

Bob Gaines, 1935 (Source Find a Grave)

automobiles in town the gas station's success was immediate. At about the same time he met a lady from Chicago, Grace Louise, who was born August 9, 1884. They were married soon after.

Around 1928, Gaines was able to buy the land under his service station and in 1933 he leased both the service and the land to Homer Campbell who remodeled and managed the station. Once that transaction was completed Bob began a fuel distribution business for Texaco and became Clark County's Texaco distributor. By 1938 he had two twelve-hundred-gallon delivery tanks and a small pickup truck he used for deliveries.

A 1931 Camas Post article reports that Mrs. Robert Stoller, Mrs. Fred Stoller and Mrs. R. N. Gaines, among others, attended the "White Shrine" in Vancouver. During the "Wild Spree of '33" held in 1933, Bob was photographed wearing mutton chop sideburns. Most of the men of town grew beards during the fifty-year celebration of Camas' beginnings.

Bob's wife, Grace Louise Gaines, died at age sixty-one in 1945. Bob gave u p   his

Gaines Service Station, 5th and Dallas 1926 (Source TRHM)

Texaco distributorship and in 1946 opened "Van's Fuel Service." That business thrived well into the 1970's. However, Gaines sold that business in 1947, just a year after he began operations. He wanted to retire and just do nothing for a change. But being Bob Gaines meant that he soon bought a sixty-acre farm in the Forest Hill community and became an active farmer that gave him more work that he had ever imagined. He sold out again and moved back into Camas purchasing a home on Garfield Street. His home had been constructed by Camas builder, John Roffler in 1910 and the fine craftsmanship demonstrated both inside and outside of the home was of great personal pride to Gaines.

Bob Gaines, center, with Camas Mill work crew sent to work in California 1915. (Source TRHM)

On March 8, 1967, when the block of land between 2nd and 3rd Streets in Camas was cleared to make room for the new Safeway store, Bob sat on the porch of his Garfield Street home and watched the demolition crew tear apart and burn sixteen old homes and apartments. He remembered each and every one of them being a part of Camas history. Although saddened by the loss of these homes, he took an active interest in the building of the new Safeway store, visiting the site daily and giving advice to the workers. Ironically in 1990, eleven years after Bob's death, his cherished home on Garfield Street was burned down to make room for yet another, newer Safeway store.

Bob Gaines died June 22, 1979, at the age of ninety-six. He had lived seventy years in Camas and was survived by three nephews and five nieces. They were Joseph Gaines, Harold Middleton, Franklin Brannan, Kay Charles, Peggy Marks, Gussie Herr, Betty Juul and Wallena Finley.

ROBERT W. CARMACK

Author's Preface: To proclaim that Oregon Trail pioneers were great adventurers would have to be an understatement. Pulling up roots on the east coast and in the Midwest, hitching their dreams to a wagon train and finding success at the end of the rainbow took not only foresight but a great deal of courage. Some of the early pioneers went west with such confidence that it seemed to be "the natural thing to do." And, changing locations once they got here was equally easy for them. Such a man was Robert Wiley Carmack who not only came west but encouraged and pestered his friends to do likewise. When things did not work out in one Washington town, he came to Camas and not only found success but happiness.

⊗⊗⊙

R OBERT WILEY CARMACK was born August 17, 1877, in California, Kentucky to George W. and Sammie E. Carmack. The Carmack family lived in Cold Springs, Kentucky, about twenty miles south of Cincinnati, Ohio. George Carmack was of Irish-Scottish descent with his spirited ancestors leaving the British Isles under duress sometime before. Robert's grandfather, George Carmack Sr., was the husband of Martha D. Washington who had her own famous roots as the niece of the first United States president, George Washington. Martha's father was George Washington's brother.

George Carmack Jr. and his wife Sammie had nine children including Robert. First was Emma born in 1872, but who died two years later in 1874. Then Richard was born in 1874, Anna Maude in 1876, Robert in 1877, Etta in 1879, Frank in 1880, Alice in 1882, Harvard in 1888 and finally, Mary Traver born in 1894. Because this was such a large family and they were living through hard times, Robert and his siblings received only rudimentary education in their early years. Thirsting for knowledge and books, Robert left home at the early age of twelve to seek his fortune and education away from Cold Spring.

Although still a child, Robert was an adventuresome sort of fellow, heading out of state to Minnesota and the farming country. He was able to get a job doing farm work in Minnesota for a couple of years and at fourteen was fortunate to meet a wealthy farming couple named Weaver who owned a large ranch in Elton, Illinois. The Weavers took to young Carmack immediately employing him on their ranch. Robert stayed with the Weavers for the next few years because they treated him like an adopted son. When he wasn't busy with farm chores, he tried to better himself educationally by reading every book the Weavers had available and soon became known as a "book hound." That began a life-long love affair with books for Robert Carmack who became a self-educated man.

Robert Carmack, 1910 (Source Camas Post)

In 1901, when he was twenty-four, Robert felt it was time to move on to higher aspirations than farming. He fondly bid the Weavers goodbye although he stayed in touch with the family throughout his life, and moved to Ceylon, Minnesota where he obtained a temporary position at First National Bank of Ceylon. It was there he met his lifelong friend, Oscar Franklin Johnson who was also employed at the bank. As their friendship grew, Oscar introduced Robert to one of his attractive young nieces, a woman who was later to become Robert's first wife.

Five years later, in 1906, Carmack, who had a restless nature, said goodbye to his friends at the bank and headed west. He had heard stories of excellent entrepreneurial opportunities in the new state of Washington and decided to try his luck there.

Success in the west did not come immediately to Carmack. Upon arrival in Mt. Vernon, Washington he took a job at an Anacortes sawmill and later joined a logging camp in the mountains. He became an engineer in a Kent sawmill south of Seattle biding his time for the opportunity to go into business for himself. The opportunity arose a few months later when he invested the money he had saved into some Kennewick land that included a small grocery store in Kent. He had finally realized his dream to "be his own boss." However, even then Bob knew that real money was to be made in real estate and in his own words in a letter to O. F. Johnson he wrote, "Land profits paid better than working."

Being a smart businessman with a broad vision, Carmack realized that the banking business in Washington State was also expanding at a rapid pace. He wrote to his friend Oscar Johnson and urged him to also come west. Johnson had done quite well at the Ceylon bank and was also engaged to Beatrice "Amelia" Bauman, the assistant teller, so it took a great deal of persuasion to talk Johnson into coming to Seattle. But Johnson finally took a leave of absence from the bank and headed west to join his friend. It took Oscar no time at all to obtain a banking position in Aberdeen, Washington making double his Ceylon bank salary. He sent notice to his Ceylon employers that he was permanently leaving his position there and set to work establishing himself at the Aberdeen bank. When he was firmly settled in his new job he sent for Amelia, and they were married in 1907.

The newlyweds rented a house at F and 3rd Street in Aberdeen and their good friend and bachelor, Robert Carmack rented a room from them for ten dollars a month. Observing the Johnson's wedded bliss, Robert felt that he too was ready for marriage. He sent for Oscar's niece and when she arrived in Kent the couple married and ran the general store together in Kent until the new Mrs. Carmack got pregnant. She gave birth to a son in 1908.

In a September 6, 1908, letter from Carmack in Kent to Johnson in Aberdeen, Robert described his new-born son, "He will soon be big enough to go to school. We have not named him yet because I can't think of a name good enough." He went on to say, "I recently sold my store for a seven-hundred-dollar profit. I also traded my Kennewick land for a store four miles east of Kent in a town called Christopher, Washington. Most of the trade at my new store will be with the Japanese with some white customers. The stock in the new store invoiced at two thousand eight hundred dollars but I had to order almost one thousand dollars in goods right away. We have a good trade in feed and flour and groceries. Also, cloth and hardware. I have the post office and have charge of the Northern Pacific Depot."

The Carmack's had moved to Christopher and the two-story general store that was called T. S. Harvey's. Bob renamed his business R. W. Carmack General Merchandise, Hardware, Flour and Feed. The fast-paced growth of the area plus Bob Carmack's talent for merchandising soon paid off with his store profits increasing each month. Unfortunately, his marriage did not fare so well. The Carmack's divorced with Mrs. Carmack gaining custody of their son. Very little is known of this marriage and the first Mrs. Carmack who when this was written in 1992 remained a mystery to the Carmack family eighty-four years later.

Alone and emotionally drained by the loss of his wife and son, Carmack poured himself into his business and by 1910 his store in Christopher was a well-known fixture in that part of the state.

Meanwhile, his friend Johnson was formulating new plans in Aberdeen. Johnson dreamed of owning and operating his own bank, so he made a list of possible cities in Washington and Oregon with his top choice being the newly incorporated town of Camas on the Columbia River. He and Amelia moved there in 1908 and with the help of Johnson's father-in-law built a new brick bank building at 4th and Cedar Streets. He called his bank Camas State Bank with Johnson the first teller and Amelia the assistant teller.

By mid-1910, Johnson's bank was doing so well that he wrote a stirring letter of invitation to his friend, Bob Carmack. He wrote "If you will move to the thriving paper mill town of Camas and enter into the grocery business, I will furnish you with a small, one hundred by one-hundred-foot store building to the west of the bank on N. E. 4th Street." The current business at that location was Camas Grocery Store and the owners were anxious to sell. Carmack promised to come and take a look-see. In a postcard dated November 20, 1910, from Christopher, R. W. Carmack wrote the Johnson's "Dear friends, will try and come to see you Wednesday night about 8:00 p.m. Don't look for me until you see me. RWC."

Although Robert Carmack was firmly established at his general store in Christopher and had been courting a young nurse from Tacoma named

Daisy Wilhite, he took his friend Oscar's advice and made a visit to Camas. When he arrived, he was impressed with the tidy building and good location plus liked the busy, bustling city. He found it impossible to resist Johnson's generous offer and knew how nice it would be to see the Johnson's on a regular basis. In May of 1911, Bob Carmack sold his store with all its' goods in Christopher and moved to Camas. He purchased the Camas Grocery renaming it Carmack's Camas Grocery and although there were other general merchandise stores in town like MacMaster's and Farrell's, Carmack decided to concentrate primarily on groceries, the freshest and best he could find.

The May 1911 Camas Post quotes, "R. W. Carmack formerly of Seattle, is one of the most recent arrivals in this city. On Monday, May 8, Mr. Carmack took possession of the Camas Grocery Store. He is an experienced grocer and businessman and will undoubtedly meet with success."

With his business off to a good start, Robert could turn his attention to unfinished business in Tacoma. The

Daisy Carmack, 1910 (Source Camas Post)   hardest part about moving to Camas had

been leaving Daisy Wilhite behind and when he left her, he resolved the parting was only temporary and he would return as soon as possible to make Daisy Wilhite his bride.

Daisy was born in Milan, Missouri, the daughter of Benjamin and Melinda Wilhite. Benjamin was a wealthy gentleman farmer from Nebraska and when ready for marriage had ordered a "mail order" bride from Louisiana. The new Mrs. Wilhite was of Cajun descent and could not speak English, only French. The Wilhite's proceeded to have eight children with Daisy being the youngest. When Daisy was born on October 3, 1890, her mother died in childbirth at age thirty-eight. Although it was difficult for forty-six-year-old Benjamin to raise the children by himself, it helped to be of "means" and that ensured good quality upbringing and education for all of the children. When he died at the age of sixty-nine in 1913, each of his children inherited a goodly sum of money.

Once Daisy had finished her schooling in Nebraska, she moved to Tacoma to live with her sister, Viola, who was married to Roy Kellum. She took a position as a nurse and when she was twenty-one, she met Robert Carmack. Her longtime pet name for Robert was "Rob," although most others called him "Bob." Daisy was a high-spirited spunky woman who enjoyed life and Robert was immediately attracted. Daisy in turn was intrigued by the handsome, adventurous Carmack. When Robert made his move to Camas, Daisy knew that this was her one true love, and it would be just a matter of time until she joined him.

The August 31, 1911, Camas Post had a front-page article that read "The friends of R. W. Carmack were treated to a surprise this week when they heard of the marriage. Tuesday, he slipped quietly away to Tacoma and there was joined by Miss Daisy Wilhite of that city. They proceeded to Vancouver where they were married on Wednesday afternoon and arrived in Camas on Wednesday night where they will occupy the house on Burton, now Cedar Street recently vacated by A. E. Heaton. Although but a recent arrival in Camas, Mr. Carmack has made many friends who wish him and his bride a long and happy life." Moving to Camas was just another bit of excitement for Daisy. Although Camas lacked the cosmopolitan atmosphere of Tacoma, she immediately liked the small, busy community.

Carmack's Camas Grocery 1911 (Source Camas Post)

In 1911, the streets of Camas were still a muddy mess as shown in a historic photo featured in the 1934 Camas Post. The ladies of the day wore long skirts, and it was a continuous battle to keep them from dragging in the muddy streets. The photo shows Carmack's Camas Grocery facing the muddy street. However, in 1912, with Mayor J. W. Duvall leading the way, the streets were widened and graveled with noticeable improvement. Then in 1913, a break in the Pittock Canal from LaCamas Lake to the paper mill flooded the business district with nine feet of water. No fatalities but much property damage to all the stores downtown including Johnson's bank and Carmack's grocery.

The Camas Post's earlier prediction of Carmack's success proved to be true. At Christmas in 1911 his grocery store gave out complimentary ceramic plates that read, "Compliments of Carmack's Camas Grocery Company, Camas, Washington, Season 1911."

With his increased business, Carmack's grocery on N. E. 4th soon became too small and a larger wooden structure was completed by Johnson to the north of the Camas State Bank on Burton Street. This larger building became Carmack's new location that he called Carmack's Camas Mercantile Company. He employed eight clerks and delivered his goods by several horse drawn wagons called "drays." He did this until automobiles came into being. Keeping up with the times, Carmack promptly went out and purchased a fine new delivery truck. His store, horse drawn delivery wagon and new delivery truck were all featured in an early Camas Post photo.

On July 24, 1912, a lovely baby daughter, Beatrice Melinda Carmack, was born to Robert and Daisy at a Vancouver hospital. Two years later, on August 6, 1914, they welcomed a son, James Robert Carmack, who was delivered on the kitchen table of their home. After the children were born it was necessary to move from the small, rented house behind the store to a larger home on N. E. 4th Street just below the cemetery and east of the downtown area.

Carmack's fortunes continued to improve, and he began to invest in real estate, buying several lots on N. E. 3rd between Garfield and Hayes. He contracted with John Roffler to build three houses on these lots and moved his family into one of them until 1920. The homes are no longer there making room several years ago for the Zion Lutheran Church.

In 1919, the Carmack's asked Daisy's brother, O. J. Wilhite who was a general contractor, to build them a home at what is now 1828 N. W. 6th. Robert purchased a large parcel of land west of town with the knowledge that the proposed North Bank Highway would soon be the main route east and west through Camas. Workmen were trying to complete the Camas to Vancouver link that ran through Carmack's new property, later known as the "Carmack's Addition." The Carmack's decided that a perfect location for their planned home would be on a knoll overlooking the highway. Their new home was a spacious two-story structure with many large windows facing north including a bay window on the lower elevation. Large trees and sweeping lawns surrounded the lovely home that still stood at its' lofty location above the highway in 1992. However, an interesting comment regarding the family home came from the Carmack's son, James, who described the house as being "one of the prettiest in Camas on the outside and one of the ugliest on the inside." He later explained why his parents had faced their home toward the highway instead of the Columbia River where they would have had an excellent view of the water. He said that before the great dams of the 1930's the river smelled so horribly from the salmon runs, that river views were both unsightly and repugnant.

Beatrice and James were often photographed in front of the house at various ages and times. James would often take the cows down the old rutty road below the house and across the railroad tracks towards the river. That was before any thoughts occurred of future freeways and the old country road provided a pleasant afternoon's meandering.

In 1923, Carmack sold his Burton Street mercantile store to W. C. Mansfield and moved with his family to Los Angeles where he intended to retire. Los Angeles proved to be a disappointment for the family who dearly missed the pleasantness of living in Camas. A few months after their California arrival, they packed up and drove to San Francisco where they caught the steamer north to Portland and then home. Upon returning to Camas, Carmack was shocked to discover that three weeks after selling his store to Mansfield half the downtown business district had gone up in smoke. A terrible fire raged through three blocks of wooden buildings burning all in its path including Johnson's corner brick bank building.

Johnson rebuilt all his buildings on 4th and Burton Streets, but this time using only the best of fire-resistant materials. A much larger and finer brick building on the 4th and Burton replaced the bank building. The first tenant to occupy this building was "W. E. Dungan, Clothing and Shoes." It later became the location of Sprouse-Reitz who occupied the building until 1993. Another brick building was constructed where the Carmack Mercantile had been. That became the location of Carmack's new endeavor "R. W. Carmack Real Estate and Insurance."

Around the same time, Carmack was persuaded to invest in a puncture-proof inner tube company with his partners Dr. Carlos Urie, the town physician, and Wilmer Swank, successful owner of the largest furniture store in town. The deal he made was that if the company failed, Carmack would get his money back.

RW Carmack "arrested" during the Spree of 33 for not growing a beard – 1933 (Source TRHM)

The business went downhill fast and when Robert Carmack wanted out, Urie and Swank didn't have the cash so the two gave Carmack a hundred foot by hundred-foot parcel of land on the southeast corner of 4th and Burton across the street from Swank's furniture store.

It was on this site that Carmack had his brother-in-law, O. J. Wilhite build a beautiful stately Carmack Building in 1923. There were six apartments on the second floor and store and office space on the ground floor. Carmack moved his real estate business into the ground floor location and Camas Home Laundry and the Camas Stage Company took over the Johnson Building on Cedar Street. During this period Robert often had to take business trips and before one trip knowing the independent spirit of his wife, Daisy, he chidingly warned her to not buy new furniture while he was away. The irrepressible Daisy promptly went out and bought a whole house full of furniture much to Carmack's dismay when he returned.

During this time, a photo was taken of Daisy Carmack and Pearl Mansfield picketing for women's rights on the steps of city hall. Many of the women of Camas including Daisy, Pearl, Gladys Carleton who was the Sprouse-Reitz manager, Hansi Michaelis who owned Ideal Corner and educators Nora Self and Irene Roffler were way ahead of their time. They made sure that the "women's rights" message was heard loud and clear in Camas during the 1920's and 1930's. Although Pearl, Daisy, Gladys and Hansi's "formidable" husbands were better known and more often written about, these early ladies were clearly the real "power behind the throne."

In 1925, Beatrice Carmack performed as a solo dance in junior high for the annual operetta according to the May 1, 1925, edition of the Post. After graduation from high school, she attended the University of Washington and then nurses training at Emanuel Hospital in Portland.

Bob Carmack had always been involved in community affairs as a member of the Kiwanis Club, on the board of Farmer's Coop Creamery and active in Camas school projects including the Garfield Auditorium that he was instrumental in building. He later became president of the Camas School Board and that was a special honor for him considering his difficult educational beginnings.

James Robert Carmack graduated from high school in 1931 and was awarded a scholarship to Whitman College. Unable to attend, he worked at the paper mill taking University of Oregon extension classes. In 1935 he was finally able to begin his Whitman studies, and the following year James entered the University of Washington.

By 1932, Carmack's real estate and insurance business was doing so well that Daisy devoted most of her time helping to manage the thriving business. The Carmack's decided to build another building next door that they also leased out. Besides owning the Carmack Addition they owned Midland Acres, an area of homes surrounding the 1992 "One Stop Shopping Center."

They also owned Weir Park where lots were sold for four hundred dollars with an agreement to build a double garage for two hundred more. Many of the double garages became permanent homes.

In 1934, the Carmack Building boasted as its' tenants Maddocks Plumbing, Northwestern Electric Company and the new Camas Mercantile Company. This Mission-Mediterranean style building was also to become the 1930's location of city hall, the library and the police and fire departments.

When Robert's health began to fail in 1935, Daisy took over management of the properties and by 1936 their son James had to quit college and return home to assume a more active role in the real estate firm.

On November 11, 1937, Beatrice married Horace W. Clear who worked for Standard Oil Company's Portland office. It was a simple but impressive ceremony at the Benson Hotel in Portland with James serving as best man at his sister's wedding. Lela Rae Rossman of Washougal sang "The Sweetest Story Ever Told" at the ceremony. An elegant wedding breakfast was served after the ceremony to twenty-four guests that were mostly relatives and then the couple left for a British Columbia honeymoon. When the wedding couple returned two weeks later, they moved into an apartment on Glisan Street in Portland. In the following years they had a daughter, Barbara Ann, but the marriage did not last, and they were later divorced.

A year after Beatrice's marriage, on October 13, 1938, Robert W. Carmack died at the age of sixty-one. He had been in ill health for over two years but had maintained his post as chairman of the Camas School Board during his period of illness. He had also continued to serve as secretary for the Camas Cooperative Creamery and was still a member of the Kiwanis Club at the time of his death. Robert suffered a heart attack and passed away quietly at his home in the Carmack Addition.

In 1943, during World War II, Daisy moved out of the family home and into one of the apartments above the store. She installed a connecting door to the adjoining flat so that when her son James returned from the service, he would have his own place to live. Although James appreciated his mother's efforts, he refused her offer. Daisy later bought a small English-style cottage at the corner of 4th and Everett next to the old city hall and current library.

Claude Knapp constructed the home in the 1930's for Mayor Duvall. Daisy shared the residence for a time with her recently divorced daughter Beatrice and her granddaughter Barbara Ann. It was in this very house that in January of 1946 James Robert Carmack married the very beautiful Juanita Corrienne "Joni" Yount, daughter of Ella and Dick Yount from Missouri.

The Yount family had moved to Camas during World War II and encouraged their daughter Joni to follow them. When she arrived, the whole town gossiped that a "Hollywood Starlet" had come to town incognito. James was immediately enraptured by Joni asking her to marry him on the second date, but she refused. He continued to pursue her, and Joni finally relented. The joyous wedding photo shows the whole family including Daisy, Beatrice, Barbara Ann, James, Joni and the Yount's standing in front of the fireplace in the living room of the 4th and Everett Street home. James and Joni raised a family of four children including April Carmack Ourso, Victoria, Lloyd, and Robert Hadley Carmack who was named after his deceased grandfather.

The Carmack grandchildren delight in telling of their visits to Grandma Daisy, as they called her. The exterior of Daisy's home was finished in thousands of pebbles imbedded in the cement. If the grandchildren picked out certain favorite stones, Daisy would go outside and pry them away with a knife giving them to the children as treasures. Daisy was an excellent seamstress and when her granddaughter Barbara Ann lived with her, Daisy would sew the child the most beautiful of dresses. Once a month Daisy's women friends met at her house to play canasta and other card games. The best china dishes would come out of the cupboard for these occasions. The ladies would laugh, talk, and puff on their cigarettes as they played cards and drank their tea.

Daisy continued to live in her "pebble house" close to friends including the Johnson's until her death on July 21, 1955, seventeen years after her husband. Although her tombstone is located next to her husbands in the Camas Cemetery there is no birth date recorded. Throughout her entire life, Daisy never divulged her age and there was always great speculation in town about just how old Daisy Carmack really was. Daisy had the last laugh on all those people who trekked to the cemetery to find out. In 1992 the "pebble house" was owned by the City of Camas and used as its' Building Department headquarters. After Daisy's death the Carmack Building was willed to her son James while the building next door was willed to her daughter, Beatrice.

James Carmack successfully continued with the business his father had begun so many years before that included real estate, insurance, and new housing developments. Another "Carmack Addition" was located between Garfield Auditorium and the middle school, and a third "Carmack Addition" was developed on Prune Hill near the old drive-in theater. Like father, like son were Robert and James. During the 1960's the business was renamed "Camas Realty and Carmack Insurance" for easier identification by new residents to the area.

Beatrice Carmack married Paul Christenson, who had a son from a previous marriage. The couple had been married for several years, losing Paul's son to an accident during that time. Beatrice and Paul later divorced, and Beatrice married Frank Masco. When she died in 1988, she was buried as Beatrice Carmack Masco between her parents at the Camas Cemetery. She was remembered by friends and family alike as a sweet, lovely lady. In 1992 her daughter, Barbara Ann Hunter, lived with her husband in Portland and had three grown children.

If you are wondering about the little son in Kent, Washington that Robert Carmack had written so proudly about in his 1908 letter to O. F. Johnson, although the Carmack family tried desperately to contact and establish a relationship with him through the years, he did not respond to their efforts. He ended up being a "lost" child to Robert W. Carmack and a missing brother to James and Beatrice.

In 1989, after the death of Joni Carmack's mother, Ella in Camas, the James Carmack's moved to Sun City West, Arizona to enjoy year-long sunshine. By that time their children were grown and had families of their own. April's son James Carroll Reinhart graduated from Camas High School and went on to graduate from law school. Her daughter, Heidi Melina Reinhart was a postulate with the Sisters of Mercy in Michigan when this account was written in 1992. Robert Hadley Carmack lived and worked in Australia.

In 1992, all that was left of the Carmack family in Camas was the old Carmack house and the Carmack Building. The house still stood regally poised about the old North Bank Highway, its' exterior beauty and graceful lawns reflecting on times past. The residents of the home in 1992 had found many porcelain doll remnants beneath the large picture window of the home. These were likely parts of Beatrice's dolls that she played with in the 1920's.

It is easy to imagine a lazy summer afternoon in 1921 with a little nine-year-old girl playing with her dolls on the sloping grassy area beneath the bay window of her new home in Camas. She is humming a tune and dreaming of a grownup world sometime in the future. In her most vivid thoughts, she could not have imagined that in 1992 her parents Bob and Daisy Carmack would be so fondly remembered as famous early Camas pioneers.

WILBER E. FARR – FARR BROTHERS

Author's Preface: During the late 1800's and early 1900's many new businesses opened in LaCamas. Some of the owners became discouraged by the rawness of the town and its' people. It was hard to compete with the stores in Portland, a major industrial hub. One gentleman who did not give up was Wilber Farr. He started a men's clothing store with his brother in 1910 and although his brother decided not to stick around, Farr Brother's Clothing did with continuous operations up into the 1950's. Farr Brothers boasted of being the oldest continuing businesses in Camas. It's been said if Wilber Farr was still alive today the store would still be going strong.

≈≈⊙

WILBER E. "BILL" Farr was born October 26, 1880, in North Branch, Minnesota. Little is known about his early life but during the month of July 1910 he arrived in Camas with his twenty-nine-year-old wife, Amy Farr of Rush City, Minnesota. Wilber was thirty at the time and was also accompanied into town by his brother, Clifford E. Farr and his mother, Anna S. Farr.

The Farr brothers apparently had a good deal of merchandising experience because they immediately purchased a lot at 4th and Clara, now Birch, and erected their first store. They originally called their new business "The Mercantile Store" but soon after it became "Farr Brothers" dealing in men's clothing, shoes and furnishing goods. They carried a large and carefully selected stock of merchandise and were welcomed to Camas with open arms by the community.

In 1912, they demolished the small wooden building and built a new much larger structure on the same site. That store served Camas and customers up and down the Columbia Gorge for twenty-two years.

Wilber and Amy constructed a two-story home at 708 N. E. 2nd Street in 1918 that still stood in 1992, but was owned by the Regan family. This home, like many others of its' time, had wood siding. It was of the American Four-Square Craftsman style with a mushroom roof. The Farr house had bell cast eaves and a hip roof dormer with a sleeping porch on the second story. In 1934 the old Farr Brothers store was demolished, and a new, much larger two-story office building was constructed. The fine new structure was built of reinforced concrete and veneered brick. It had four storerooms downstairs and six office rooms and two apartments upstairs. In 1938, Farr Brothers was advertised as being the oldest existing business in Camas.

As storekeepers, the Farrs were known throughout the area for being quite thrifty. When a customer came into the shop the Farr's would be sitting in the dark. If the customer wanted to look at shoes, Wilber would turn on a forty-watt bulb in the shoe department and would turn it off when they moved on to the coat department where he would turn on another forty-watt bulb. When the customer left the store, it was lights out again.

Wilber Farr served a term as mayor of Camas and was responsible for providing real sidewalks in the downtown area, to the delight of the ladies who did not like wading in the mud. He was known as an outdoor man who loved to hunt and pick huckleberries. In the 1930's, Wilbur served as city clerk while Wilmer Swank was mayor.

Farr Brothers Building 236 NE 4th Built 1934, remodeled 1975 (Source TRHM)

Anna S. Farr, Wilber's mother, was quite active in the WRC in 1916. She died in 1929 at the age of seventy-six and was buried in the Camas Cemetery. Wilber died in October of 1958, and it was the talk of the town that only twelve people showed up for his funeral. It is possible that those grateful ladies of the early 1900's were also deceased so could not pay their respects. His wife Amy died September 22, 1967.

In 1992, both Wilber's house on 2nd Street and the Farr Brothers building downtown were still standing. At that time, it was being used by LaCamas Credit Union who did major remodeling in the 1970's.

This is a short chapter because no other information could be found on these early Camas pioneers and businessmen.

STATEHOOD AND THE GOOD LIFE

POETS AND PROFESSIONALS

JESSIE D. BELKNAP

Author's Preface: Most towns or cities aren't lucky enough to have a poet laureate, but Camas was the exception. A young woman had arrived in LaCamas around 1890 while still in her early twenties. She quickly developed a love affair with the small community nestled in the forests at the north side of the Columbia River. In the early 1900's she expressed her feelings for the beauty of the area through a series of poems submitted to the local paper. Although not specifically called a town leader, Jessie Belknap was dear to all who knew her, and we would like to recognize her contributions here.

～～～

JESSIE D. "ELIZABETH" Belknap was born December 21, 1870, in Milwaukee, Wisconsin. After spending some time in California Jessie moved to the new community of LaCamas and met Edgar Levi Belknap who was born July 8, 1869, in St. Clair, Michigan. The Belknap's married around 1890 and bought a home at 540 Beeson Street, now Dallas, from the Sass family. The home was located where the AAWPW building was in 1992.

At the turn of the century Jessie quickly became renowned as the "town poet" submitting many of her verses to the "Poet's Corner" section of the LaCamas Post. Although others in town contributed poems to the newspaper, Jessie had the greatest poetic talent and was published frequently. Jessie and other LaCamas Post poets became known as "Corner Friends."

Jessie's most noteworthy poem appeared in the May 11, 1911, LaCamas Post and was entitled "Do you want a home near Camas?" The poem expressed the feeling and love we all have for this southwest Washington town.

A few of Jessie's poems were "You'd better get off at Washougal," "Houses," "Winter," "Garden Gossip," and "Reminiscence." The last poem was dedicated to her late husband Edgar.

Reminiscence

When the distant hills
Are a misty grey
And the summer is growing old,
When the winding trail
Through the canyon woods
Is sprinkled with red and gold.
Then, with my shawl around my shoulders thrown
While the old hearth fire burns low
I am seeing again the merry groups
And the holly and mistletoe.
Then out beneath the twinkling stars
Where sparkles the evening dew,
I wander down through memory lanes
Searching, my dear, for you.

Jessie always kept her latchkey out for her "Poet's Corner" friends who happen to come out this way. It was her expressed wish that she would have the pleasure of knowing all the "Corner Family" and she issued a standing invitation for folks to drop in on her. Jessie always had a warm welcome and a cup of hot tea.

Edgar died June 24, 1941, at the age of seventy-two and Jessie died September 9, 1964, at the age of ninety-four. After twenty-three years of searching, Jessie finally found Edgar.

ARCHIE E. BIRD, M.D.

Author's Preface: In the early 1900's the professional doctor had to be a man or woman for all seasons. Dedication to the patient and their profession was the key to a successful career. House calls were the norm regardless of location or time of day. The early doctor really had no personal life and he or she would drop everything to travel across mountain roads or choppy waters in the dead of night to attend to the sick. Such a physician was Archie Edward Bird, M.D., who was not only a remarkable doctor in the early Camas community but a friend to all who lived there as well.

❧

ARCHIE EDWARD BIRD was born in Rio Dell, Humboldt County, California February 11, 1894, the son of James B. Bird and Catherine O'Rouke. James' parents had immigrated to America from Northern Ireland settling in Mobile, Alabama. James was born in 1868 in Springfield, Illinois. His early years were spent happily growing up with a brother and a sister plus loving parents in Springfield. James' father was a master mechanic on the Illinois Central Railroad. However, tragedy struck in 1876 when James was just eight years old. Both of his parents died of yellow fever. Being orphaned at such a young age was indeed a hardship but James Bird was a strong young man who worked hard to learn the railroad trade just like his father. He first worked for the Santa Fe Railroad, and then moved to California. Through ambition and effort, he held the positions of fireman and engineer on the railroads in California.

Twenty-year-old James was described by his friends as being a quiet and gentle man. His diligent ways and kind nature were attributes that attracted a lovely sixteen-year-old Irish girl named Catherine Jane O'Rouke. Catherine's Irish ancestors had first settled in Canada then later moved to Table Bluff, California where she was born in 1875.

When James met Catherine in 1891, he was attracted to her outgoing, gregarious, and friendly nature. In just a matter of time they were married and established residence in Rio Dell, California. In 1894 their first son, Archie, was born. James was twenty-six and Catherine was nineteen at the time. Five years later in 1899 another son, Vernon James Bird, arrived. The family continued to make Rio Dell their home until the early 1900's.

Because James worked for the railroad the family moved often after Vernon was born. They went from Rio Dell to South Bay, then to Alton and Scotia, California. From there they moved to Kellogg, Idaho and Phoenix, Arizona. Finally in 1905 they moved to Brush Prairie, Washington and settled permanently in Vancouver, Washington in 1911. The family was Catholic and became faithful members of St. James Catholic Church in Vancouver. James got a job tending the boilers at the high school. James and Catherine purchased a home at the corner of 12th and Daniels across from the post office in Vancouver. The home was still there in 1992 when this chapter was written but was used for offices occupied by attorneys.

Archie and Vernon grew up in this wonderful old home, graduated from high school and went to work to get themselves through college. Archie dreamed of being a doctor and toiled at various odd jobs including delivering ice, to take pre-med at the University of Oregon. Vernon joined the Merchant Marines as a radio operator, saving his money to attend dental college. He graduated from North Pacific College of Dental Medicine in 1927 and set up an office at the Medical Arts Building in downtown Vancouver.

Like his father Archie was a man of quiet nature but very sociable when in a group. While attending the University of Oregon he came to love football and attended as many games as possible. He especially liked the rivalry of football games between the University of Oregon and Oregon State College. Through the years Archie would place friendly bets that his alma mater would emerge victorious in the "Civil War" battle each year. When he could no longer attend the games in person, he became an avid TV football fan.

Towards the end of his schooling in Eugene, Archie came home one weekend and was introduced by a mutual friend to twenty-year-old Adeline "Ad" Blair. That introduction began a romance that ended in marriage on

August 25, 1917, in Eugene, Oregon. Ad was the daughter of Robert Blair who began his life in Polk County, Missouri on January 16, 1861. Her mother was Lucy Jane Coffman Blair, born on Christmas Day 1865 in Missouri. Although the Blair family made their home in the Fisher area of Clark County, they were well known in Camas. Baby Ad arrived on June 17, 1897, in Camas, one of seven Blair children. Her four sisters were Dona Blair Ostenson, Nora Blair Owen, Olive Blair Duback, and Jessie Blair Phillips. Her two brothers were Otis Blair and Walter J. Blair. Adeline grew up in Clark County and graduated from Mill Plain School.

After Adeline and Archie got married, Ad stayed with her mother-in-law Catherine Bird in Vancouver while Archie continued his studies at the University of Oregon Medical School in Portland, Oregon. Finally, Archie realized his long-time dream of achieving his Doctorate in Medicine. The Archie Birds settled in Camas where Archie set up practice as a physician and surgeon on the second floor of the MacMaster Building. The MacMaster Building was constructed in 1916 on the southwest corner of 4th

Dr. Archie Bird and Adeline "Ad" Blair-Bird – 1920 (Source *Camas Post*)

and Clark Streets. Although the ground floor of the building was used to sell general merchandise and food, the upper floor contained professional offices and apartments.

Dr. Bird's practice grew by leaps and bounds because he was compassionate to his patients and dedicated to his profession. At that time doctors made house calls when there was an illness, and the patient was unable to leave home. These house calls were often made after hours, on weekends, and in the black of night. One such visit was made to a sick patient on Government Island. Dr. Bird was met at the shore by a man in a rowboat. The water going across the Columbia was rough and Dr. Bird had to help bail out the boat as they went along. Although they successfully reached their destination and he tended to the patient, Dr. Bird had only mild enthusiasm about that trip.

Often in winter, Dr. Bird would travel up the steep and icy Columbia Gorge highway to Skamania County to visit those who were ill. It was this kind of caring for the sick, risking his own safety, that won the respect of the community and built up his practice.

On August 5, 1922, the Bird's welcomed a daughter, Patricia at St. Joseph's Hospital in Vancouver. Five years later another daughter arrived. Mary was born at a maternity home located between Camas and Washougal. In 1992 the maternity home was still there to the left of the telephone building on N. E. 3rd Avenue.

Adeline Bird's mother, Lucy Coffman Blair, died in 1923 at the age of fifty-eight. Her bereaved father, Robert, later married Mrs. Harriet Fisher of the renowned Fisher family in Clark County.

Around 1925, Dr. Bird moved his medical practice to the second floor of the new Farrell Building. The first floor was occupied by J. C. Penney's at that time. Dr. Bird's offices were in the upper front of the building and the family's living quarters were in the rear. The Bird's soon grew tired of apartment living and in 1927 Dr. Bird built a lovely new home on the North Bank Highway, now S. E. Sixth Avenue. The design was California Mission style with a flat roof.

Archie and Adeline lived in this spacious home for many, many years. Although Patricia and Mary Bird were raised in the new house on the outskirts of Camas, Archie and Adeline had the girls attend Central School in the downtown area. In 1992, the building was used for Highland Terrace, a nursing home facility. Pat Bird remembers that on hot, summer evenings she and her friends often slept on the flat roof of the Bird's new home.

During the Depression years times were tough for everyone and those who became ill or hurt often could not pay their bills. They would offer produce, eggs, vegetables, meats, and other things in payment of services. Years later many bills were still uncollected due to "patient hardship" and Dr. Bird's kindness and generosity. By 1934 Dr. Bird was considered one of

Camas' leading physicians advertising his services in the Professional Directory of the Camas Post. His partner at the time was Dr. Lewis H. Carpenter who was also a physician and surgeon. They shared an office in the "Medical Building."

A funeral notice in the April 14, 1936, Camas Post tells of the death of Archie's father, James Bishop Bird. The notice states "Mr. James Bird of Vancouver was survived by his widow and two sons, Dr. A. E. Bird of Camas and Dr. J. B. Bird of Vancouver. Father Egan officiated at the services and interment was in the Park Hill Cemetery." Adeline's father Robert Blair passed away in November of 1936 in Harmony at the age of seventy-five and was buried next to his first wife, Lucy, at Park Hill Cemetery.

The Bird's "unusual for Camas" styled home was featured in the 1938 Industrial Edition of the Camas Post still with its' original flat roof. Sometime during the 1940's Dr. Bird remodeled the house adding a pitched tile roof. Later owners removed the tiles switching to a more traditional style of roofing materials. Dr. H. W. Andreson DDS was the Bird's next-door neighbor and also had his home featured in the same 1938 Post edition.

Life wasn't all work for the Bird family who had a cabin at Klipsan Beach where they could escape for weekends of rest and relaxation. They would often go with Dr. Andreson and his family. Dr. Andreson was an avid sportsman and would try to convince Dr. Bird that fishing and clamming were the two best things to do on those weekends away. Dr. Bird was never convinced of the fact.

In 1938, Dr. Bird built the "Adeline Building" at 5th and Cedar naming the new $25,000 medical building after his beloved wife. This beautiful building was a one and a half story Italianette style with a Roman brick exterior and brick veneer interior. It had a red clay roof and prominent chimney. D. W. Hilborn was the architect and Frank McKever did the plumbing and heating. Swank and Stoller's furniture stores were responsible for the interior furnishings. The 1938 Camas Post described the building as "One of the most prominent public structures in Camas. It has the very latest arrangement and is furnished with moderntype equipment."

Being of two stories, the ground floor is occupied by the offices of Dr. Bird, Physician and Surgeon, including a beautiful reception room and the offices of Dr. H. E. Andresen, Dentist. Three apartments modernly equipped occupy the rest of the building." It was reported by old timers that longtime resident of Camas, Hilda Boch, rented out one of the lovely new apartments.

During the 1940's, Dr. Sheppard became a medical partner of Dr. Bird at the N.E. 5th and Cedar location. Also, Archie Bird built a four-plex located close to the corner of N. E. 6th and Garfield. He soon had all four units rented out.

Pat Bird graduated from Camas High School in 1940 and attended Marylhurst College in Portland, majoring in Sociology. She also helped in her dad's medical office. After graduation from Marylhurst, she worked in Seattle for a year doing social work. Mary Bird graduated from high school in 1945 and attended Marylhurst. She went on to become an X-ray technician in Vancouver.

In 1945, Pat Bird married Tom Richardson, and they moved to Camas. Tom worked in real estate with James Carmack and later became a partner at City Investment. Tom was well known throughout the county for his land transactions and went on to work in real estate sales for several different offices. He later became a city councilman. The Richardson's had six children, Thomas, Steve, Nick, Mark, Patrick and Mary.

During the 1950's, Dr. Bird bought the old wooden McKever Building between 3rd and 4th on Adams from the estate of Morris Riback. The old building was built in 1908 by an early pioneer, A.D McKever on the southeast corner of 4th and Clark, now Adams, but was moved in 1922 to an empty lot next door. Dr. Bird also purchased the brick McKever Building built in 1924 on the same corner after the old building was moved. When Dr. Bird purchased the two buildings, the basement of the brick building was being used by the Carpenter's Local Union for their meetings. In 1958 the City of Camas determined that the wooden McKever building constituted a fire hazard and because of that Dr. Bird had the building demolished to make room for a new structure on that site.

In the 1960's, the Birds sold their home on S. W. 6th and moved to a fine new home at N. E. 6th and Garfield in downtown Camas. That home was built by Leo McEny and is located just east of the Bird's four-plex. In 1967, the Bird's noted fifty years of marriage in a celebration at their new home.

Two years later, Dr. Archie Bird passed away at the age of seventy-three. He had faithfully served the people of Camas for over fifty years as the town's resident doctor and premier surgeon. He had also invested in the community he loved so much through the buildings he constructed and purchased and the real estate he developed over the years. He was remembered by many of the old-timers I interviewed in 1992 as being a fine, dignified man even in emergency situations. During Archie's long, full life his favorite hobby was playing poker with his friends that included Dr.

Dr. Archie Bird (Source The Columbian Dec 1969)

Andreson, Ernie Krieger, Harold Blake, Lloyd Hochin and others. They formed a poker club in the early days and played weekly poker games together for over thirty years.

At the time of this writing in 1992, Adeline Bird was in her nineties, living in Vancouver where she resided with her daughter, Mary Bird. Pat and Tom Richardson continued to live in Camas and had a lovely, older home in the southwest part of town just a few blocks from the Bird's original residence. Vernon Bird whose career as a successful Vancouver dentist spanned forty years died on August 31, 1983, at the age of eighty-four. He left a daughter, Diane Belisle and two grandchildren.

In 1992, the Bird and Andresen homes stood side by side on S. W. 6th Avenue like two old friends who have weathered many decades together. Both homes clearly showed their age at the time. The Adeline Building was being restored by the LaCamas Credit Union who planned to occupy it as soon as the restoration was completed.

As a historic preservationist it is inspiring to me that instead of tearing down the old buildings, Camas is a rare town that has restored much of its downtown to make it a unique blend of new and old. Many have described it as a "Norman Rockwell" painting because it depicts all that is good and well in America's past.

WILLIAM BAZ

Author's Preface: Early Camas was a melting pot for all races, religions, and immigrants from many countries worldwide. It was a dream fulfilled whether you were Scotch, Irish, Syrian, German, English or whatever, you had a chance for success in this little paper mill town. All it took was a little money, quite a bit of intelligence and a lot of determination. An early settler who possessed all of these qualifications was William Baz. The young man came into town and began a real estate dynasty that continues to this day. "Where the land is green, the trees are tall, and the river swiftly flows, that is utopia. That is Camas."

◈

WILLIAM BAZ WAS born August 7, 1888, in Baskinta, Syria. This handsome young man came to Camas with his mother, Syrian born Christina Baz. William's dark good looks and successful business manner attracted young Julia who was born in 1901 and thirteen years younger. They were married and in 1919 built a fine, large family home at 133 N. W. 12th Street. At that time William gave Julia a framed romantic poem entitled "Evening And You." He wrote on the back "Dad to Mom, first day in our new home, 1919 Jan." In the next few years William and Julia had three children, Walter, Paul, and Virginia.

William worked hard to establish his own business in the rapidly developing town. William Baz Enterprises was originally located at 231 NE 4th Street in a wooden building that he owned. He was a dealer in used furniture and because many of the people moving into town could not afford to buy new furniture, he flourished in his secondhand business. Even though selling used furniture was a successful endeavor for Baz, he had always professed a love for dealing in property, namely real estate. So, in 1923 he sold the old wooden building complete with all the furniture to the town mortician, Fred Stoller. Fred determined that selling used and new furniture would blend well with his mortuary business.

Julia and William Baz (Source Penny Baz and TRHM)

Stoller continued with Baz's used furniture business but ended up splitting the business into two entities, Stoller Mortuary and Stoller Furniture. Fred moved his furniture business to 415 N.E. 4th, the location of the Chamber of Commerce in 1992 and relocated his mortuary business to the location of Coast of Coast in 1992. Baz's old store, at 231 N.E. 4th, became the home of Camas Public Market. In the meantime, William Baz was not sitting still. Taking the profits from his furniture store he set up a real estate and insurance office in a small wooden building located where Cameo Costumes was in 1992. Business flourished and, in 1925, he purchased the large corner lot at 3rd and Clara, now Birch, and began excavation for a grand, brick two story building. The dirt was initially hauled out of the excavation pit by teams of horses. Later they used Model T's. While the building was being excavated, police were chasing a robber, a Mr. Weidman, who was shot dead and fell into the excavation hole.

Finally in 1929, after four long years of construction, the beautiful Baz Building was completed. William moved his real estate business that he called City Investment Company into part of the building and leased out the rest. One of his early tenants was Clark County Savings and Loan that in 1992 was Riverview Savings and Loan. The top floor of the building was originally called Baz Apartments and although they were small in size they were considered quite modern for those times. They were later renamed The Clara Street Apartments. Julia Baz was active during the 1920's and 1930's in the Camas Order of the Eastern Star,

Baz-Stoller Store (Source Penny Baz and TRHM)

eventually rising to the group's most exalted position of Worthy Matron in 1932.

A 1934 ad in the May 14 Camas Post had a listing for a four-room house, lot, woodshed, and garage for sale in Forest Home for $750.00. The listing agent was City Investment Company at 307 Clara Street. One of the tenants that year in the Baz Building was Bruce Thurber Insurance Company.

In September 1934, William's mother, Christina died at the age of seventy-two. The Baz family attended St. John's Presbyterian Church when John Phipps was pastor. Young Paul Baz was president of the young people's Tuxis Club in 1938.

On October 23, 1942, William Baz died in Vancouver. He was just fifty-four years old. Two years later Julia Baz remarried, this time to Arthur H. Repman. According to an article in the May 4, 1944, Camas Post, the marriage took place at the home of Julia's sister, Mrs. Lawrence Kelly in Washougal. The couple was attended by Mr. and Mrs. Gus Lorenz.

William's son Paul Baz joined the firm of City Investment Company and together with his partners, Robert W. Peery and J. I.

Paul and Belva Baz (Source Penny Baz and TRHM)

Pollock operated two offices in the 1950's. An ad for the company in the May 14, 1953, Camas Post lists several interesting and inexpensive properties for sale. In 1992 Paul was continuing to carry on his father's love of Camas real estate. He was semi-retired and was spending time at Stan Wiley Real Estate in downtown Camas. The real estate office was located at the site of J. J. Harrington's old house. Harrington was Camas' first mayor and lived in the home back in the early 1900's. The home was later moved to 12th and G Streets in Washougal where it had been restored.

When I interviewed Paul Baz, he was living with his wife Belva in northwest Camas. They had a daughter Penny. He loaned me three photos, one of the Baz homes in 1919, and one of the Baz Building in 1929. The third photo was of William Baz aged twenty-nine in 1918. Plus, a framed poem "Evening and You."

Unfortunately, I was not able to complete my interviews with Paul about his father, William, in 1992 so this chapter was never completed to my satisfaction. However, I do know that in 1992 the Baz Building was owned by Bob Angelo and that the old family home at 133 N.W. 12th stood at that time with an addition on one side and a gazebo in the yard. There was a huge cedar tree in the front yard that was most likely planted by William Baz back in 1919. The home was no longer owned by the Baz family.

THE CAMAS MILL

A CONSTANT THEME
IN COMMUNITY LIFE

A s you can see by this account of early Camas pioneers, the paper mill played a huge part in the development of the original city of La Camas that became Camas, Washington. Aside from farming and early sawmills, the paper mill was the first industry in town. Like a rippling effect, people came from all over the world to work at the mill, houses and businesses sprang up with each owner and resident interacting in some way with the paper mill. There are other industries in Camas today, but the paper mill is still going strong as a constant theme in community life.

In 1883, Henry Lewis Pittock needed a new source of paper for his rapidly expanding Portland, Oregonian newspaper. His representative, D. H. Stearns, negotiated a deal with Horace Belding and others to purchase twenty-six hundred acres of prime land ten miles east of Portland on the north side of the Columbia River in the area we now call Camas. The land contained three lakes, a creek, and a powerful river close by. LaCamas Colony Company was formed, paper mill buildings were constructed, dams and an aqueduct were built, and a town was platted. Articles of Incorporation were filed in Portland in 1884 naming the new paper mill business Columbia River Paper Company. The name La Camas was selected for the town because of the Camas roots used by the Native Americans for food in the area. It was later changed to just Camas.

In 1905, the Columbia River Paper Company of Camas and the Crown Paper Company of West Linn, Oregon merged to form Crown Columbia Paper Company. In 1914 Crown Columbia merged with Willamette Pulp and Paper from Oregon becoming Crown Willamette Paper Company. In 1928

Crown Willamette Paper Company merged with Zellerbach Paper Company becoming Crown Zellerbach Paper Company. During all this time the company continued to flourish, employing more and more people, and drawing more and more businesses and residents into Camas.

In the spring of 1985, in a series of corporate maneuvers, Crown Zellerbach Paper Company became James River Corporation. In 1992, James River continued as a powerful influence in Camas and employed many Camas residents. The pulp and paper industry still plays a huge roll in Camas life with the company in 2011 now Georgia Pacific Corporation.

EPILOGUE – CAMAS TODAY

IT IS INTERESTING to write this epilogue in 2011 because I finished my book on "Camas Pioneers" in 1992. But, because my book was not published at that time, I had the opportunity to edit it in 2011 and to add this epilogue of Camas today. I have not lived in Camas since 1998, and things have really changed quite a bit. Here is an update provided by the City of Camas and their Chamber of Commerce websites and I wish to thank them for this opportunity to use their information.

The City of Camas is currently home to approximately 16,700 residents and several large hi-tech manufacturing industries. Because of its' location along the Columbia River, what was once a small city has become a perfect location for international companies. The paper mill that was at one time the one and only driving industrial force in Camas is now called Georgia Pacific Corporation. However, it is just one of many major companies that include Wafer Tech, Linear Technology, Logitech, Sharp Microelectronic, Underwriter's Laboratories, Camas Power Boiler, Bodycote IMT Inc., Industrial Materials Tech, Heraeus Shin-Etsu America, Bruzzone 4th Street, LLC, and others. These companies employ many workers and that is a bonus for the area.

What were once prune orchards on Prune Hill and rolling timothy fields in Grass Valley now contain beautiful homes with vista views of the Columbia River and east Clark County. As a prelude to my chapter on the Knapp family I express my feelings about what was then and what was to come. It was inevitable that developers would discover the lush hills and serene valleys of the Camas area with its' pristine lakes and rushing streams. Careful planning with open space, parks, and recreation areas are very important to everyone's quality of life.

Most important to me as a historic preservationist was keeping downtown Camas as an example of how preservation can be utilized in older buildings, each with a history of its' own. In writing this book I have tried to express what each new building constructed in Camas back in the early 1900's meant to these early pioneers and how retaining and restoring them continues to be beneficial to the whole community. The current downtown core with its trees, planters and sitting areas nestled among the old beautiful buildings is truly a sight to behold. The downtown area remains like a Norman Rockwell painting and that is a joy for newcomers and old-timers alike.

Camas has had its' ups and downs with the 1890's and 1930's depressions, terrible fires in the early blocks of wooden buildings, and good and bad economic times. But, with good city management, the city overcame the obstacles, continued to grow and is thriving today. The early pioneers described in this book and their descendants played a big part in the development of this once little paper mill town on the Columbia River called "Camas."

ACKNOWLEDGMENTS

Author's Preface: Because so much research went into this book and each chapter had so many sources and contained so many interviews, I am listing and thanking each of my sources and photograph contributors by how the pioneers are listed in this book, beginning with the Knapp's and ending with the Baz's. I wish to thank each and every contributor, although many are no longer with us since 2011. I also extend my deepest appreciation to each and every source listed because without their help I would not have been able to write this book. In the many years of bringing this book to publication many photos were unfortunately lost. If I've omitted anyone, I sincerely apologize.

KNAPP SOURCES:

Clark County Genealogical Society: Camas Cemetery Records, Fisher Cemetery Records, Fern Prairie Cemetery Records, Clark County Pioneers, Clark County Land Records. The Vancouver Columbian Newspaper: February 25, 1980 edition, Sunday May 21, 1989 edition, April 20, 1986 article on Fisher Cemetery, Bob Beck Columbian article on Ida Fisher Dewey, Ted Van Arsdol Columbian article on Grass Valley School May 13, 1965.

Camas Post Record (LaCamas Post and Camas Post): 1976 Cenaqua-Bicentennial Issue, Camas Post-Washougal Record December 7, 1934, Camas Post April 1, 1932, Camas Post Record May 7, 1959, Camas Post Record Shopping Guide May 27, 1970, Camas Washougal Post Record's Buyer's Bonus January 15, 1985. Milt Bona article on mail service Camas-Washougal history. Clark County Census Records: 1850 Census, 1860 Census, 1871 Census, 1880 Census.

Camas-Washougal Historical Society: Various articles from their historic records. Books: "Clarke County" by B. F. Alby and J. P. Munro Fraser, copyright 1885. "Looking Back" by Mark Parsons, copyright 1983, "Camas Early Days" by Ted Van Arsdol, "Clark County History Volume One", copyright 1960. Oral Interviews: By Dora: Cecil I. Knapp November 16, 1988. By Sally Alves: Donald Knapp June 13, 1992, Hugh Knapp December 21, 1991

Miscellaneous Resources: Birth Records of Dr. Carlos Urie Volume One, Territorial Suffrage Speech by Henry Monroe Knapp 1881, Diary of Deborah Woolf. Photos Loaned Courtesy of the Knapp Family: 1887 Washington State Legislature with Henry Monroe Knapp, 50th Wedding Anniversary of Henry Adelbert Knapp and Deborah Woolf,

Deborah Woolf and her sisters after trip on the Oregon Trail, Claude Adelbert Knapp, Diary of Deborah Woolf, Four Generations of Knapp's/Briggs photo, Historic Knapp Home at 637 N. E. Everett Street in Camas.

COFFEY SOURCES:

Clark County Genealogical Society: Camas Cemetery Records, Fern Prairie Cemetery Records, Clark County Pioneers, Clark County Land Records.

Camas Post Record: Camas Post March 7, 1919, Camas Post February 2, 1911, Camas Post Record December 7, 1934, Story of Lewis Van Vleet.

Clark County Census Records: 1860 Census.

No Oral Interviews or Photos Available

VAN VLEET/WRIGHT SOURCES:

Clark County Genealogical Society: Fern Prairie Cemetery Records, Camas Cemetery Records. Vancouver Columbian Newspaper: Vancouver Daily Columbian May 31, 1913, The Columbian October 2, 1990.

Camas Post Record: Articles printed on November 8, 1929, March 20, 1941, December 6, 1919, May 27, 1970, May 28, 1976, September 27, 1978, July 10, 1958, May 14, 1953, December 7, 1934, and May 27, 1970. Camas Washougal Post Record 1976 Cenaqua-Bicentennial Issue, Camas Post Record Centennial Issue 1988.

Clark County Census Records: Census 1860, Census 1871

Camas Washougal Historical Society: Various articles from their historic records.

Parkersville Landing Committee, Port of Camas Washougal: Interviews, articles and old photographs.

Books: "Portland, the Rose City" S. J. Clarke Publishing Co. 1911, "Clark County Washington Territory" B. F. Alley and J. P. Munro-Fraser 1885, "Camas Twin Mill Towns Clark County History" Beverly Woods 1987, "Clark County History" 1976, "Panther Tales" Martha Grimani and Wanda Berry, "Clark County History 1978 Louisa Wright M.D." by Winnie Shinn.

BELDING/PAYNE SOURCES:

Clark County Genealogical Society: Clark County Pioneers, Clark County Land Records.

Camas Post Record: Articles December 7, 1934, September 14, 1934. Camas Post Record 1976 Cenaqua-Bicentennial Issue.

Clark County Census Records: 1870 Census and 1880 Census.

Clark County Death Records: 1891-1903 Clark County Cemetery Records, Fisher Cemetery

Northwest Farm News "Camas A Story of Pioneers and Paper" September 1944

Books: "Clark County History 1988, History of the Camas Mill" by Janet Hall.

Abstract of Titles: Abstract of Title and Bill of Sale property of W. H. Payne to George K. Bafus, loaned to author by Ruben Bafus. Abstract of Title from Knapp Family Camas.

Miscellaneous: Research material furnished by Barbara Payne Jones. Research material furnished by Lorraine Knapp Thompson. Research material and photos submitted by Ruben Bafus of Camas/Grass Valley.

Oral Interviews: Ruben Bafus of Grass Valley, Edgar Duman of Vancouver, Lorraine Knapp Thompson, Barbara Payne Jones.

PITTOCK/LEADBETTER SOURCES:

Clark County Genealogical Society: Camas Cemetery Records

The Vancouver Columbian: May 1984 Article by Wendy Reif. November 11, 1989 reprint of March 21, 1925 Article, Article by Bob Beck.

Camas Post Record: Article by Margo Knight July 1982 Interview with Mabel Pickett, Article by Chris Clohessy September 1989 Interview with Mabel Pickett, Article February 19, 1979, Article July 10, 1958, Camas Post Record Centennial Edition May 27, 1970, Article by Margo Knight, Camas Post Record Centennial Edition November 11, 1988, Article July 10, 1958, LaCamas Post January 25, 1908.

Camas Washougal Historical Society: Various information from their historic records.

Books and Brochures: "Clark County Washington Territory " By B. F. Alley and J. P Munro-Fraser, Edited by Mark Parsons, "Columbia River Valley, Volume II", "Paper Maker, Donnelly 1958, Volume I", "A Brief History of Camas" Welsh 1941, "Pittock Mansion" brochures 1991, "Camas Washougal Soroptimist's Historical Home Tour 1989" brochure.

Camas Public Library: "Camas History" files.

Other Articles: East County News April 27, 1977 Article, Columbia Willamette Business Hall of Fame Article October 22, 1990.

TIDLAND SOURCES:

Clark County Genealogical Society: Camas Cemetery Records

The Vancouver Columbian: Clark County History, 15th Anniversary Issue 1984, Ted Van Arsdol.

Camas Post Record: Articles September 14, 1934, December 7, 1934, October 13, 1938, November 11, 1988.

Camas Public Library: "Camas History" files.

Oral Interviews: Bessie Tidland taped interview with Jon Larson 1985, Bob Tidland interview with Sally Alves March 1993, and Barbara Gist interview with Sally Alves March 1993.

Miscellaneous Sources: Vivian Scott, Maxine at Tidland's re: Scrapbook on Tidland Corporation, Roberta Tidland.

HARRINGTON SOURCES:

Clark County Genealogical Society: Camas Cemetery Records

Camas Post Record: Articles May 11, 1911, July 31, 1953, LaCamas Post 1908.

Other Print Sources: "Camas Early Days" Ted Van Arsdol, "The Paper Maker Number Two" Donnelly 1958, "A Brief History of Camas" Welsh 1941, "Crown Zellerbach Spotlight" July 1983.

LORENZ/KARNATH SOURCES:
Clark County Genealogical Society: Camas Cemetery Records
Camas Post Record: "At Your Leisure" August 15, 1989, "Shopper's Guide" May 27, 1970, Article December 10, 1959, "Buyer's Bonus" October 1, 1985, Camas Post Record Centennial Edition November 11, 1988.
Camas Washougal Historical Society: Various News Clippings.
Oral Interviews: Several interviews with Howard Lorenz Spring 1993 by Sally Alves. Photos provided courtesy of Howard Lorenz and Steve Lorenz.

MCKEVER SOURCES:
Clark County Genealogical Society: Camas Cemetery Records.
Camas Post Record: LaCamas Post January 25, 1908, Camas Washougal Post Record Cenaqua Bicentennial Issue 1976, Articles on December 7, 1934, July 9, 1915, September 14, 1934, June 22, 1939, and December 5, 1940. Post Record 1970 McKever Building photo and caption, Post Record August 7, 1958 article on McKever Building demolition.
Camas Washougal Historical Society: Article on Charles McKever. Profile on Charles McKever.
Other Print Sources: Book "Looking Back" Parsons 1983, "Lackamas Yearbook" 1930.
Oral Interviews: Interview by Sally Alves with Nadine Smith April 1993. Photographs furnished by Nadine Smith at that time. Interview by Vincent Ast with John Aubrey "Jack" McKever July 16, 1987, text edited by Ceil Kirchner, printed in a Centennial Letter, Fall 1989.
Other Information Sources: Charles Daniel Buslach, Lonnie McCoy, Jack Keel, Michael McKever, Cinda Busch, Michael Burden.

AENEAS MACMASTER SOURCES:
Clark County Genealogical Society: Clark County Cemetery Records.
The Vancouver Columbian: Article Sunday May 21, 1989, Clark County History 15th Anniversary Issue 1984 Ted Van Arsdol.
Camas Post Record: Washington Centennial November 121, 1988, Camas Washougal Post Record Centennial Edition May 27, 1970, Cenaqua-Bicentennial issue 1976 Camas Washougal Post Record, Articles December 7, 1934, May 14, 1953, and June 10, 1970.
Camas Washougal Historical Society: Aeneas MacMaster file.
Fort Vancouver Historical Society: Clark County History 1981.
Books: "Clarke County" by B.F. Alby and J. P Munro-Fraser copyright 1885, "Looking Back" Parsons 1983, "A Brief History of Camas" Welsh June 1941.

Other Print Sources: "Camas A Story of Pioneers and Paper" Northwest Farm News September 1944, "Camas-Washougal Twin Mill Towns" Beverly Woods 1984 Clark County History, "The Paper Maker" Donnelly 1958, "The Farmer Out Front in Clark County" Clark County History 1961, "History of St. John's Presbyterian Church" Bona 1983.

Oral Interviews: Interviews by Sally Alves with Betty Rose Matthews and Glenn Blake April 1992. MacMaster family photos loaned by Betty Rose Matthews and Glenn Blake.

DUFFIN SOURCES:

Clark County Genealogical Society: Camas Cemetery Records

Camas Post Record: Article on Elizabeth Duffin February 24, 1944, Obituary Elizabeth Duffin 1945, Articles on Duffin April 1, 1932, October 1, 1959, January 18, 1924, December 7, 1934, February 24, 1944, and June 24, 1927. Camas Post Record Cenaqua-Bicentennial Issue 1976, Post Record Washington Centennial Edition November 11, 1988, 1970 Post Record Centennial Edition.

Books and Other Print Sources: "Looking Back" Parsons 1983, "Camas Early Days" Ted Van Arsdol, "The Coast Magazine" 1909, "A History of St. John's Presbyterian Church" Bona 1983, "A Brief History of Camas" Welsh June 1941, 1918 Lackamas Yearbook, 1922 Lackamas Yearbook.

Oral Interviews: April 1992 Interview with Betty Rose and Wally Matthews by Sally Alves, April 1992 Interview with Glenn and Alice Blake, Sandy Powell information fall 1992.

Photos Courtesy of Matthews: Allan Duffin Letter of Introduction dated October 1, 1872, Harold Blake trotting track, Ella and Hugh MacMaster photo by A.B. McAllpin, Ella and Hugh MacMaster mid age photo by Redmond & Jenks, Old photo of St. John's church, family photo of Elisabeth Duffin, Maysie Duffin, Kent Chappell, Leila Duffin Chappell and Marjorie Duffin Blake, photo of Elisabeth Duffin with Maysie age three, and Marjorie, age six or seven on postcard, Book "A Short History of Business" regarding MacMaster Store, photo Ella and Hugh MacMaster Golden Anniversary, Photo of MacMaster Store with Harold Blake name on back.

COWAN SOURCES:

Clark County Genealogical Society: Camas Cemetery Records, Book: "Clark County Pioneers".

Camas Post Record: Articles re: Cowan September 14, 1934, January 18, 1924, July 10, 1958, January 25, 1908, December 7, 1934, May 11, 1911, March 15, 1912, June 24, 1927, April 1, 1932, and May 14, 1953.

Camas Washougal Historical Society: Various historical materials.

Books and Other Print Sources: "Camas Early Days" Ted Van Arsdol, "A History of St. John's Presbyterian Church" by Bona, "Columbia River Valley", "A Brief History of Camas" Welsh 1941, "Looking Back" Parsons 1983.

Oral Interviews and Photos: October 31, 1992 Interview with Ruth Ginder Freeman and Bill Ginder by Sally Alves, Photos courtesy of Ruth Ginder Freeman, Information and photos furnished to Sally Alves by James Freeman of Eugene, Interview with Annice Sampson November 11, 1992 by Sally Alves, and photos furnished courtesy of Annice Sampson.

Other Sources: Sandy Powell, Lowell Bobbitt.

HUGH MACMASTER SOURCES:

Clark County Genealogical Society: Camas Cemetery Records, Book "Clark County Pioneers".

The Vancouver Columbian: Articles dated May 21, 1989 and May 1984.

Camas Post Record: 1938 Industrial Edition, Camas Post Cenaqua-Bicentennial Issue 1976, Camas Post Record Centennial Edition November 11, 1988, Camas Post Record Centennial Edition May 27, 1970, Articles re: Hugh MacMaster printed December 07, 1934, June 10, 1970, May 11, 1911, May 1, 1925, April 1, 1932 and September 14, 1934.

Camas Library: Clark County Death Records

Camas Washougal Historical Museum: Historical Records.

Fort Vancouver Historical Society: Clark County History 1981, Clark County History 1961.

Book and Other Print Sources: Book "Clarke County", "Northwest Farm News" September 1944, "Camas Early Days" Ted Van Arsdol, "Clark County History 15th Anniversary Edition" 1984 Sterns, "The Paper Maker" Donnelly 1958, Milt Bona Letter dated August 1, 1966, "The Paper Maker Number II Donnally 1958, Book "Columbia River Valley", "Looking Back" Parsons 1983, "Coast Magazine" 1909, "A Brief History of Camas" Welsh June 1941, "A History of St. John's Presbyterian Church" by Bona 1983, "A History of the Columbia River from the Dalles to the Sea, Vol.II" Trail Breakers, 1988, "A Short History of Business" MacMaster & Company 1916.

Oral Interviews and Photos: March 1992 with Betty Rose Matthews and Glenn Blake by Sally Alves. Photographs and news clips provided courtesy of Matthews and Blake. Photos of Blake property on Columbia River, the Duffin family in living room, St. John's church, Elizabeth, Maysie and Marjorie dressed up with flowered background, Allan Duffin Letter of Accreditation October 1872, Hugh and Ella MacMaster early marriage photo, mid-marriage photo and Golden Anniversary photo.

Other Sources: Betty Rose Blake, E. Sandy Powell, Renee Norman, Grace Snoey, Mildred Benedict.

FARRELL SOURCES:

Clark County Genealogical Society: Camas Cemetery Records

The Vancouver Columbian: Article re: Farrell May 21, 1989.

Camas Post Record: 1976 Cenaqua-Bicentennial Issue, May 1938 Industrial Edition, Washington Centennial Issue November 1, 1988, Obituary Notice August 15, 1930

Articles re: Farrell's May 11, 1911, December 7, 1934, June 7, 1956, December 20, 1967, September 4, 1984, March 15, 1912, July 10, 1958, April 1, 1932 and October 9, 1931.

Camas Washougal Historical Museum: "Charlie Farrell's Home Fact Sheet".

Camas Washougal Soroptimist's: "Historical Home Tour 1989."

Books and Other Print Sources: Book "Columbia River Valley", 1917 Lackamas Year Book, 1926 Lackamas Year Book, 1927 Lackamas Year Book, "Looking Back" Parsons 1983, "Camas Early Days" Ted Van Arsdol.

Oral Interviews and Photos: With Irene Roffler by Sally Alves, with the Farrell family of Camas by Sally Alves. Photos courtesy of Irene Roffler and the Farrell family.

SELF SOURCES:

Clark County Genealogical Society: Camas Cemetery Records

Camas Post Record: 1976 Cenaqua-Bicentennial Issue, 1938 Industrial Edition, 1958 Obituary Notice Nora Self, Articles re: Self family printed May 27, 1970, January 25, 1908 LaCamas Post, May 1, 1925, October 9, 1931, December 7, 1934, February 18, 1936, November 14, 1940, February 1, 1941, February 15, 1942, February 15, 1946.

Birth Records: Dr. Urie, Volume One

Books and Other Print Sources: Washougal Newspaper February 18, 1936, "Camas Early Days" Ted Van Arsdol, 1922 Lackamas Year Book, "A History of St. John's Presbyterian Church" by Bona.

Oral Interviews: Interview with Jim Pillette by Sally Alves November 17, 1992. Sally Alves phone conversations with Jim Pillette September 24 and September 25, 1992. Any photos are courtesy of Jim Pillette.

STOLLER SOURCES:

Clark County Genealogical Society: Camas Cemetery Records

The Vancouver Columbian: 1957-1958 Clark County Directory

Camas Post Record: "Peeryodicals" by W. K. Peery 1951 Post Record, May 1938 Camas Post Record In-dustrial Edition, Articles re: Stoller's printed March 29, 1935, September 26, 1940, May 13, 1943, March 15, 1912, December 7, 1934, May 1, 1925, October 9, 1931, April 1, 1932, September 14, 1934, October 13, 1938, August 4, 1938, 1959 Camas Post Record. 1958 Crown Zellerbach 75th Anniversary Edition Camas Post Record.

Clark County Death Records: 1891-1903

Print Sources: Camas Historical Walking Tour by Justin Shewell, 1917 Lackamas Yearbook, 1921 Lackamas Yearbook.

Other Sources: Dorothy Ryan, Steve Stoller, Beverly Richardson Stoller, Alan Stoller and Steve Stoller.

SWANK SOURCES:

Clark County Genealogical Society: Book "Clark County Pioneers".

The Vancouver Columbian: May 21, 1989 "Columbia River Valley"

Camas Post Record: Articles on Swank printed: January 25, 1908, May 14, 1953, January 18, 1924, Sep-tember 14, 1934, June 1933, December 7, 1934, March 12, 1937, October 13, 1938, and April 9, 1959.

Book: "Camas Early Days" by Ted Van Arsdol

Oral Interviews and Photos: September 1993 interview with Dr. Roy Swank by Sally Alves. Photos courtesy of Dr. Roy Swank.

JOHNSON SOURCES:

Clark County Genealogical Society: Camas Cemetery Records

The Vancouver Columbian: Article August 31, 1982.

Camas Post Record: Camas Post Industrial Edition 1938, Bicentennial Issue 1976, LaCamas Post January 25, 1908, Article February 11, 1960.

Camas Washougal Historical Society: Miscellaneous articles and O.F. Johnson House.

Camas Washougal Soroptimist's: "Historical Home Tour 1989".

Books: "Camas Early Days" by Ted Van Arsdol, April 1909 Coast Magazine.

Oral Interviews: April 3, 1992 personal interview with Winston Ellis by Sally Alves, 1967 taped interview Don Ellis and Oscar Franklin Johnson, 1979 "My Life Story" by Oscar Johnson and Winston Ellis.

Photos: Courtesy of Winston Ellis: Beatrice Amelia Bauman, Aberdeen 1907 in long dress. Johnson and his Imperial car 1912, Beatrice and Winston Johnson 1915 first day of school, Johnson at eighteen bust profile in suit, Beatrice graduating from college white dress with flowers, Emil Bauman's house 506 N.E. Hayes, Johnson photo by Witzel age thirty five. North Bank Highway Committee January 25, 1921, Winston's birth home 713 N. E. 4th Street, 1907 Johnson's newlywed photo in Aberdeen, Johnson building 1920's, Johnson in Scottish Rite outfit, Beatrice and Winston in Franklin automobile 1916, house on N.E. 4th with board sidewalk in front, Winston age five at Hayes home. Johnson aged twenty three in checked jacket, Johnson and new Franklin automobile, Winston age four in 1914 with ax, Emil Bauman early 1900's, Perry Johnson aged sixty eight, Beatrice in 1906 hair piled high, Katherine Bauman age fifty years, 1965 Moody and Johnson, Johnson's Bank, Johnson in 1934, Johnson's 50th Wedding Anniversary, Beatrice and Winston dressed up 1911, Ann Fletcher in Beatrice's wedding dress 1988, Don Ellis and horn, Johnson home in snow, 1911 Johnson home, Johnson home in 1920.

BLAKE SOURCES:

Clark County Genealogical Society: Camas Cemetery Records.

Camas Post Record: 1976 Cenaqua-Bicentennial Issue, May 27, 1970 Centennial Edition, 1938 Industrial Edition, Centennial Edition November 11, 1988, Articles re: Blake printed on April 1, 1932, September 14, 1934, February 11, 1943, April 10, 1990.

Camas Washougal Historical Museum: Historic Records.

City of Camas Building Department: Building Department records.

Books: "Looking Back" Mark E. Parsons 1983, Lackamas Year Book 1921.

Oral Interviews and Photos: April 1992 interview with Glenn Blake family by Sally Alves, Interview by Sally Alves with Leighton Blake and Grace Snoey on August 8, 1992, Phone conversation with Grace Snoey by Sally Alves on July 1, 1992. Photos courtesy of Glenn Blake family: Blake family photo with Frank, Maude, Hard, Edna, Ralph, Albert, Rose, Rozina. A.M. Blake and Rozina, Harold Blake photo, another family photo, color photo of Harold Blake home, Aerial photo of Harold Blake's Columbia River property before Highway 14. Other photos, negatives and articles loaned by Leighton Blake August 8, 1992.

GAINES SOURCES:

Clark County Genealogical Society: Camas Cemetery Records.

Camas Post Record: Post Record Obituary June 27, 1979, Post Record 1976 CenaquaBicentennial Supplement, October 9, 1931 Post Record.

Other Source: C. F. Herr

CARMACK SOURCES:

Clark County Genealogical Society: Camas Cemetery Records.

Camas Post Record: R. W. Carmack Obituary October 14, 1938, Articles on Carmack printed December 7, 1934, May 14, 1953, December 7, 1934, May 1, 1925, November 11, 1937, April 1, 1932, August 31, 1911, October 13, 1938.

Camas Washougal Historical Society: "Centennial Project", Carmack House Survey.

Books and other Print Sources: "Looking Back" Mark Parsons 1983, Letter from Carmack to Johnson September 8, 1908 provided by Winston Ellis, Letters dated March 10, 1992 and April 2, 1992 from R. H. Carmack, Australia.

Oral Interviews: Interview with April Carmack Ourso March 1992 by Sally Alves, Interview with Barbara Ann Hunter April 1992 by Sally Alves.

Photos: Courtesy of April Ourso, James Carmack, Winston Ellis, and R. H. Carmack: 1910 Carmack Store Christopher Washington, 1927 Carmack Building, 1920's Carmack Home, Beatrice and James Carmack aged five and three 1911, R. W. Carmack twenty years old, Carmack at 40 years old, North Bank Highway Committee 1921, James Carmack's Wedding, Articles from Post Record November 31, 1911 and October 13, 1938, Lackamas yearbook 1932, Camas High Commencement Program 1932, In remembrance Daisy Carmack July 15, 1955, Harvey Store Photo, Victoria BC James and Joni Carmack, James Carmack with fish, Join Carmack with flowers in hair, Carmack House 1930's, Carmack's Mercantile Truck, Carmack Home early 1920's Westco Water System, James and Beatrice Carmack 1930's, Carmack Home distant view.

FARR SOURCES:

Clark County Genealogical Society: Camas Cemetery Records

Camas Post Record: Articles on Farr Brothers September 14, 1934 and 1911 Camas Post

Oral Interview: With Vincent Ast 1991 by Sally Alves

Photo of Farr's: Courtesy of Vincent Ast given to Sally Alves

BELKNAP SOURCES:

Clark County Genealogical Society: Camas Cemetery Records

Camas Post Record: Camas Post Poet's Corner, LaCamas Post Article May 11, 1911, Camas Post articles February 18, 1970 and Camas Post Washougal Record article December 7, 1934.

BIRD SOURCES:

Clark County Genealogical Society: Book "Clark County Pioneers"

Camas Post Record: Industrial Edition 1938, Articles printed on Bird's October 13, 1938, November 10, 1936, September 14, 1934, April 14, 1936 and August 7, 1958.

Camas Washougal Historical Society and Museum: Historic files

Oral Interview: With Pat and Tom Richardson by Sally Alves on October 31, 1992.

Photos: Courtesy of Pat Richardson: Archie and Adeline Bird 1917 in front of home, 1902 photo of James Bird, Vernon Bird, Archie Bird and Catherine Bird, 1917 photo of Archie and Adeline Bird in front of car, Archie Bird in 1914, Dr. Bird in surgery at St. Joseph's Hospital in 1920's, Catherine Bird 1902 and James Bird 1902.

Other Source: Mary Bird of Vancouver

BAZ SOURCES:

Clark County Genealogical Society: Camas Cemetery Records

Camas Post Record: Articles on Baz printed April 1, 1932, September 14, 1934, May 4, 1944, May 14, 1953, and the 1938 Camas Post Industrial Edition.

Oral Interview: With Paul Baz fall 1991

Photos: Courtesy of Paul Baz: William Baz home taken when built 1919 with Paul and brother Walter Baz, William Baz Building in 1929 photo by Nelson Studio, photo of William Baz aged 29 in 1918, framed poem entitled "Evening and You"

ABOUT THE AUTHOR

As an avid historic preservationist and lover of history, author Sally Alves spent five years researching and writing this book.

Designated the gypsy in her family, she has traveled the United States and Europe, most recently living eight years in Mexico, and writing two additional books in the process. A loving wife and mother of five children, she is currently living in Southern Arizona.